THE OTHER PATH

THE
OTHER
PATH

THE INVISIBLE REVOLUTION
IN THE THIRD WORLD

Hernando de Soto
in collaboration with the Instituto Libertad y Democracia

Foreword by
Mario Vargas Llosa

Translated by June Abbott

1817

HARPER & ROW, PUBLISHERS, New York
Cambridge, Philadelphia, San Francisco
London, Mexico City, São Paulo, Singapore, Sydney

This book was produced with the cooperation and support of the International Center for Economic Growth (ICEG), a nonprofit public policy organization founded in 1985 to sponsor and promote research on sound economic policies. ICEG promotes an international discussion on economic policy, economic growth, and human welfare issues through research, publications, and conferences. Through a network of more than one hundred correspondent institutes in fifty-four countries, ICEG distributes books and monographs on economic development to leading policymakers, academics, businesspeople, and journalists throughout the world.

For more information, write to the International Center for Economic Growth, 243 Kearny Street, San Francisco, CA 94108.

Designed by Karen Savary

Library of Congress Cataloging-in-Publication Data
Soto, Hernando de, 1941–
    The other path.

    Translation of : El otro sendero.
    Includes index.
    1. Informal sector (Economics)—Peru.   2. Bureaucracy—Peru.   I. Instituto Libertad y
Democracia (Lima, Peru).   II. Title
HD 2346.P4S6713   1989   381   88-45572
ISBN 0-06-016020-9

89   90   91   92   93   AC/RRD   10   9   8   7   6   5   4   3   2

To Latin America's competitive workers and entrepreneurs,
formal and informal, who through their efforts are
tracing the other path.

And, of course, to my left-wing friends,
whose ideals I share, in the hope that we might
also agree on ways to achieve them.

Editor's Note

This book reproduces in many instances the results of economic research, calculations, and estimates made directly by the Instituto Libertad y Democracia (ILD).

We have chosen not to include in this volume the technical and statistical foundations of such, for this would have altered the purpose of the book and perhaps also discouraged readers who might not be drawn to these disciplines. We have therefore reserved the detailed methodology and economic calculations for a separate volume titled "Technical and Statistical Compendium to *The Other Path*," which includes the methodology for estimating the magnitude of informal economic activity in Peru.

To obtain this material, contact the editor of *The Other Path* by Hernando de Soto, Harper & Row, Publishers, Inc., 10 East 53rd Street, New York, N.Y. 10022.

Reader's Guide

When *The Other Path* became a best-seller in Latin America, some commentators pointed out that the greatest contribution of the book is the astonishing revelation of how the economic underground of an underdeveloped country operates; for others, the fundamental contribution of the book is its political analysis, which alters the terms of debate concerning the prerequisites for economic development, effective democratic institutions, and appropriate foreign policy toward the Third World.

These considerations show that besides the reader who is attracted by the subject matter of the book as a whole, there are two other types of readers of *The Other Path*: we recommend that those readers who are especially interested in the detailed narrative on how the underground emerges and operates concentrate on chapters 1, 2, 3, and 4; those readers who are predominantly interested in the political proposal derived from the foregoing analysis should concentrate on chapters 1, 5, 6, 7, and 8.

Contents

Foreword

Economists occasionally tell better stories than novelists. *The Other Path* by Hernando de Soto is a perfect case in point. His story, based entirely on Peruvian reality, reveals an aspect of life in the Third World that is traditionally obscured by ideological prejudice.

Unlike good literature, which teaches us indirectly, *The Other Path* preaches an explicit lesson about contemporary and future Third World reality. And unlike run-of-the-mill economic and sociological essays on Latin America, which seek to be abstract and end up distanced from any specific society, *The Other Path* never strays from the real world. It focuses on a hitherto little-studied and even less-understood phenomenon—the informal economy—and then offers a solution to the economic plight of underdeveloped countries. This solution is completely different from the economic projects the majority of Third World governments, progressive or conservative, have devised, but it is—and this is the book's main thesis—the very solution the poorest sectors of Third World societies have already put into practice.

The Other Path is an exhaustive study of the informal economy, or black market, in Peru and reveals startling information about its magnitude and complexity. But the book is much more than an exposé: After describing the magnitude and complexity of economic activities carried out outside the law in Peru, Hernando de Soto—with the assistance of his researchers at the Institute for Liberty and Democracy—examines the origins of social injustice and economic failure in Latin America. As he delineates the problems of underdevelopment, he explodes many myths about the Third World that pass for scientific truths.

The Informal Economy

The "informal economy" is usually thought of as a problem: clandestine, unregistered, illegal companies and industries that pay no taxes, that compete unfairly with companies and industries that obey the law and pay their taxes promptly. Black-marketeers are brigands who deprive the state of funds it might use to remedy social problems and strengthen the very structure of society.

That kind of thinking, as Hernando de Soto proves, is totally erroneous. In countries like Peru, the problem is not the black market but the state itself. The informal economy is the people's spontaneous and creative response to the state's incapacity to satisfy the basic needs of the impoverished masses. It is, of course, paradoxical that this study, carried out by an institute that defends economic freedom, constitutes an indictment of the Third World state unrivaled in its severity and force, while at the same time it reduces most radical or Marxist critiques of underdevelopment to mere rhetorical posturing.

When legality is a privilege available only to those with political and economic power, those excluded—the poor—have no alternative but illegality. This is why the informal economy comes into being, as Hernando de Soto demonstrates with incontrovertible proof. To find out just what the "cost of legality" is in Peru, the Institute for Liberty and Democracy set up a fictitious clothing factory and went through the procedure—the bureaucratic maze—of establishing it legally. The institute decided to pay no bribes, except when not paying them would bring the entire process to a standstill.

On ten occasions bribes were solicited, but the institute was obliged to pay only twice. To register the imaginary factory took 289 days and required the full-time labor of the group assigned to the task, as well as $1,231 (including expenses and lost wages). At that time—summer 1983—the amount was the equivalent of 32 minimum monthly wages. This means that the process of legally registering a small industry is much too expensive for any person of modest means. It is certainly no coincidence that this is the kind of person who founds "informal" industries in Peru.

If setting up a legal shop is a costly and time-consuming task for the poor, it is even more expensive and difficult for them to obtain legal housing. The institute found out that if a group of low-income families petitioned the state to cede them a vacant lot on which they might build, they would have to work their way for six years and eleven months through ministries and municipal offices and spend approximately $2,156 (56 times the minimum monthly wage at the time) per person. Even to get a license to open a street kiosk or sell from a pushcart is a task of Kafkaesque proportions: forty-three days of commuting between bureaucrats and $590.56 (15 times the minimum monthly wage).

The statistics that accompany the study are devastating and bolster the institute's analyses with implacable logic. The kind of country we see in these numbers is tragic and absurd: tragic because the legal system seems designed to favor those already favored and to punish the rest by making them permanent outlaws; absurd because a system of this kind condemns itself to underdevelopment. It will never progress and will slowly drown in its own inefficiency and corruption.

The Other Path's description of the origins and extent of injustice in a Third World nation is pitiless, but it does not leave us demoralized and skeptical about a remedy for these problems. The informal economy—a parallel and in many ways more authentic, hardworking, and creative society than the one that hypocritically calls itself legitimate—appears in its pages as an escape hatch from underdevelopment. Many of the victims of underdevelopment have already begun to take advantage of it and are revolutionizing the nation's economy. Curiously enough, the vast majority of those who write and theorize about the backwardness and iniquity of life in the Third World do not seem to be aware of its existence.

All over Latin America, the poor have fled from the countryside to the cities. When these poor people, driven off the land by drought, flood, overpopulation, and the decline of agriculture, reached the city, they found that the system had already closed its doors to them. They had no money and no technical training. They had no hope of getting credit, no chance to obtain insurance, and could expect no protection from the police or the judicial system. They knew their businesses would always be threatened from all sides. All they had was their will, their imagination, and their desire to work.

To judge by the four areas studied by the Institute for Liberty and Democracy—business, manufacture, housing, and transportation—these entrepreneurs have not done badly. To begin with, they are infinitely more productive than the state. The statistics in *The Other Path* are shocking. In Lima alone, the black market (excluding manufacture) employs 439,000 people. Of the 331 markets in the city, 274 have been built by the black-marketeers (83 percent). It is no exaggeration to say that it is thanks to them the citizens of Lima are able to get around, because 95 percent of public transportation belongs to them. The black-marketeers have invested more than a billion dollars in vehicles and vehicle maintenance. As to housing, the figures are equally impressive. Half the population of Lima lives in houses built by black-marketeers. Between 1960 and 1984, the state constructed low-income housing at a cost of $173.6 million. During the same period, the black-marketeers managed to construct housing valued at the incredible figure of $8,319.8 million (47 times what the state spent). Economic freedom existed only on paper before the poor of our nations began to put it into practice independently.

These numbers speak eloquently of the productive energy that restrictive legality has pushed into the black market. But that vigor also reflects the true nature of the Third World state, which is almost always grotesquely caricatured. In this respect, Hernando de Soto offers some evidence that will shatter myths.

Underdevelopment and Mercantilism

One of the most widely accepted myths about Latin America is that its backwardness results from the erroneous philosophy of economic liberalism adopted in almost all our constitutions when we achieved independence from Spain and Portugal. This opening of our economies to the forces of the market made us easy prey for voracious imperialists and brought about internal inequities between rich and poor. Our societies became economically dependent (and unjust) because we chose the economic principle of laissez-faire.

Hernando de Soto attacks that fallacy head on and rebuts it. The institute's thesis is that Peru never had a market economy, and that it is only now, because of the black market, beginning to get one—a savage market economy, but a market economy nevertheless. This concept applies to all of Latin America and probably to the majority of Third World nations. Economic freedom is a principle emblazoned in our constitutions that has no more reality than the principle of political freedom, to which our politicians, especially our dictators, traditionally render hypocritical tribute. De Soto calls our economic system, which has been masquerading as a market economy for generations, mercantilist.

The term is confusing, since it defines a historical period, an economic school, and a moral attitude. Here, "mercantilism" means a bureaucratized and law-ridden state that regards the redistribution of national wealth as more important than the production of wealth. And "redistribution," as used here, means the concession of monopolies or favored status to a small elite that depends on the state and on which the state is itself dependent.

The state, in our world, has never been the expression of the people. The state is whatever government happens to be in power—liberal or conservative, democratic or tyrannical—and the government usually acts in accordance with the mercantilist model. That is, it enacts laws that favor small special-interest groups—the study calls them "redistributive combines"—and discriminates against the interests of the majority, which has marginal power or token legality. The names of the favored individuals or consortia change with each new government, but the system is always the same: not only does it concentrate the nation's wealth in a small minority but it also concedes to that minority the *right* to that wealth.

"The system" includes not only that hybrid monster I mentioned earlier—the state government—but also the entrepreneurs who work within the law. *The Other Path* does not pull any punches in its criticism of this entrepreneurial class which, instead of favoring an egalitarian and dynamic system in which the law would guarantee free competition and reward creativity, has adapted itself to the mercantile system and dedicated its best efforts to obtaining monopolies. Even today, when the comfortable house that class has been inhabiting for generations is falling down around it, it continues to view industrial activity as a sinecure instead of a way to create wealth.

This system is not only immoral but inefficient. Within it, success does not depend on inventiveness and hard work but on the entrepreneur's ability to gain the sympathy of presidents, ministers, and other public functionaries (which usually means his ability to corrupt them). In chapter 5, on the cost of legality and informality, Hernando de Soto reveals that, for the majority of formal or legal businesses, the single greatest expense, in both money and time, is bureaucratic maneuvers. This blights our economic life at its very roots.

Instead of favoring the production of new wealth, the system, owned, in effect, by the closed circle of those who benefit from it, discourages any such effort and prefers merely to recirculate an ever-diminishing amount of capital. In that context, the only kinds of activity that proliferate are nonproductive, parasitic activities—our elephantine bureaucracies. To justify their own existence, these monsters decree, for example, that in order to register a small-scale factory, a citizen has to fight for ten months through eleven different ministerial and municipal departments and, just to keep things moving, bribe at least two people. Is it any wonder that most Third World businesses are technologically backward and have tremendous difficulty competing in international markets?

At the same time that the mercantilist system condemns a society to economic impotence and stagnation, it imposes relations between citizens and between citizens and the state that reduce or eradicate the possibility of democratic politics. Mercantilism, as described by Hernando de Soto, is based on laws that mock the most elementary democratic practices.

The Legal Tangle

It is said that the number of laws and executive orders—decrees, ministerial resolutions, procedures, and so forth—in Peru exceeds half a million. This is only an approximate figure because, in point of fact, there is no way to determine the exact number. We live in a legal labyrinth in which even a Daedalus would get lost. This cancerous proliferation of laws reflects the bizarre ethical conditions that prevail in our legislative process. Laws work for special interests, not for the general interest. A logical consequence of this uncontrolled growth is that for every law there is another law that emends, attenuates, or negates it. In other words, anyone involved in this morass of legal contradictions, like it or not, is at some time or another breaking the law. By the same token, anyone deliberately breaking the law can find a law that will render his or her actions lawful.

Who legislates these laws and decrees? Hernando de Soto's study shows that only the tiniest number—1 percent—of our laws emanate from the body created to make them: the Parliament. The other 99 percent derive from the executive. That is, they flow from government departments that conceive them, draw them up, and have them promulgated—with no interference, no debate, no criticism, and often without even the knowledge of those affected by them. Laws presented in Parliament are publicly discussed, so it is conceivable that the media may inform the public about them and that their beneficiaries or victims may possibly influence their final form.

But this never happens with the majority of our laws. They are cooked up in bureaucratic kitchens (or in the private chambers of certain lawyers) in accordance with the dictates of the redistributive combine whose interests they serve. They are promulgated at such a rate that not only the ordinary citizen but even lawyers are unable to keep abreast of them and react appropriately.

Whenever a Third World nation returns to democracy, it holds more or less honest elections and permits freedom of the press. Political life takes shape and is carried on without too many impediments. But behind that facade, and particularly with regard to legal and economic life, democratic practices are conspicuously absent. The reality behind the facade is a discriminating, elitist system run by the smallest of minorities.

Black-marketeering is the masses' response to the system, which has traditionally made them victims of a kind of legal and economic apartheid. The system invents laws to frustrate the legitimate desires of the people to hold jobs and have a roof over their heads. What should the masses do?

Stop living, in the name of a legality which in many ways is unreal and unjust? No. They have simply renounced legality. They go out on the streets to sell whatever they can, they set up their shops, and they build their houses on the hillsides or in vacant lots. Where there are no jobs, they invent jobs, learning in the process all they were never taught. They turn their disadvantages into advantages, their ignorance into wisdom. In politics, they act in a purely pragmatic way: they turn their backs on fallen idols and hitch their wagon to any rising star. In Peru, they were behind General Odría when he was in power, behind Prado when he governed, with Belaunde when he ran things, and firm supporters of Velasco when that general was their leader. Now they are—simultaneously—Marxists with Mayor Barrantes and followers of the Popular Revolutionary American Alliance (APRA) with President Alan García.

Hernando de Soto's book shows clearly what they really are, despite these transitory, tactical alliances: men and women who through almost superhuman hard work and without the slightest help from the legal country (in fact, in the face of its declared hostility) have learned how to create more jobs and more wealth in the zones in which they have been able to function than the all-powerful state. They have often shown more daring, effort, imagination, and dedication to the country than their legal competitors. Thanks to them, our throngs of thieves and unemployed are not larger than they are. Thanks to them, there are not more hungry people wandering our streets. Our social problems are enormous, but without the black-marketeers our situation would be infinitely worse.

But what we should thank them for most is that they have shown us a practical and effective way of fighting against misfortune which belies the preachings of Third World ideologues who cling to their worthless doctrines with baffling tenacity. The path taken by the black-marketeers—the poor—is not the reinforcement and magnification of the state but a radical pruning and reduction of it. They do not want planned, regimented collectivization by monolithic governments; rather, they want the individual, private initiative and enterprise to be responsible for leading the battle against underdevelopment and poverty.

Who would have said it? If we listen to what these poor slum dwellers are telling us with their deeds, we hear nothing about what so many Third World revolutionaries are advocating in their name—violent revolution, state control of the economy. All we hear is a desire for genuine democracy and authentic liberty.

These are the ideas Hernando de Soto convincingly defends in *The Other Path*. The concept of liberty, in all its senses, has never been seriously applied in our countries. Only now, in the most unexpected way, through the spontaneous action of the poor, is it beginning to gain ground, showing itself to be a more sensible and effective solution than any undertaken by our conservatives and progressives as ways of overcoming underdevelopment. Extremists of both persuasions, despite their ideological differences, agree to the strengthening of the state and its interventionist practices, which does nothing but perpetuate the system of corruption, incompetence, and nepotism that is the recurring nightmare of the entire Third World.

Freedom as an Alternative

That freedom should be the alternative the poor choose in their struggle with the elite will probably surprise many. One of the most commonly accepted truisms of recent Latin American history is that liberal economic ideas are characteristic of military dictatorships. Didn't the "Chicago Boys" put them into practice with Pinochet in Chile and Martínez de Hoz in Argentina, with the catastrophic results we know so well? Didn't those politicos make the rich richer and the poor poorer in both countries? And didn't they precipitate both countries into unprecedented disasters from which they still have not recovered?

There is only one kind of liberty and it is obviously incompatible with authoritarian or totalitarian regimes. The economic liberalism they can bring about—or rather *impose* from above—will always be relative and will always be weighed down, as in Chile and Argentina, by a complementary lack of political freedom. But it is precisely political freedom that permits the evaluation, perfection, or rectification of any measure which does not work in practice. Economic freedom is the counterpart of political freedom, and only when the two are united—two sides of a single coin—can they really function.

No dictatorship can be really liberal in economic matters, because the basic principle of economic liberalism is that it is not the politically powerful but the independent and sovereign citizens who have the right to take action—to work and sacrifice—to decide in which kind of society they are going to live. The function of political power is to guarantee that all obey the rules of the game, so that action will be fairly and freely chosen. That requires a consensus, the support of the people who desire those principles, and it can take place only in a democracy.

Within liberalism, there exist extremist tendencies and dogmatic attitudes. They are usually expressed by those who refuse to change their ideas when those ideas fail the acid test of all political programs: reality. It is natural that, in a Third World country with huge economic inequities, no cultural cohesion, and tremendous social problems, like so many Latin American nations, the state has a redistributive function. Only when those huge differences have been reduced to reasonable proportions is it possible to talk about truly impartial rules of the game, identical for all. With the imbalances we have today between poor and rich, urbanites and peasants, Indians and those who live in the Western tradition, the best conceived and purest measures tend in practice to favor the few and harm the majority.

It is essential that the state remember that before it can redistribute the nation's wealth, the nation must produce wealth. And that in order to produce wealth, it is necessary that the state's actions not obstruct the actions of its citizens, who, after all, know better than anyone else what they want and what they have to do. The state must restore to its citizens the right to take on productive tasks, a right it has been usurping and obstructing. The state must limit itself to functioning in those necessary areas in which private industry cannot function. This does not mean that the state will wither away and die.

By the same token, a large government is not necessarily a strong state, as the majority of Latin American nations shows. Those immense organisms that in our countries drain the productive energies of society to maintain their own sterile existence are in fact giants with feet of clay. Their gigantism makes them torpid, and their inefficiency deprives them of the respect and authority without which no institution can function well.

The Other Path does not idealize the informal market—to the contrary. After showing their accomplishments, de Soto describes the limitations that living outside the law imposes on informal businesses: they cannot grow, they cannot plan for the future, they are vulnerable to theft, extortion, and any crisis. The report also shows the desire for legality that many of the actions of the black-marketeers betray: the street vendor's desire to get a stall in a market, the neighborhood group that improves sanitary and aesthetic conditions as soon as it gains legal title to its homes. But the study, even though it does not embellish or overvalue the informal economy, does allow us a glimpse of the black-marketeers' spirit and imagination. It shows us what might be hoped for if all that productive energy could be put into practice legally in an authentic market economy in a government which, instead of harassing the black-marketeers, would protect and stimulate them.

By calling this book *The Other Path*, Hernando de Soto challenges

the movement that sprang up in the Andes in 1980 and proclaimed a
Maoist utopia. It counters that program with a social project which,
although totally contrary to Marxist-Leninist fundamentalism, requires a
transformation of society no less radical than the one demanded by the
Shining Path. It means uprooting an ancient tradition which, through
the inertia, greed, and blindness of a political elite, has blended with the
institutions, customs, and traditions of the official nation. But the
revolution this study analyzes and defends is in no way utopian. It is
already under way, made a reality by an army of the current system's
victims, who have revolted out of a desire to work and have a place to live
and who, in doing so, have discovered the benefits of freedom.

Mario Vargas Llosa
Translated by Alfred J. McAdam
London, August 1988

Preface

The methods and research which went to make up this book evolved from my doubt about at least three fairly widespread assumptions concerning the situation in Peru.

The first assumption is that informality—slums and shantytowns, small industry and, in general, many activities which Peruvians carry on illegally—represents only poverty and marginalization.

The second assumption is that Peruvian culture, that which we associate with Peru's rural areas—*el Perú profundo* or "the unknown Peru"—is incompatible with the entrepreneurial spirit and economic systems of the world's more advanced countries.

The third assumption is that all the evils which assail Latin America are generally not our fault but almost always the result of some external force.

In other words, from the very outset I questioned the positions of those schools of thought which claim that, in Latin America, the poor are so poor, income differences are so great, foreign exploitation is so perverse, and the legacy we have inherited is so different from that of the advanced countries, because the mechanisms and institutions which have permitted development in other parts of the world are unable to function in our societies.

I was convinced that no serious research could be conducted on the basis of the prejudices, which no one had been able to substantiate fully and which instead reflected an inability to understand or appreciate Peruvians' true potentialities.

I did not start out by trying to separate the "good guys" from the "bad guys" in order to conveniently attribute everything good to the former and blame everything bad on the latter. Any society, like any individual, has its good and bad sides. The interesting thing, rather, was to see whether the incentives offered by our society encouraged the bad to the detriment of the good.

My aim, therefore, was to gain a picture of informality in Peru which was based on reality and on the actual experience of those engaged in informal activities. This drew my attention to certain types of information and certain methods of obtaining and analyzing the relevant data. It also demonstrated the importance which my informants, advisors, and colleagues were to have. With this in mind, the research was conducted as an ongoing process of analysis, testing of assumptions, and further analysis—described in greater detail in the "Technical and Statistical Compendium to *The Other Path*"—until, by a gradual process of refinement, we arrived at the observations and conclusions described in this book.

I would never have embarked on this task were it not for Mario Vargas Llosa: it was he who suggested that it take the form of a book, challenged me to do it, and gave me constant encouragement. It is he who is definitely to blame for everything.

Between 1979, when I began my frequent personal contacts with informal business owners and workers, and 1982, when I began to write the book, I used my spare time to conduct on-the-spot interviews and observations. As I gathered more information and began to grasp the significance of the phenomenon I was studying, I realized that I needed a team if I was going to make a thorough study, not only because the subject was too vast for one person to handle but, above all, because I needed the assistance of professionals in various disciplines to perform the proper research and analysis. An interdisciplinary approach was needed—the surveying techniques of anthropologists; the analyses, theories, and reasoning of lawyers and economists; the interdependent research systems which are the province of project engineers; and the writer's knack of saying things in a way that everyone can understand.

My contribution was that of the businessman: I set my goals, identified my limitations, and obtained the resources to achieve the first and offset the second. First, I organized two symposiums and used the profits to finance the first studies and prepare proposals to foundations. Then, once I had obtained funding, I did what I have always considered my strong points: I recruited the magnificent team which today is the Instituto Libertad y Democracia (ILD) and contacted excellent advisors. All of them are the real authors of this book.

Manuel Mayorga La Torre was the most important figure in this whole task. As general manager of the ILD, and with a background as a project director, he organized all the teams and saw to it that they produced results. In particular, he took charge of obtaining data, processing them on computers, and preparing them for analysis. He also took charge of handling all the institute's operations, giving me the time I needed to devote myself increasingly to the book, above all from 1985 onward. I sometimes believe him when he says that there is no big difference between directing the construction of an electric power station and directing the ILD's activities.

Luis Morales Bayro conducted most of the economic research and, in particular, the cost-benefit analyses on which this book is based. His energy, imagination, and competence as the head of our economic department were invaluable to the book and provided the technical basis for the "Technical and Statistical Compendium to *The Other Path*." I should also mention the special contributions made by the distinguished economists Jorge Fernández Baca, Keta Ruiz, Fernando Chávez, and César Burga.

In the actual writing of the book, my closest collaborator was Enrique Ghersi Silva, a brilliant twenty-five-year-old lawyer who began to work with me more than four years ago. Enrique is a self-taught expert in the logic of economic reasoning. All my ideas were discussed with him before being written down. He is my fiercest and most outspoken critic. He also has a view of things, an educational background, and a capacity for research and analysis so special and enriching that this book would not be the same without his contribution. I am sure that Peru will come to know him better and confirm his merits.

My second collaborator was Mario Ghibellini, a young man of twenty-six. He is a man of letters, the winner of a number of literary prizes, and the writer of successful television screenplays. He is not only an artist but also an ideal team player, flexible and with a unique ability for conveying meaning with a minimum of words and technical jargon. There is no sentence in the book which he did not revise, reshape, or approve.

Nelly Arakaki organized our work as no one else could have, and efficiently and patiently took charge of typing successive versions and filing hundreds of documents. I think she must be the best administrative assistant in the world.

Daniel Herencia and his team took charge of the computing, verifying the accuracy of figures and methods of calculation. María Murillo, Mariano Cornejo, Alberto Bustamante, and their colleagues and advisors designed many of the concepts used in the sections on housing and in the section "An Agenda for Change" in chapter 8. Iván Alonso continued and developed the research on street vendors and discovered

Lima's informal markets. Orlando Eyzaguirre and his group of surveyors conducted polls and gathered valuable data in informal settlements.

All the publications produced by the ILD, including this book, were reviewed and corrected by Roberto MacLean Ugarteche, Renato Vázquez Costa, Alberto Bustamante, and Franco Giuffra. I have the salutary habit of consulting them about my ideas because they know how to evaluate them. Franco edited the final version of the book with me.

Dozens of people who do not belong to the ILD also gave us the benefit of their valuable knowledge. It would be inappropriate to mention them all here by name, or our hundreds of informants: because of their ties with informality or the state authorities, many would prefer not to be mentioned. However, I can and should mention the special contributions made by Carlos Ferrero, Ruben Cáceres Zapata, José Yi Li, Ricardo Talavera Campos, Lucrecia Maisch Von Humboldt, Alfredo Cossi Bunsen, Victor Carrasco, Tomás Unger, Carlos Aramburú, Folke Kafka, Luis Pásara, Reynaldo Susano, Fernando Iwasaki, Victor Montero, Jaime Robles, Luis Oliveros, Angel Rivera Marca, Jesús Elías, Eduardo de Rivero, Juan Carlos Tafur, Elio Távara, and Raúl Saco.

A number of foreign professionals also contributed to the book by giving advice or writing memoranda on specific subjects. I should particularly like to mention anthropologist Douglas Uzzell of the Social Science Consortium, who taught me what little I know about anthropology and launched our field work, and Warren Schwartz of Georgetown University, who did the most to instruct us all in law and economics. Robert Litan of the Brookings Institution and Saul Levmore of the University of Virginia also worked with us in this area, as did Paul Rubin of the City University of New York. Our main advisor in estimating the magnitude of the informal economy and the legal system's effect on it was Michael Block of the University of Arizona, while the work done by Steven Salop of Georgetown University and Pete Reuter of the Rand Corporation was particularly useful in determining the costs of informality.

Douglass C. North of Washington University in St. Louis, Joe Reid and Gordon Tullock of George Mason University, and Francisco Cabrillo of the Universidad Complutense de Madrid answered questionnaires which gave us a better understanding of the history of mercantilism.

I should like to extend my thanks and gratitude to all my colleagues, advisors, and informants without whom this book would not have been possible. At the same time, I should like to make it clear that I alone am responsible for its contents. Despite the extremely valuable technical support they gave me, I cannot implicate them in the authorship of a book which, to a large extent, contains a personal political message.

I do not think it presumptuous to make a recommendation to my readers: although this book will be controversial because it proposes an end to the status quo—and the status quo suits a lot of people—I do not want it to be viewed as unnecessarily aggressive. First, its explicit aim is to substitute, for change that is left to chance, a peaceful and deliberate alternative. Nor is it an attack on public officials; it has never been my intention to belittle the efforts which many of them make to improve the country's situation honestly and honorably. Last, I am not trying to label other business people "mercantilists": in a mercantilist society, all of us who do business—and I include myself—are forced to behave like mercantilists in one way or another. It will be very clear that what I am criticizing is not people but the system.

What is the purpose of this book and why did I write it? A single answer suffices. I wrote it because I want a free and prosperous society in which people's intelligence and energies are used for productive purposes and to bring about beneficial political changes, and because I refuse to accept a society in which effort is wasted on obtaining legal privileges and in which an arbitrary state fiercely punishes us for our hopes. These are the obstacles that block the path to liberation.

PART
ONE

Introduction

In the period since the Second World War, Peru has undergone the most far-reaching change in its history as a republic. This change has not been an isolated or planned event, but a succession of millions of incidents which have gradually transformed a seemingly immutable order.

Peru's cities have ceased to be small familiar places and become impersonal, heavily populated metropolises with new, unfamiliar neighborhoods.

In the past forty years, indigenous migration has quintupled the urban population and forced cities to reorganize. New activities have emerged and gradually replaced traditional ones. Modest homes cramped together on city perimeters, a myriad of workshops in their midst, armies of vendors hawking their wares on the streets, and countless minibus lines crisscrossing them—all seem to have sprung from nowhere, pushing the city's boundaries ever outward. Daily, a medley of smoke and odors from the fried food cooking on the streets blends with strains of Andean music. A steady stream of small craftsworkers, tools under their arms, expand the range of activities carried out in the city. Ingenious local adaptations add to the production of essential goods and services, dramatically transforming certain areas of manufacturing, retail distribution, building, and transportation. The surrounding desert and hills have ceased to be a passive landscape and themselves become part of the city, and the city's European style has yielded to a noisy, tawny-skinned personality.

But the cities have also conferred individuality on their inhabitants. Individual effort has come to predominate over collective effort. New business owners have emerged who, unlike their predecessors, are of popular origin. Upward mobility has increased. The patterns of consumption and exclusive luxuries of the old urban society have been displaced by other, more widespread, ones. In entertainment, for instance, opera, theater, and zarzuela have been replaced over the years by the cinema, soccer, folk festivals and, most recently, television. Likewise, consumer goods such as beer, rice, and table salt have been brought within everyone's reach, while consumption of the more expensive items, such as wine and meat, has declined over the decades.

There have been significant changes in the Peruvians' religious habits, too. Catholicism, identified with the traditional order, has lost ground to newer religious movements such as Protestantism, the Charismatics and, more recently, such vernacular and syncretic expressions as the Asociación Evangélica de la Misión Israelita del Neuvo Pacto Universal. Popular saints like la Melchorita or Sarita Colonia, who are not recognized by the Church, are replacing Santa Rosa de Lima and other traditional saints in local devotions.

The result is a new cultural identity which needs to be portrayed in social terms. The emergence of *chicha* music, which is replacing Andean folk music and Creole music, and the success of certain forms of communication—radio programs and television soap operas which refer to or reflect definite elements of this new identity—are clear examples of this change. Society pages and television programs devoted to the life-style of the upper classes have gradually disappeared, and crime series and programs featuring popular entertainment, which the nostalgic dismiss as vulgar, are now preferred viewing.

People have also begun to invest more in their education. The proportion of students of popular origin in secondary schools and schools of higher education has increased significantly, and in the former mansions of the aristocracy all kinds of academies and institutes offer cheap, practical training in an endless variety of subjects.

The upper classes have discovered that they must henceforth rub shoulders with people of popular origin in restaurants and airplanes, on beaches, on boards of directors, and even in the government. Many of them have chosen to retreat into their own, steadily shrinking, world and console themselves with memories of a bygone age. There are those who entrench themselves in exclusive residential neighborhoods, frequent clubs where time seems to have stood still, drive whenever possible only on tree-lined avenues, and preserve customs which consign them to de facto social and racial segregation.

New organizations have emerged in an attempt to restore or reformulate some of the values and attachments that were being lost. Over the years, regional, church, and sports clubs, neighborhood committees, street vendors' associations, and even transport operators' committees have tried to secure the well-being of their members. In the cities, the extended family has been transformed into a network of commercial or productive relations: economic activities conducted among "cousins" and "uncles" are now commonplace.

As the economic activities with which they are associated have grown, these organizations have also begun to play a dominant role in relation to the state. Thus, the provision of such basic infrastructures as roads, water supply, sewage systems, and electricity, the construction of markets, the provision of transport services, and even the administration of justice and the maintenance of law and order have, to varying degrees, ceased to be the exclusive responsibility of the state and are now also offered by these new organizations. And as the state's role has diminished, so too has that of traditional society. With new organizations gardually gaining ascendancy, the old unions have lost ground and membership in trade unions has dropped steadily, today accounting for only 4.8 percent of the economically active population.

What is disturbing is that only part of the ground relinquished by the state has been occupied by these new organizations. The rest appears to have been taken over by violence. Attacks, kidnappings, rapes, and murders have coincided with increasingly aggressive driving habits and unsafe streets. The police have gradually lost control of the situation and some of their members have been involved in scandals and become seasoned criminals. Overcrowding and promiscuity in the prisons foster bloodshed and increased criminality which spreads throughout the city when prisoners escape, sometimes with the complicity of their guards. The resulting violence has forced people to defend themselves as best they can: all kinds of weapons, including machine guns and automatic shotguns, watchmen in various uniforms, and even inscrutable bodyguards, are now commonplace. With each day that passes, we come closer to resembling the offensive movie stereotype of the banana republic.

People have gradually grown used to living outside the law. Theft, illegal seizure, and factory takeovers have become everyday occurrences and do not greatly disturb people's consciences. Thanks to constant whitewashing, some criminals have become public figures.

A complete subversion of means and ends has turned the life of Peruvian society upside down, to the point that there are acts which, although officially criminal, are no longer condemned by the collective consciousness. Smuggling is a case in point. Everyone, from the aristo-cratic lady to the humblest man, acquires smuggled goods. No one has any scruples about it; on the contrary, it is viewed as a kind of challenge to individual ingenuity or as revenge against the state.

This infiltration of violence and criminality into everyday life has been accompanied by increasing poverty and deprivation. In general terms, Peruvians' real average income had declined steadily over the last ten years and is now at the level of twenty years ago. Mountains of garbage pile up on all sides. Night and day, legions of beggars, car washers, and scavengers besiege passersby, asking for money. The mentally ill swarm naked in the streets, stinking of urine. Children, single mothers, and cripples beg for alms on every street corner.

Civilian interest in public matters has also begun to grow. Such issues as inflation, devaluation, and the external debt are no longer mysteries to which certain members of the elite hold the key, but have become topics of discussion on which everyone has something to say. Governments must now submit their actions to public opinion and the public's acceptance or rejection has become a political force which can affect government stability.

Certain new attitudes toward the state have emerged. The bureaucracy has lost social standing. Citizens have resigned themselves to the fact that they must corrupt public officials if they want their needs to be satisfied. The traditional centralism of our society has proved clearly incapable of satisfying the manifold needs of a country in transition. The inefficiency of the law courts has given rise to a growing disenchantment with, and loss of confidence in, law-enforcement mechanisms. This in turn has led to increasing dissatisfaction with the status quo, which, coinciding with a gradual increase in new activities, has steadily reduced the state's social relevance.

In this situation, more Peruvians have learned to negotiate with the state for all manner of privileges which will enable them to overcome their difficulties, something which has led to an increasing politicization of our society. Small interest groups fight among themselves, cause bankruptcies, implicate public officials. Governments hand out privileges. The law is used to give and take away far more than morality permits. Many media of information are dependent on state assistance or state banks and therefore bow to the powers-that-be, surrendering their ability to denounce abuses or even describe events objectively. Increasingly, more than one source of information is needed to obtain a true idea of the facts.

This state of affairs has brought about a sharp change of attitude toward society. Terrorism has emerged as a violent alternative to the present situation, but a new attitude to things Peruvian has also emerged. It is as though the country's intelligentsia were seeking refuge in the idyllic innocence of the Andean people, a people uncorrupted by all this decadence. The terrorist movement itself proposes to wage "popular warfare from the countryside to the cities," as if the regenerative force for change has to come from Peru's inner depths.

Things have changed in Peru. Although life goes on as it has for centuries in some parts of the country, it is in the cities that today's history is being written. It is there, rather than in the countryside, that we must look for the meaning of, or the answer to, the changes that have taken place. The present has finally prevailed. Nothing will be as it was; the past will not return.

Migration

All these changes began when the population of self-reliant farming communities began to move to the cities, reversing the long historical trend that had kept them in isolation. As we have already seen, between 1940 and 1981 Peru's urban population increased almost fivefold (from 2.4 to 11.6 million), while its rural population increased barely a third (from 4.7 to 6.2 million). Thus, while 65 percent of the population lived in rural areas and 35 percent in urban areas in 1940, these percentages had been reversed by 1981. To put it more simply, in 1940, two of every three Peruvians lived in the countryside, but by 1981 two of every three lived in the city.

If we consider that, in 1700, the rural population was 85 percent of the total population and the urban population accounted for only 15 percent, and that, by 1876, the population living in rural areas still accounted for 80 percent as against 20 percent in the cities, the dramatic change of the last forty years becomes even more striking. The historical predominance of the rural population has been reversed in favor of the urban population, housing conditions have altered dramatically, and the transition has been made from an agricultural to an urban civilization.

Generally speaking, Peru's urbanization dates back to the mass migrations from the countryside to the city, which began to be recorded in the national statistics in 1940 but actually started a little earlier. This urbanization coincided with a rapid growth of the population throughout the country. Growth had hitherto been fairly slow. While not entirely accurate, the national censuses of the last two centuries reveal an average growth of 0.6 percent. In this century, on the other hand, the total population grew more than two-and-a-half times between 1940 and 1981, from 7 million to almost 18 million.

The increase was substantially greater in Lima. The population of the capital city multiplied by 7.6 times during this period. In 1940, it housed 8.6 percent of the country's population; it now contains 26 percent. The number of migrants to Lima increased 6.3 times over, from 300,000 to 1,900,000, between 1940 and 1981.

The numerical impact of migration on the growth of the capital city was greater than the actual number of migrants, however, since the fertility rate was higher among migrant women than among city-born women, and their children's mortality rates were lower than they would have been in the countryside. This can be illustrated by an example: in 1981, Lima would have had a population of only 1,445,000, instead of the 4 million recorded by the census, if there had been no migration after 1940. Or, to put it another way: in 1981, two-thirds of Lima's population were migrants or children of migrants, while the remaining third were actual natives of the city. Migration is thus a key factor in explaining the changes that have occurred. But we still have to explain why these migrations took place. Like most social phenomena, it has many causes.

The most visible one is the building of highways. After the War of the Pacific a century ago, a complete reorganization of Peru was undertaken, which included providing the country with a highway system instead of improving railways or coastal facilities that had been the traditional modes of transport. At the beginning of this century, Peru had only 2,500 miles of highway; by 1981, it had roughly 37,500 miles. In the intervening period, the Highways Conscription Act, adopted in 1920, and plans for a national highway, among other policies, transformed the unconnected roads built over old Inca and colonial paths into a proper highway system that became the material base essential for mass migration and which also awoke, in the rural population, an increasing desire to move to the cities.

The subsequent development of other means of communication provided an additional incentive for increased migration. By publicizing, from thousands of miles away, the opportunities, amenities, and comforts of urban life, radio in particular aroused all kinds of enthusiastic reactions—above all, expectations of increased consumption and income.

Civilization was, so to speak, being offered to anyone with the courage to take it.

There is also fairly widespread agreement in academic circles that the agricultural crisis of 1940 to 1945 was another decisive factor. The modernization of agriculture and the uncertain market for sugar and cotton following the Second World War triggered massive layoffs of farm laborers on the traditional mountain estates and the large industrialized farms of the coast, unleashing a vast contingent of people who were prepared to leave in search of new horizons.

The impact of the agricultural crisis on migration can also be traced to the problem of property rights in the countryside.[1] The traditional difficulties of acquiring agricultural land were compounded—and ultimately exacerbated—when, in the 1950s, there began what would prove to be a long, continuous, and unstable process of agrarian reform. Unable to own land or find work in the countryside, many people chose to migrate to the cities in an attempt to acquire the property hitherto denied them and thereby satisfy some of their material aspirations.

The lower infant mortality rate in Lima was also a powerful incentive to leave the countryside. Over the decades, mortality rates had always been lower in the capital city than in the rest of the country. While in 1940 the national infant mortality rate was 181 per 1,000 children, Lima's rate was 160. This gap widened as medical services expanded; by 1981, the national infant mortality rate was 98 per 1,000, while in Lima it was 44. This incentive to migrate thus increased with time.

Better wages were also an important incentive. By 1970, people leaving the countryside to take up semiskilled employment in Lima could, on average, triple their monthly income. Salary earners could quadruple their previous income, and professionals or technicians could earn six times as much. Higher pay offset the risk of unemployment: an average migrant who had been unemployed for a year could recoup the lost income by working for two and a half months in the city. A migrant unemployed for two years could recoup the lost income in a little over four months, and so on.

Last, but not least, the growth of the government bureaucracy and the possibility of obtaining a better education were also powerful incentives for moving to the city. The centralization of redistributive power, the feeling

[1] Throughout this book, we shall use the concept of property rights in a broader economic sense than it normally has in Peruvian law. By "property rights," we mean those rights, personal or real, which confer on their holders inalienable and exclusive entitlement to them. For a fuller explanation, see "The Cost of Not Having Property Rights" in chapter 5.

of being close to political decision making, the urban location of most of the government offices competent to provide advice, answer requests, or issue permits, and the possibility of finding employment in its ranks, turned the burgeoning government bureaucracy into an added incentive for abandoning rural life.

And, until recently, 45 percent of secondary school graduates, 49 percent of students enrolled in vocational training centers, 46 percent of those enrolled in schools and institutes of higher education, and 62 percent and 55 percent, respectively, of university applicants and entrants were to be found in Lima. To peasants whose only capital is themselves, education seems a valuable and productive investment.

These concurrent facts suggest that migration was not an irrational act undertaken on a whim or out of a herd instinct, but rather the result of a rational assessment by the rural population of the opportunities open to them. No matter how rightly or wrongly, they made their decisions in the belief that migration would benefit them.

A Hostile Reception

When they arrived in the cities, however, migrants encountered a hostile world. They soon realized that, while formal society had a bucolic vision of Peru's rural world and acknowledged its right to happiness, no one wanted that other world to descend on the cities. Assistance and development programs for rural areas were designed to ensure that the peasants improved their lot where they were, well away from the cities. Civilization was expected to go to the countryside; the peasants were not expected to come looking for it.

The hostility was extreme. In the 1930s, a ban was imposed on the construction of cheap apartments in Lima. There are those who recall that, in the early 1940s, President Manuel Prado considered a curious proposal for "improving the race" which involved encouraging the migration of Scandinavians to the country's cities. In the 1946 legislature, the senator for Junín, Manuel Faura, presented a bill that would have prohibited people from the provinces, particularly from the mountains, from entering Lima. In the next legislature, Representative Salomón Sánchez Burga submitted a request, with the House's approval, which would have required people wishing to enter the capital from the provinces to carry an entry passport. All these proposals failed, but they show that, even then, there was a clear desire to deny migrants access to the city.

Nor was it strange that these politicians should react thus. From their beginnings, Peru's cities had been administrative and religious centers whose mission was to bring order to a wild and rustic land. Cities represented the cosmos in the midst of chaos. As a result, their latter-day inhabitants, heirs to the old Andean and Spanish tradition, could not react with anything but horror to the migration from the countryside, for chaos was finally invading their cosmos. Moreover, each person who migrates to the capital is in some way a potential competitor and it is natural inclination to try to avoid competition.

However, the greatest hostility the migrants encountered was from the legal system. Up to then, the system had been able to absorb or ignore the migrants because the small groups who came were hardly likely to upset the status quo. As the number of migrants grew, however, the system could no longer remain disinterested. When large groups of migrants reached the cities, they found themselves barred from legally established social and economic activities. It was tremendously difficult for them to acquire access to housing and an education and, above all, enter business or find a job. Quite simply, Peru's legal institutions had been developed over the years to meet the needs and bolster the privileges of certain dominant groups in the cities and to isolate the peasants geographically in rural areas. As long as this system worked, the implicit legal discrimination was not apparent. Once the peasants settled in the cities, however, the law began to lose social relevance.

The migrants discovered that their numbers were considerable, that the system was not prepared to accept them, that more and more barriers were being erected against them, that they had to fight to extract every right from an unwilling establishment, that they were excluded from the facilities and benefits offered by the law, and that, ultimately, the only guarantee of their freedom and prosperity lay in their own hands. In short, they discovered that they must compete not only against people but also against the system.

From Migrants to Informals

Thus it was, that in order to survive, the migrants became informals. If they were to live, trade, manufacture, transport, or even consume, the cities' new inhabitants had to do so illegally. Such illegality was not antisocial in intent, like trafficking in drugs, theft, or abduction, but was designed to achieve such essentially legal objectives as building a house, providing a service, or developing a business. As we shall see later, it is more than likely that, economically speaking, the people directly involved in these activities (as well as society in general) are better off when they violate the laws than when they respect them. We can say that informal activities burgeon when the legal system imposes rules which exceed the socially accepted legal framework—does not honor the expectations, choices, and preferences of those whom it does not admit within its framework—and when the state does not have sufficient coercive authority.

The concept of informality used in this book is based on empirical observation of the phenomenon itself. Individuals are not informal; their actions and activities are. Nor do those who operate informally comprise a precise or static sector of society; they live within a gray area which has a long frontier with the legal world and in which individuals take refuge when the cost of obeying the law outweighs the benefit. Only rarely does informality mean breaking *all* the laws; most individuals disobey specific legal provisions in a way that we shall describe later. There are activities for which the state has created an exceptional legal system through which informals can pursue their activities, although without necessarily acquiring a legal status equivalent to that of the people who enjoy the protection and benefits of the entire Peruvian legal system; these are also informal activities.

This is a book which tells the story of the migrants who have become informals during the past forty years and which attempts to show why we have come to be a country in which 48 percent of the economically active population and 61.2 percent of work hours are devoted to informal activities which contribute 38.9 percent of the gross domestic product (GDP) recorded in the national accounts. It is a book which tries to explain the reasons and the prospects for the change which is taking place in Peru by analyzing the vanguard of this change, the informals. It also tries to explain why our legal institutions have been unable to adapt to this change, with the result that, despite an average productivity equivalent to only a third of that of the formal sector, informal economic activity will continue to grow and by the year 2000 can be expected to generate 61.3 percent of the GDP recorded in the national accounts. It also shows how the new institutions developed by the informals provide a coherent alternative on which a different order, open to all Peruvians, can be based. It is also, of course, a book which proposes solutions.

In the first part of the book, consisting of this chapter and the three that follow, we describe the world which we gradually discovered in the past six years as we visited, in turn, informals and their formal counterparts. On the basis of these observations and the findings of other researchers, we describe how, in three specific sectors—housing, transport, and trade—where the Instituto Libertad y Democracia (ILD) has been able to complete its research, the informals have won a space for themselves and are gradually taking over most of the market, appropriating land on which to live and produce, setting up on the streets as vendors in order to work, or invading the cities' main thoroughfares in order to provide transport services. In all these cases they have openly disobeyed the law and defied institutions, creating a breach through which the rest of society is also deserting the formal sector. As the informals have advanced, the Peruvian state has fallen back, viewing each concession as temporary, "until the crisis is over," when in fact it is being forced to adopt a strategy of steady retreat, a retreat that is gradually undermining its social relevance.

The first part of this book describes how *el Perú profundo*, "the unknown Peru," began a long and sustained battle to integrate itself into formal life, a battle so gradual that its effects are only just beginning to be seen. We appear to be witnessing the most important rebellion against the status quo ever waged in the history of independent Peru.

The early chapters are devoted to Lima. In the first chapter, we show how, through invasions or illegal acquisitions of land, neighborhoods sprang up which today account for 42.6 percent of all housing in Lima and are home to 47 percent of the city's population. Such housing, built by illegal settlers at a cost of years of sacrifice, is today valued at $8,319.8 million. It demonstrates only part of the informals' tremendous ability to generate wealth.

In the second chapter, we describe how Lima's 91,455 street vendors dominate the retail distribution of popular consumer goods in the capital and how they maintain a little over 314,000 relatives and dependents. In addition, in order to move off the streets, and in the face of countless restrictions, 39,000 other vendors have managed to build or acquire 274 informal markets valued at $40.9 million.

In the third chapter we show how, by invading routes, informals have managed to gain control of 93 percent of the urban transport fleet, and 80 percent of its seats. We also describe how these informals spontaneously designed the transport routes which now serve Lima.

The first part of this book contains other information as well. We describe how the informals, rather than surrender to anarchy, developed their own laws and institutions, which we call the "system of extralegal norms," to make up for the shortcomings of the official legal system. They created an alternative order to that of the formal sector. We also recount the epic struggle waged by the informals in recent decades, their confrontations and alliances with the state, their relationships with politicians, and their incorporation into the landscape of our city.

Lastly, in these chapters we analyze how the informals have converted invasion into an alternative means of expressing the value of things and how their apparently superficial decisions are based on a fairly complex rationale. In short, in these chapters we try to explain the logic implicit in the functioning of informality.

The second part of the book is an analytical exercise which shows how the different costs in our society are a result of the way the law is conceived and made, as if wealth were a stock whose shares are to be redistributed by the state to different pressure groups. This way of governing suggests a significant historical parallel with mercantilism, the system which guided European economic and social policies from the fifteenth to the nineteenth century.

The most difficult pages in this part of the book are those devoted to identifying, measuring, and classifying existing costs. They describe the costs of enjoying the protection of the law and the way in which these costs affect people's access to and ability to remain in different economic activities. They also describe the costs and losses to the country when people do not enjoy the protection of this law. These pages thus show the importance of legal institutions in explaining the poverty and violence, the new cultural trends, informality, and the retreat of the state—in other words, in explaining the changes in our society.

Chapters 6 and 7, on the redistributive tradition and mercantilism, enable us to present one of the key arguments of this book, namely, that mercantilism—and not feudalism or the market economy—constituted Peru's economic and social system after the arrival of the Spaniards. The emergence of a growing and thriving informality is a revolt against mercantilism and is hastening its ultimate demise. In the final chapter, we offer some conclusions about Peru's future and possible ways to solve its present crisis.

It will be easy to judge the accuracy of the account given in the pages that follow, for everything happened as we were observing it. There is nothing in this book that needs to be confirmed by complex laboratory experiments. You have only to open the window or step into the street.

Nonetheless, since we lack the distance in time to judge fully what has happened, this book cannot be called a scientific history. It is a political book which is based on evidence and will doubtless need to be rewritten some years from now. But this does not make it any less a book which seeks to offer guidance and, above all, to show that there is hope amidst all the apparent disaster, a hope based on the creativity and energy of Peruvians who have yet to find an appropriate legal and institutional framework for their development.

CHAPTER TWO

Informal Housing

In the last four decades, Lima's urban area has grown by 1,200 percent. While this is amazing, what is even more so is that this tremendous growth has been essentially informal. People have in fact acquired, developed, and built their neighborhoods outside of or in defiance of state laws, by setting up informal settlements.[1]

In the course of time, some of these settlements have come to be governed by an exceptional legal system which can be regarded as the authorities' improvised response to the problem, with the result that, while residents may receive title to the land—but not ownership of the buildings—they are also subject, for a period of time, to a number of limitations of the exercise of their rights. Some settlements have been created by political decision of the government, but their subsequent development has not differed significantly from the rest, except in that they have perhaps been less successful.

In informal settlements, the various stages of traditional urban development are reversed. First, the informals occupy the land, then they build on it, next they install infrastructures, and only at the end do they acquire ownership. This is exactly the reverse of what happens in the formal world, which is why such settlements evolve differently from traditional urban areas and give the impression of being permanently under construction.

---

[1] By "informal settlements" we mean all those settled areas which in Peru are known variously as neighborhoods, marginal neighborhoods, similar areas, publicly owned popular urban developments (UPIS), reception areas, shelters, young towns, marginal human settlements, municipal human settlements, associations, and cooperatives.

Having said this, we must point out that of all the housing in Lima in 1982, 42.6 percent were in informal settlements, 49.2 percent in formal neighborhoods, and the remaining 8.2 percent in slum areas within these neighborhoods. This means that, for every ten formal dwellings in the capital city, there are nine informal ones. Of the capital city's total population in 1982, 47 percent lived in informal settlements, 45.7 percent in formal neighborhoods, and the remaining 7.3 percent in slum areas. There are districts like Comas, Independencia, San Juan de Miraflores, and Villa María del Triunfo, which are almost completely informal, and others like Carabayllo, El Agustino, San Juan de Lurigancho, and San Martín de Porres, which are largely informal.

Today, Lima's landowners are no longer just the traditional families living in comfortable, ornate residences, but also migrants and their descendants, who have taken by storm a city which denied them access and have had to violate the law in order to build homes and develop neighborhoods.

Lima's newest residents have also created considerable wealth over the years by causing land values to rise and investing in the building of their own homes, thereby dispelling a myth fairly widespread, even in the country's supposedly more progressive circles, that Peruvians of humble origin are incapable of satisfying their own material needs and must be provided for, guided, and controlled by the state. According to the assessment made by researchers for the Instituto Libertad y Democracia (ILD)—on a house-by-house basis, using replacement cost as of June 1984—the average value of an informal dwelling was $22,038 and the total value of the buildings located in Lima's informal settlements came to $8,319.8 million, an amount equivalent to 69 percent of Peru's total long-term external debt in that same year.

One way of assessing the importance of this investment is to compare it with the state's efforts. In the same period in which the investment was made—roughly between 1960 and 1984—the state also built housing for settlers whose socio-economic characteristics were similar to those of the informals. The state's investment in housing amounted to $173.6 million, a mere 2.1 percent of the informal investment. Total public investment in housing as of 1984, including investments in middle-class housing (some $862.2 million), came to only 10.4 percent of the informal investments.

In order for informals to build, outside the law, neighborhoods that housed approximately 47 percent of Lima's population, accounted for 42.6 percent of its dwellings, and had a value of $8,319.8 million, however, first formality had to decline and informality gather strength until it was able to create an alternative system of urban development. In the pages that follow, we shall try to explain this process. We shall begin by describing how the informal acquisition of property takes place, in order to identify the extralegal norms to which it is subject and the logic implicit in its functioning. We shall then describe the development of informal settlements and the steady defeat of formality, which has been gradually losing ground. Last, we shall describe how informality has ultimately succeeded in establishing a new system of property rights to land.

The Informal Acquisition of Property

In the course of its research, the ILD found no evidence to bear out the charge that life in informal settlements is anarchic and disorganized. On the contrary, it found a set of extralegal norms which did, to some extent, regulate social relations, offsetting the absence of legal protection and gradually winning stability and security for acquired rights.

These rules are what the ILD has termed the "system of extralegal norms." Consisting essentially of informal customary law and of rules borrowed from the official legal system when these are of use to informals, the system of extralegal norms is called on to govern life in the informal settlements when the law is absent or deficient. It is the "law" that has been created by informals to regulate and order their lives and transactions and, as such, is socially relevant.

We have identified at least two ways of acquiring property informally for housing purposes. The first is invasion; the second is the illegal purchase of agricultural land through associations and cooperatives. In both of these, we have observed the functioning of some elements of the system of extralegal norms.

Invasion

State or private land is occupied illegally in essentially one of two ways, which we have called "gradual invasion" and "violent invasion."

The first kind of invasion occurs gradually in already existing settlements. Such settlements are generally farmworkers' huts attached to farms or estates, or to mining camps, the owners of which have a special relationship with the occupants (who are generally employees or tenants) and therefore, to start with, are not interested in evicting them. The owners generally attach very little value to the land, which minimizes its importance in relation to their overall assets and the efforts they are prepared to make to hang onto it. As times goes on, new groups of people who do not have any relationship with the owner gradually join the settlement, either because they have relatives there, acquire a piece of land, rent it, or simply take it over. In this way, they gradually occupy the land adjacent to the original settlement until they effectively own the entire area. Settlements formed by gradual invasion take on a definite shape only after a lengthy process.

In order to succeed, these takeovers nonetheless require a critical mass which enables the settlers to exert pressure on and negotiate with the owners in order to dissuade them from trying to recover the land. They also have an internal rationale very similar to the one we shall observe in the case which follows.

In the second kind of invasion, there is no prior link between the settlers and the owner of the land. It is for precisely this reason that the invasion must be violent and unexpected. This does not, of course, mean that it does not require complex, detailed planning. According to the ILD's observations, the violent invasion begins with a meeting of a group of people who come from the same neighborhood, family, or region, and have a shared interest in obtaining housing. This group plans the invasion at one or more closed meetings. There is often also decisive intervention by professional invaders—generally trade unionists, politicians, or simply business people—who offer their expertise in the organization of invasions in exchange for certain political or economic concessions.

After the original nucleus has been established, preparatory meetings are held to discuss which locations meet the requirements for a potential settlement. At these meetings, the suitability of the site and the ease with which it can be invaded are evaluated. The frequency with which public or private land is invaded differs, showing that invaders choose between the two types of land according to the chances of success which each of them offers. It is calculated that, throughout the years, 90 percent of violent invasions have occurred on state land, especially waste or unoccupied land. It is easier to invade state land than private land for, when no particular individual is affected, there is less incentive to react. There are also political considerations which may make the government sympathetic to an occurrence which, although it amounts to the illegal seizure of property, may appear to be a spontaneous act of redistributive justice.

Once the land has been chosen, the original group tries to show interested parties that they stand to gain more by joining an invasion than by acting on their own. In this way it begins to assemble the critical mass essential to reducing the possibility of police repression or reinvasion of the settlement by new individuals who try to occupy the free areas. A plan is then drawn with the help of engineers or engineering students. Individual lots in the settlement are distributed. The areas which will in future be occupied by public buildings (schools, health centers, or municipal authorities) and recreation areas (parks or sports grounds) are marked off. A census is taken of the invaders and the contribution they will make to common costs is approved. Responsibility for negotiating with the authorities, preserving law and order in the settlement, and organizing resistance to any attempted eviction (by forming settlers' pickets) is assigned. Sometimes lawyers are hired and a formal request for adjudication of the land to the settlers is filed with the competent department so that any authorities can be shown a copy of the request and proof that it is being processed: in this way, leaders can argue that they are not robbing the state of its assets, but have legally requested that the land be adjudicated to them and that they have been forced to occupy it in order to prevent other potential—and often nonexistent—invaders from occupying it illegally.

Once these preparations have been made, the invasion is carried out. It takes place at night or in the early hours of the morning. The date generally coincides with some civic anniversary, in order to reduce the possibilities of a rapid response by the forces of law and order. Whether they are a hundred or forty thousand, the invaders arrive at the agreed place in rented trucks or minibuses, bringing with them poles, rush matting, and everything they need to erect their first dwelling. They enter the land and put up numerous Peruvian flags to show that they are not committing an offense but making a patriotic bid for their rights and for social justice. Immediately after this, pickets demarcate the settlement with powdered chalk, in accordance with the plan. Women and children clear the land and, in a matter of hours, lots have been distributed and rush mats erected on each of them in the form of an "igloo."

At the same time, the communal kitchen which will feed the invaders during these early days is organized. A makeshift child-care center is set up; there, a group of mothers take care of all the invaders' small children so their parents are free to carry out their assigned tasks. Depending on what has been decided or on the size of the settlement, its leaders may also receive and install people who come to join the invasion, thus strengthening the critical mass. Simultaneous negotiations are also frequently launched with the nearest minibus operators' committee to get it to extend its route to the new settlement, making transportation readily available to the invaders. And once the land has been taken over, street vendors soon appear and take charge of supplying the settlers with food and other provisions. Vendors of building materials come equipped with everything needed to build the first homes.

The invaders also take various precautions for avoiding repression and maintaining law and order inside the settlement. Defense pickets are formed, ready to repel any eviction attempt with stones, sticks, and other suitable objects, and also to punish anyone who commits an offense. Another way of avoiding repression or reducing its effectiveness is to name the settlement after the current president, his wife, or some other prominent political figure, in an attempt to persuade that person to intervene on the settlement's behalf. This happened at the María Delgado de Odría, Clorinda Málaga de Prado, Pedro Beltrán, Juan Velasco Alvarado, Victor Raúl Haya de la Torre, Villa Violeta, and Pilar Nores de García settlements, among others.

Finally, if the police try to intimidate the invaders, women and children are placed in front in order to arouse the sympathies of the authorities and make the troops feel like bullies.

The invasion contract

Stripped to its essentials, the invasion has a clear and strict operating logic. Nothing is left to chance; everything is planned. This requires that negotiations take place among the future invaders before the invasion, once an original group, generally more dynamic than the rest, has identified shared interests. It is in this sense that we can speak of an "invasion contract" as being the source of the system of the extralegal norms that govern informal settlements and the residents' organization.

The different agreements needed to carry out an invasion become the provisions of this contract. Such provisions fall into two groups: those relating to the establishment, demarcation, and distribution of the actual settlement, and those identifying functions and responsibilities and assigning them to the informal organization responsible for executing the terms of the contract.

The provisions relating to the actual settlement are the agreements establishing the plans, distributing the land, and taking the initial census of the invaders. The provisions relating to the informal organization are the agreements establishing mechanisms for the election of the organization's leadership, putting it in charge of negotiations with the authorities or, when necessary, with those whose land has been invaded, allocating its budget and stipends, recommending that it update censuses, and entrusting it with the maintenance of law and order, the administration of justice, and even the mobilization of resistance.

Such contracts are not exclusive to violent invasions. They also exist in gradual invasions whenever the original occupants decide to remain on the land and establish among themselves a system of relations and a procedure for admitting new residents. There have been cases where the original nucleus tried to limit new members and triggered other invasion contracts hostile to its own. Mirones Bajo, Reynoso, and San José de Tres Compuertas, formed gradually before 1961 at the initiative of the Federation of Sand Workers, which claimed for its members public land acquired at the source of the Rímac river after the channel was improved in the 1940s, are examples. There an unusual dispute arose between the different settlers' organizations, which sought to obtain official blessing for their members and to exclude members of the other group. However, since they demanded public utilities which no one could be barred from using—for instance, water, sewage systems, and electricity—they ended up benefitting each other. Such confrontations do not normally occur because the invasion contract is usually open-ended, this being the key to assembling a critical mass, invoking social need over the requirements of the law, and preventing the owner from reacting effectively.

In general, an invasion contract is improved through the free consent of the interested parties, does not necessarily take the form of a written document, and is open to the inclusion of new parties.

The expectative property right

The execution of the invasion contract has the immediate effect of establishing a right to the land which has no specific equivalent in the legal world and which we have called the "expectative property right." The idea of establishing a real right by one's own initiative and in contravention of established norms may seem strange. However, the ILD found that this right is becoming increasingly predominant in Lima: of every 100 houses built in the capital city in 1985, 69 were governed by the extralegal system and only 31 by the formal legal system.

The expectative property right does not, however, confer on its holders all the benefits offered by the formal legal system. It applies temporarily, until such time as the government confers definite ownership on the members of the informal settlement or until, with the passage of time, popular organizations become able to defend it as effectively as the state. As a result, it builds up gradually. At first, the expectative right is based solely on the presence of the invaders on the land. Next, it comes to be based also on the censuses which the invaders begin to conduct to certify their possession of the land and thus reduce the need for their constant physical presence. Later, the expectative right is based also on the authorities' own activities. Each of the 159 bureaucratic steps which residents must complete in order to legalize their settlement, receive title to their lots, and incorporate the neighborhood into the city—a process which takes an average of twenty years—enhances the security and stability of the rights acquired. Nevertheless, this enhanced security does not signify complete integration into the formal legal system, but rather an exceptional recognition which the settlers regard as decisive for increasing their investment. Thus, as soon as it becomes clear that the state will not remove the settlement, the invaders begin to build with proper materials instead of rush matting. These buildings in turn provide powerful support for the expectative right, for in Peru it is politically unacceptable to demolish properly built housing. The result is that such buildings can be regarded as the first title to the land. The level of investment in housing is thus determined by the measure of legal security which the state confers on the settlement. The greater the security, the greater the investment and vice versa.

To illustrate this situation, the ILD chose the Mariscal Castilla and Daniel Alcides Carrión informal settlements, built adjacent to one another during the same period and inhabited by people with the same socio-economic characteristics. The only difference between them lay in their legal security: the former had been classified as permanent, and the second had been classified as removable. As a result, the value of a typical dwelling in the legally secure settlement was 41 times greater than in the other settlement. Even taking the value of the land, and not just the buildings, into account, the value of a dwelling in the legally secure settlement was still 12 times greater than in the other settlement. Using a larger sample, thirty-seven settlements covering the entire range of possibilities and areas in Lima, ILD researchers found that the average value of buildings whose owners had received title was 9 times that of buildings whose owners had not.

The above examples show that, while the expectative property right creates sufficient security and stability to possess land and build a house on it, it does not provide the necessary incentives to invest large sums of money in that house. People are at least 9 times more prepared to invest when they are given some measure of protection by the formal legal system.

The imperfection of this expectative right is demonstrated by the fact that it does not confer on invaders the same rights to the buildings as traditional ownership. As long as there is no definitive title, selling the land and renting out the buildings resulting from an invasion are prohibited by law. Residents may use, enjoy, lay claim to, and dispose of the land, but they are always relatively vulnerable, which forces them to take a number of costly precautionary measures. The situation is particularly difficult when it comes to disposing of the property.

If they want to sell, for instance, informals resort to the stratagem of claiming that they are transferring the buildings but not the land itself, in order to disguise the fact that they are actually selling the entire property, for, while there is no question as to the ownership of the buildings, legally the land does not belong to the seller. Moreover, as there are still no definitive rights and the system of extralegal norms protects only those who have devised it, the transfer must be approved by the residents of the settlement, especially in its early stages. Buyers must demonstrate to the residents' assembly that they are prepared to adhere to the invasion contract and any supplementary agreements. Later, when the settlement enjoys greater legal security, the informal sale takes place simply by agreement between the parties, as happens in formal society, and there is no need to go to the assembly for approval. The sale of the land is always registered, however, in the rudimentary real-estate register kept by the informal organizations.

Eventually, when the authorities grant final title to the settlers, they do so on the basis of the information contained in this register, with the result that, in the end, the extralegal system also manages to satisfy the expectation of ownership.

Renting is equally tricky. Because the tenant occupies the dwelling, informals fear that the authorities will come to recognize the tenant as the owner of the land. As a result, informals often prefer to disguise the tenancy as a lodging arrangement, and the owner stays in the building with the actual tenant.

Thus we see that, despite the ingenuity of the extralegal system by which the settlement dwellers protect themselves, they must assume a number of costs as a result of having acquired property informally. These costs include organizing the invasion and carrying it out physically, running the risk of eviction or relocation, putting up with a long period of insecure occupation, and living without the benefit of basic services or infrastructure. The settlers are also forced to immobilize or waste a sizable proportion of their resources because they have to be physically present on the land to ensure their rights. Finally, they acquire a property over which they can exercise only reduced rights.

Therefore, contrary to what one might believe, invaders pay a very high price for the land they occupy. Since they have no money, they pay for it with their own human capital. We are living in a costly society, one which forces its members to assume countless burdens, not only if they want to enjoy the benefits of formality but also if they prefer informality.

Informal organizations

Informal organizations are the organs which the settlers themselves elect and designate to execute the invasion contract. Over the years, these organizations have been given different official titles: urban development associations; settlers' associations; settlement organizations; residents' boards and communal committees; and settlers' organizations.[2] Whatever name they have been given, however, all the informal settlements have always had democratic organizations, with a basic, clear-cut organizational structure consisting of a central leadership—the executive body—and a general assembly—the deliberative body. This is in marked contrast with formal society where, over the same period of time, legislative and executive powers have been consistently concentrated in the cabinets of de facto governments. In times of dictatorship, not even local governments can boast the democratic origin and functioning of the informal organizations.

The organizations resulting from the invasion contract are not the only ones that exist in informal settlements. There are many others which concern themselves with satisfying a very wide variety of settlers' interests and which are very similar to those in formal society. These include mothers' clubs, parents' associations, school boards, sports clubs, and church centers.

The ILD's research shows that the basic aim of the informal organizations resulting from the invasion contract is to protect and increase

---

[2] Supreme Decree of 26 June 1956; Act 13517; Directive 01-70-PND; Legislative Decree 051; Ordinance 192; respectively.

the value of the property acquired. To this end, they perform a whole range of functions, from negotiating with the authorities, preserving law and order, and trying to provide services, to registering the properties in the settlement and administering justice within it.

The informal organizations' first task is to negotiate with the authorities for, while the extralegal system allows them to possess the land, build on it, and even use it for economic purposes, it confers only imperfect, expectative, and relatively vulnerable rights. It is therefore essential that the settlers reinforce those rights by dealing with the government. The negotiations cover different issues, such as the recognition of acquired rights, the provision of basic services and infrastructure, and any other problems that may arise because of their illegality. These negotiations, which have to be conducted in the political and bureaucratic spheres, require cultivating contacts, gathering information, and investing time. Accordingly, informal organizations try to find competent leadership and sufficient political or bureaucratic contacts to be able to win support, and settlement dwellers have no qualms about replacing their leadership if it loses access to the authorities. This has given rise over the years to a pragmatic political flexibility.

In maintaining law and order, the organizations take action against ordinary criminals at two specific stages. During the actual invasion, when pickets are designated to defend the invaders, they keep watch, provide security, and receive new invaders. Once the settlement is established, the residents themselves or specially appointed committees perform these tasks. In either case, if an attack occurs, whistles, lights, or lamps sound the alarm, and residents armed with sticks, lamps, pickaxes, and other objects respond by helping to catch the offender.

Since informal organizations want to improve the standard of living of their members and increase the value of their properties, they also try to provide public services for their settlements. To do so, they set up committees of settlement dwellers to undertake specific tasks such as obtaining a water supply, sewage system, electricity, roads, and sidewalks. These committees base their budgets on the income received from settlers' dues less expenditures on such items as stipends for the organization's leaders, public works, the cost of complying with bureaucratic procedures, and a fund for bribing public officials. Once prepared, these budgets are submitted to the assembly for approval.

Public works are often carried out by settlement residents, as a way of reducing costs. Depending on the negotiating skills of the leaders or the receptiveness of the authorities, the state or some private institution may be persuaded to do the work free of charge, or to cover the cost. Often, the work is contracted out to formal businesses.

Another of the informal organization's tasks is to keep a register of the land in the settlement, indicating who owns the different lots. This register is often in notebooks or even in the books of minutes of assembly meetings. To keep the list of owners and lots up to date, censuses are carried out repeatedly in the period preceding eventual legal recognition. Each new census is designed to adjust the informal register to actual occupancy of the land. All censuses are therefore temporary and, in the event of discrepancies, generally corrected according to actual physical presence on the lot.

Since it is the only source of information, the titles eventually conferred by the state after a lengthy bureaucratic process are usually based on this register. Unlike what happens in the rest of the urban society, most land in informal settlements is not registered by the state, but in informal registers. If at any point the state were to decide to establish a compulsory registration system for property transfers, most of the necessary data would exist in informal settlements before it did in traditional urban areas.

Finally, informal organizations are responsible for administering justice on their own account and do so essentially in two areas of jurisdiction: land disputes and criminal offenses. Jurisdiction over land disputes is largely a response to the absence of official intervention. Over the years, the formal judicial system, overwhelmed by numerous problems, has tended to ignore individual disputes over land in informal settlements. A number of provisions have thus transferred jurisdiction over these disputes from the judiciary to the government bureaucracy.[3] However, the bureaucracy has been overtaken by the initiative of settlement residents and forced to formalize decisions adopted by informal organizations or to intervene only at a very late stage in the dispute. There have even been cases where unresolved disputes have been taken informally to justices of the peace for arbitration, instead of to the competent government authorities. These justices of the peace tend to rely on extralegal norms to resolve the disputes, since it is the extralegal system which is the socially relevant one and there is often no formal law on which to rely.

[3] Act 13517, Act 14205, Act 15016, Decree 16762, Decree 14476, and Supreme Decree 19 of 10 February 1962.

All of this has encouraged the development of informal justice to resolve disputes over land. The leadership and the general assembly of the informal organization function as courts of the first and second instances, respectively, and resolve disputes over competing rights, breaches of sales contracts or tenancy agreements, boundary lines, and even family disputes about who owns the land. However, according to the ILD's calculations, 13 percent of the lots recognized in informal settlements are in litigation—evidence that the lack of coercive authority reduces the effectiveness of this system of justice.

Since informal organizations have to preserve law and order, they inevitably develop practical criteria for administering justice in criminal matters also. If an offense is committed, for instance, both accused and plaintiffs are allowed to appear, the accused defend themselves, certain evidence is allowed (including the testimony of residents, to which great value is attached), and a jury consisting of heads of family settles the case. On the other hand, the Peruvian judicial system does without juries and prefers the professional administration of justice, keeping alive a long-standing prejudice that the average Peruvian lacks the education in civics and the responsibility to decide whether an accused is innocent or guilty.

A number of penalties are invoked, depending on the nature of the offense. The penalties for ordinary criminals are beating, forced nudity, or expulsion, the last of which is enforced by members of the settlement who evict the culprits from their lot. If they resist and the expulsion cannot be carried out, it is customary to allow a new member to settle on the free areas of the lot so that sooner or later the outcasts lose all or part of their expectative property right.

Homicide is usually dealt with by handing the culprit over to the police, unless the nature of the crime triggers a lynching. Raping a child is often punished by death. Rapists, referred to as "monsters" in popular speech, are usually lynched if they fall into settlers' hands. When the police discover the body, they learn little or nothing from the residents and generally limit themselves to taking the body to the morgue, in an unusual tacit recognition of the informal system of justice. All the punishments are governed by custom, however—there are no written penal regulations in informal settlements.[4]

---

[4] SINAMOS, a state organization created during the last military government, tried to introduce such regulations at Villa El Salvador in 1975. The experiment failed because it corresponded more to the wishes of the public officials than to those of residents.

Illegal land sales

Invasion is the first informal way of acquiring property for housing; the second is to buy agricultural land illegally through associations and cooperatives.

As part of the agrarian reform of the 1970s, the government called for farmland to be expropriated and distributed among the peasants. Ironically, this made agricultural land cheaper: the threat of expropriation reduced its value and prompted many owners to sell, vastly increasing the supply. At the same time, the informal economy had substantially improved the incomes of large sections of the population (minibus operators, street vendors, and clandestine industrialists) who were now able to buy land. This gave rise to a second method of informal acquisition, in which settlers colluded with owners of agricultural land on Lima's outskirts who foresaw imminent expropriation, to organize the transfer of this land under the table and set up new informal settlements.

Different subterfuges were employed. The first was to organize associations and cooperatives in order to bring interested buyers together in legal entities that would arouse no suspicion, would enjoy state protection as formal organizations for obtaining housing and, in the specific case of cooperatives, would enjoy sufficient social standing to make violent repression politically unthinkable. Another subterfuge was for owners and informals to simulate invasions. Once the deal had been struck, the members of an association or cooperative entered as if they were invading it while the owners offered no resistance. In the eyes of the authorities, it was only another violent invasion.

In this way, some private owners partially avoided the adverse effect of agrarian reform. They transferred their land to associations or cooperatives for more money than expropriation would have brought but less than the normal price. The associations acquired magnificent land at reduced prices, saved themselves some of the cost of invasion, and acquired slightly more secure property rights. Nor was it politically expedient for the military government to clamp down on the cooperatives, which it had itself extolled as vehicles for social change.

In 1976, the state tied its own hands. That year, the law prohibited the government from expropriating agricultural land for urban development.[5] This gave owners a grace period in which to negotiate the sale of their land and gave the informals sufficient time to organize. Moreover, that same year the state revised the National Building

[5] Decree 21419.

Regulations, for the first time allowing land to be developed gradually, subject to far simpler requirements than in the past. This made it possible for associations and cooperatives to develop neighborhoods and build housing legally, without arousing suspicions that the land was illegally occupied.

Thus began the biggest boom in agricultural land sales and urban development in Lima's recent history; and it continued. Impoverished by price controls, subsidized imports, and the lack of adequate rights to property in the countryside (among other reasons), the beneficiaries of agrarian reform went on selling their land to associations and cooperatives, as landowners had done before them, despite the ban imposed by the Agrarian Reform Act.

This second informal method of acquiring property for housing is no less complex than invasion. It requires that future residents first set up an association, which may be "for housing" or "of housing," or a cooperative, identify a piece of agricultural land suitable for the new settlement, formalize contracts with the owners of the land, put together the necessary critical mass and sufficient money, and even simulate a violent invasion.

According to a field study carried out by ILD researchers, 269 organizations engaged in concluding sales of this kind in 1985: 105 associations "for housing," 88 associations "of housing," and 76 cooperatives—and they had incorporated approximately 3,400 hectares of agricultural land into the city through this new informal process. This is about 34 million square meters, approximately half the area of the young towns proper. The ILD was also able to determine that at least 60 percent of the settlements created by associations and cooperatives postdated agrarian reform and that, if their rate of growth were maintained, they could become the predominant model of informal urban development in the capital city.

In practice, there are few differences between these newer informal settlements and those resulting from invasions, to the point that the state authorities often agree to recognize as "young towns" or "marginal human settlements" groups of settlers that are, in fact, associations or cooperatives. Any difference between them are legal ones which are not readily discernible. Associations and cooperatives are legal entities whose existence predates the sale of the land and even the simulated invasion. However, the legal basis of each is different: their internal organization, their statutes, and the requirements for setting them up all differ. Associations "for housing" and cooperatives enjoy tax benefits and are therefore subject to control by different government offices, while associations "of housing" are not subject to any kind of control because they enjoy no benefits.

To sum up, what happened was that a radical change in the rules governing ownership of agricultural land, combined with other changes in the law, created a demand for an alternative means of converting land to urban use. This gave rise to collusion between associations and cooperatives, on the one hand, and the owners—whether original landowners or beneficiaries of the agrarian reform—on the other, and the outcome of this collusion was a second way of acquiring property informally for housing. This served two purposes: using the land for housing prohibited by law and avoiding expropriation.

Informal real estate brokers

Professionals are usually more involved in illegal sales of agricultural land than in invasion. A group which organizes an association or cooperative is often made up of business people who can assemble the information needed to enter into this kind of transaction—the kind of information that is difficult to obtain. These people, commonly known as "speculators," are unquestionably informal real estate brokers.

The first thing these informal brokers do is to try to match supply to demand. To do this, they have to set up an association "for housing" or "of housing," or a cooperative. They must then identify a piece of land suitable for the settlement. This is a complex business: the transaction is costly, and it is essential to obtain certain information before one can make a proposal and present it for consideration to the people who will populate the settlement.

The numerous entrepreneurial functions include negotiating with the owners of agricultural land. Such negotiations are especially tricky since the parties must agree not only on the lot and the price, but also on how they will conceal the transaction. This is why they must often deal with the authorities before undertaking the operation.

Next, the informal brokers have to assemble the critical mass essential for organizing the transaction, as in violent invasions. The most widespread method is to try to identify and emphasize the shared interests of potential participants. To do this, the brokers must determine whether participants will be prepared to maintain their occupation in the initial stage, when acts of violence may occur, or at least live in a rudimentary dwelling for some time; next, whether they will be prepared to commit themselves, in the long term, to improving their property and helping to build the necessary infrastructure; and, last, whether they constitute a homogeneous group capable of cooperating peacefully among themselves. The plans for the settlement are drawn up with the necessary technical assistance. The possibility of obtaining such services as water, sewage systems, electricity, and transportation as soon as possible is studied. Members of the association or cooperative may be offered existing plans for their dwellings or the possibility of having a professional design them.

Once the essential number of people has been brought in and individual contributions established, the brokers put together the money to buy the land, close the deal with the owners, and proceed to organize the occupation within the agreed-upon period. Since the owners are legally prohibited from selling their farmland and the associations or cooperatives are prohibited from converting it to urban land, they risk governmental intervention. To avoid this, the informal brokers may organize an invasion: on the agreed-upon day, the future residents occupy the land with Peruvian flags, rush matting, and other implements, as if staging a violent invasion.

None of the many services provided by informal brokers is free, however. In payment, they take part of the dues paid by members, a number of lots which they will sell when the settlement is developed and its value has increased, or both. This often arouses the hostility of the authorities, who prosecute them relentlessly. But none of this detracts from the importance of the work of these informal brokers or from the rationality of their decisions. An illegal sale of agricultural land involves costs which no one could pay individually and the future settlers need professionals to organize them into associations and cooperatives and handle the operation for them.

The Historical Evolution of Informal Housing

Over the years, the development of informal settlements has steadily advanced by a succession of unexpected actions, mass movements, political intrigues, and exchanges of favors. In order to describe this development more clearly, therefore, we have organized our account into ten successive historical stages, each of which shows how the formal structure has gradually yielded the ground necessary for the growth of informal housing.

The birth of informality

The formals themselves first gave informality room to develop when, in the early decades of this century, they violated the laws governing urban development and sought arrangements wherein these general rules were replaced by class privileges, bribes, and other shady dealings.

Around this time, formally established businesses began to develop residential neighborhoods on the land of former estates or villages, basically to meet the housing needs of the upper and middle classes. This was how Lince was built in 1921, Jesús María in 1923, Magdalena Vieja in 1924, and San Isidro in 1926. In urbanizing these neighborhoods, the formal business people, landowners, and contractors failed to comply with a number of laws. They did not obtain permits, they left public works incomplete, they did not provide services, and they hid behind contracts of questionable legality. In other words, they urbanized the city's traditional neighborhoods informally.

Later, before the mass migrations began, the same formal businesses began to develop neighborhoods for the popular classes. They used the same methods they had used earlier to develop residential neighborhoods—building outside or in violation of the laws. This led to the emergence of such urban developments as Chorrillos in 1926, Manzanilla and Chacra Colorada in 1928, and the Las Cabezas area of the Rímac in 1929. The popular neighborhoods organized by the formals were developed as informally as Comas, Ciudad de Díos, Villa María del Triunfo, or Las Flores were subsequently developed by the informals.

A contemporary writer, Carlos Alberto Izaguirre, described the earlier process:

> . . . none of the contracts concluded transfers ownership, or even civil possession. They do, however, enable the buyer to build on the lot as he sees fit. This provision is enough for thousands of houses, some of them meeting not even the most elementary standards of hygiene, to spring up alongside swampland, close to murky water courses filled with the detritus of older areas, and without water and sewage systems, sidewalks or paved roads. The streets are usually filled with piles of rubble. Every corner and open space has become a public latrine. In the midst of these conditions, the "holder" of the lot, since contractually speaking he is not the owner, makes his clay bricks, or buys them if he is unable to make them, and little by little, with the help of his wife and children, in the late afternoon of each day after leaving his job at the factory or other place of work, builds his house as a refuge from the rental system.[6]

[6] Carlos Alberto Izaguirre, *La Legislación y la Compraventa de Lotes de Urbanizaciones* (Lima: Compañia de Impresiones y Publicidad, 1943), pp. 307–308.

If we did not know that Izaguirre was referring to the early development of Chorrillos, Chacra Colorada, or certain parts of the Rímac, we would think he was describing the beginnings of the informal settlements we know today.

The authorities also tried to get into the act. In 1915 the Provincial Council adopted an ordinance requiring that permits be obtained before land could be urbanized and prohibiting the sale of lots in urban developments where no basic infrastructure existed. Seven years later, when it became apparent that this provision could not be enforced, President Augusto B. Leguía issued a decree reiterating that the infrastructure must be in place before land could be sold.[7] Two years later, in 1924, the same president promulgated the first regulations governing urban development in the country's history, in an attempt to standardize and enforce existing regulations. In 1928, however, Congress was forced to intervene, adopting two acts which, respectively, emphasized the obligation to install infrastructure before selling land, and ordering state intervention.[8]

The failure of the 1915 ordinance was followed by that of the 1922 decree, the 1924 rules and, finally, the 1928 acts. The increasing involvement of the authorities—first municipal, then executive, and finally legislative—revealed the state's growing concern about the problem, but also the unworkability of the measures taken to deal with it.

The government finally lost patience and, in September 1931, declared that all areas—whether upper, middle, or lower class—in which the urban development work required by law had not been carried out were rural and hence not urbanized.[9] In other words, San Isidro, Jesús María, Chacra Colorada, and Manzanilla, among others, were declared rural areas and the houses and buildings erected on them nonexistent. Of course, such a declaration had no effect.

But it had now become possible to negotiate the applicability of state laws, with the result that their enforcement might totally contradict the letter of each of their provisions. Formal business people with the requisite political influence, economic resources, or social standing negotiated the urbanization of upper and middle-class residential neighborhoods with the authorities responsible for overseeing them and, prompted by the substantial profit they made, decided to develop, and later sell, lower-class

[7] 21 June 1915; 6 October 1922.

[8] Acts 6159 and 6186.

[9] Supreme Decree of 30 September 1931.

neighborhoods. What counted was not the letter of the law or regulation, but rather the terms of the agreement reached between public officials and the formal business owners interested in developing such neighborhoods. Such agreements became the new law for the parties who entered into them. It is no exaggeration, therefore, to say that the handful of people who had the necessary political influence, economic resources, or social standing could choose to ignore the law.

Apparently Lima's inhabitants were not overly bothered by such behavior. Lima was still a relatively small city, with only a half million inhabitants, and no one could predict that lawbreaking would become a problem that would transform the very foundations of society. The real-estate operators did not know that the way they had found of negotiating the production and enforcement of laws would be used on a massive scale by the informals to "exacerbate the contradictions of the system," in the common Marxist-Leninist jargon of the extreme left agitators as successive waves of migration brought Peruvians from the countryside to the city.

Recognition by relocation

Having arrived in Lima, the migrants took advantage of the law's negotiability and the long tradition of lawbreaking to organize their first settlements, except that now they did so as part of a boom in the city's growth that would overturn centuries of tradition.[10] The second historical stage was reached when the state implicitly recognized expectative property rights by taking responsibility for relocating some informal settlements.

The decades from the late 1920s to the late 1950s were a period of gradual invasions. Wherever there was a group of farmworkers' huts, a roadside inn, or an old mining camp, people and dwellings began to proliferate as if by spontaneous reproduction. The hills close to the center of Lima, old orchards, the edges of irrigation ditches—even garbage

[10] Researchers disagree about when the first informal settlement appeared. According to a study made by the Health and Social Welfare Fund in 1959, the oldest settlement dates back to 1910. A later study, by José Matos Mar, dates the first settlement from 1924. A more recent study by the Multisectoral Program for Basic Infrastructure Works in Young Towns with Community Participation and Food Support (PIBA) maintains that the first informal settlement was established in 1906. Other studies claim that the oldest settlement in the history of the republic is the city of Sullana, recognized by act of Congress following an invasion at the Zuyana estate in 1839. Any attempt to clear up these differences would be of purely academic interest, however, since prior to the mass migrations the number of people living in settlements was very small.

dumps—were gradually settled. As early as 1920 and throughout the decade that followed, the city began to fill with people and yet nothing was done to make it easier to acquire land. The emergence of informal settlements was the response, and the state was gradually forced to recognize gradual invasion as a way of acquiring property.[11]

The first such recognition came indirectly, when a settlement damaged by natural disaster was relocated on publicly owned land. In 1915, a settlement known as Cantagallo had begun to spring up on the banks of the Rímac river, roughly at the level of the Plaza de Acho. Around 1932, the river flooded, destroying part of the settlement and injuring a considerable number of settlers.

The situation posed an acute problem of conscience for the government, which until then had simply ignored the informal settlements, hiding behind the fact that they were neither very numerous nor very densely populated. Caught in a dilemma, the government of Commander Sánchez Cerro, which was doing everything it could to be receptive to popular demands in order to show how it differed from the overthrown government of Augusto B. Leguía and compete with the emerging American People's Revolutionary Alliance (APRA), agreed to relocate the victims temporarily in an area near the Cerro San Cristóbal. The area was given the name Leticia, in honor of the conflict that arose with Colombia around that time over the Amazonian city of the same name. Leticia's first occupants settled in the foothills, the next ones settled a little higher up, and so on, until the entire area was covered. A settlement thus came into being through a combination of relocation and gradual invasion. The decision by Sánchez Cerro's government was a turning point, for it was the first time that the state had recognized the residents of an informal settlement as having acquired rights which could be protected and even replaced at the state's expense.

It appears that settlers' organizations, as we would come to know them later, did not exist at that time. Since the relocation was carried out officially, the residents felt relatively secure in their ownership of the land and did not need an organization to promote and defend their rights. Moreover, since in those days there was little hope of obtaining urban services, the residents had little reason to organize.

The Leticia episode, however, made it clear to the people that an informal alternative to the slums now existed. By 1940, informal settlers

[11] A study in 1960 by the National Health and Social Welfare Fund, entitled "Neighborhoods of Metropolitan Lima" and printed by Tipografia Santa Rosa, states that of the 157 neighborhoods existing at that date, 130 had been formed gradually and only 24 by violent occupation.

had already carved out a small place for themselves in the city: of every 100 dwellings that year, 4 were informal and 96 were formal.

Political recognition of invaders

The third stage began when different political groups began to compete for the sympathies and support of the dwellers in the informal settlements, offering in exchange a measure of recognition or at least a pledge that they would not be evicted. First APRA, then Manuel A. Odría, and last, in the 1950s, politician and journalist Pedro G. Beltrán transformed the informal settlements and their inhabitants into increasingly important protagonists of urban society. Since then, no government or political party has been able to do without them.

Invasions increased steadily after 1940, although settlements were still not massively populated. The movement picked up sharply, however, after the 1940 earthquake, which added to the growing need for housing the displacement resulting from the destruction of a large part of the city. Thus, although still numerically insignificant, informal housing began to arouse increasing interest among politicians, especially since a mass of people who were unhappy with the present state of affairs and were demanding improvements was becoming visible. Some politicians began to vie for the support of settlement dwellers, offering them all kinds of benefits, but the movement also aroused concern among others who felt that this mass was potentially revolutionary. The representatives of formal society suddenly began to view these groups, who appeared to have little more than their audacity in settling on the city's outskirts, either as a threat or an opportunity: a threat of civil disobedience and possible uprising or an opportunity to win electoral backing and political support.

Settlers, for their part, gradually became aware of their shared interests and the possibility of satisfying them by exploiting their electoral strength or their political support. The outcome was that politicians offered them the recognition that state law denied. The basis of the understanding was clear: the settlers needed to halt the repression against them and improve their negotiating position with the authorities; the politicians needed to increase their base of support in order to win votes or make converts to their revolutionary cause. Moreover, the opening of the political arena offered the informals the possibility of negotiating with the authorities for the provision of services and assistance and even recognition of their rights to the land, as well as for an end to reprisals by the police.

This exchange generally favored the settlement dwellers, for they never felt bound to the politicians who sponsored them, while the latter had to provide service in advance in order to receive some show of support. Generally speaking, the settlement dwellers have always viewed political alliances as just another tool. As a result, although they may appear to enjoy the sympathy of the settlement dwellers at a given moment, politicians have been unable to retain their support for very long. The backing they have received from the settlers has always been proportional to what they have been able to offer them at that particular moment.

This attitude has affected the election of the leaders of informal settlements and their duration in office. As a general rule, settlers back leaders who have, or may have within a reasonable period of time, some kind of access to the government. When they realize that a leader is losing this access or potential access, the leader is immediately removed from office.

The first significant wave of politically organized invasions followed the election of José Luis Bustamante y Rivero as president of the Republic in 1945. It may have begun as long as a year before he officially took office. By then, of every 100 houses built in Lima, 15 were informal and 85 were formal.

The APRA, which had thrown the full weight of its electoral strength behind Bustamante, was a declared enemy of the existing order. Originally Marxist in inspiration, this party had developed a corporate organization which sought to represent the interests of the emerging urban groups, as part of a movement toward a class alliance in Peru. As a result, it sympathized almost instinctively with the informal settlers and viewed them as a potential base of support for its political ambitions and revolutionary plans. Accordingly, at the initiative of its trade-union cells, it helped organize some of the violent invasions which began to take place at that time. Other left-wing groups began to follow the APRA's example, and interest in representing the settlement dwellers politically soon lent invasion the appearance of a bid for social justice.

This form of political involvement was extremely successful during the constitutional government of President Bustamante. None of the invasions carried out with political protection were actually undone by the police, although more evictions were attempted in that period than in any previous period. The politicians' involvement in the invasions succeeded in minimizing the effect of evictions by the police and in maximizing the effect of popular initiative. And the presence of the informal sector grew.

By 1948, the year in which President Bustamante was deposed by General Manuel A. Odría, of every 100 dwellings built in Lima, 19 were informal and 81 were formal.

General Odría proclaimed himself president and hastened to compete with the APRA and the Marxist left for political ground in the informal settlements. Since he had been minister of the interior in the year before the coup, Odría had firsthand knowledge of the problem and was able to devise a strategy that combined massive efforts to win the sympathies of the settlement dwellers with his desire to please pressure groups interested in preserving the status quo. At that time, gradual occupation of the land was still the predominant model, although violent invasions were gathering momentum, giving rise to more and more densely populated settlements. The main such settlement was San Martín de Porres, originally called "27 October Industrial Workers' District" in honor of the date on which General Odría staged his coup d'état.

Through its relations and dealings with the popular classes, the Odría regime was able to offer formal society the apparent loyalty of the informal settlements—the government was in a position to assist the settlers by helping in the acquisition of land and the provisions of services—and, at the same time, to reduce political unrest by allowing poor people to put up their own homes without major cost to the national treasury. Each time he provided assistance, Odría won a little more political support, or at least neutrality, from the pragmatic settlement dwellers.

Odría's policies also benefitted real-estate owners in the city and landholders in the countryside. He helped the real-estate owners by supporting the esablishment of informal settlements, which encouraged settlement on the city's outskirts. The settlements either led to the vacating of slums in the city center, which were then demolished to make way for new buildings or shopping centers, or increased the value of private land near the settlements. He helped the rural landowners by implicitly encouraging migration, thus helping to sustain traditional structures in the countryside. Some specialists have interpreted the urban development of this period as a deliberate governmental strategy of transferring the most determined and enterprising people to Lima in order to lessen conflict in the countryside. [12] The Odría regime also calmed the private landowners' fears of invasion by benevolently encouraging the takeover of state-owned, rather than private, wasteland. It also stepped up the construction of

[12] See David Collier, *Barriadas y Elites de Odría a Velasco* (Lima: Instituto de Estudios Peruanos, 1976), p. 76.

low-income housing—the "community housing projects" conceived during the Bustamante regime—in order to lessen social pressures.

Settlement dwellers viewed Odría's policies favorably because, after all, the dictator's benevolence increased their chances of gaining access to housing and enabled them to steadily reinforce their expectative property rights. According to David Collier, under the Odría regime only 15 percent of takeovers were resisted by the police, and only 10 percent resulted in eviction.[13] In other words, 9 out of every 10 invasions could be sure of success. Again according to Collier, there is evidence of some collusion or connivance between the Odría government and invasion leaders during this period. Of course, the meetings did not take place with the president himself, but with representatives or leaders of his political group. The very fact that such negotiations took place showed the informals not only that political forces regarded them as an attractive base of support, as the APRA and the Marxist left had earlier, but that they themselves could give a dictatorship such as Odría's the "legitimacy" it needed.

It should be pointed out, however, that the Odría regime never relied completely on the support of the informals, probably remembering that on an earlier occasion settlement dwellers had given their backing to the APRA and then abandoned it as soon as it lost power. Accordingly, Odría adopted a paternalistic attitude and never offered them title to the occupied lots, thereby keeping them dependent on the state and forcing them into a more lasting loyalty.

The government's opponents did not allow it to monopolize this political space, however. As early as 1954, when 28 out of every 100 dwellings built in Lima were informal, Beltrán encouraged and publicized the Ciudad de Díos invasion in his newspapers *La Prensa* and *Ultima Hora*—presumably to annoy the Odría regime, compete for some of its popular support, and draw attention to the crisis that the migrants' arrival was creating in the city. Beltrán's employees planned the invasion in *La Prensa*'s own print shops, winning the political support of his friends and the journalistic backing of the printers who worked with them. Four years later, during Manuel Prado's second government and, more specifically, after Beltrán was appointed president of the Council of Ministers, he pursued his efforts to provide popular housing, this time through the creation of satellite cities like Ventanilla as an alternative for the country's urban future.

[13]Collier, *Barriadas y Elites de Odría a Velasco*, p. 62.

It was already rather late to try to change things, however. By 1961, the year in which Beltrán left office, informals could take credit for having built 41 of every 100 dwellings in Lima. Formals had built the remaining 59.

Legislative recognition

The fourth stage began when society gave informal housing its first legislative recognition, accepting the existence of settlements and attempting to subject them to a set of exceptional rules.

The active participation of politicians and the parallel growth of settlements had to be resolved in some way, for it was becoming increasingly obvious that the use of violent invasions to exert pressure was causing a tremendous waste of social resources. The solution was the legal recognition of existing settlements, which took place in February 1961 with the promulgation of Act 13517. Relatively insignificant sixteen years earlier, the settlements became the subject of arduous debate in the halls of Congress, a debate in which all political parties participated.

Basically, Act 13517 sought to make a fresh start. It recognized settlements in existence at the time of its promulgation, made it possible for their residents to formalize their possessions, and established future government policy for urban development. However, it attached very unusual conditions to each of these concessions.

Although the Act stated that it was in the national interest to remodel, clean up, and legalize informal settlements existing as of 20 September 1960, it tried to be as stringent with those who had already invaded land as it was with the formal sector, forcing them to conform to a compulsory standard.[14] As a result, it did not attempt to solve the problem of invasions or access to housing, but limited itself to imposing the conditions which existing settlers would have to meet in order to gain legal recognition. Act 13517 must be seen as the price set by formal society for eventually granting the informals some kind of legality.

Likewise, while the Act provided access to formal ownership of property, it set forth a set of blatantly discriminatory rules. On the pretext of protecting settlement dwellers from speculators, it defined the settlement as inalienable, so that the settlers could not sell, rent, or subdivide it until

---

[14] By "remodel" the Act meant conforming the settlement's ground plan to official urban standards; by "clean up" it meant clearing the land, removing garbage, and installing water and sewage systems; and by "legalize" it meant recognizing the new neighborhood once the two previous conditions had been met and then issuing titles to lot holders.

five years after they had received title. Since the ILD has calculated that informals have to wait twenty years for their titles, this limitation lasts for at least a quarter-century. Although they were to receive title eventually, the informals would thus be property owners with reduced rights—barred from the real-estate market and therefore unable to compete on an equal footing with formal society.

Similarly, while the Act recognized the existence of informal organizations in the settlements, it did not place them on an equal footing with the organizations existing in formal society. Instead, it promulgated a compulsory model of organization called the "settlers' association," which had to obtain administrative authorization before it could function. All organizations set up before 1961 had to conform to this new model. The Act prevented informals from choosing any other form of organization by prohibiting them from belonging to more than one association and announcing that, when the time came to assign lots legally, preference would be given to members of the official associations. Thus began the history of a legal apartheid which would henceforth characterize most government provisions for and attitudes toward the settlements.

Last, in establishing future government policy, Act 13517 prohibited future invasions, depriving any subsequent settlements of the possibility of official recognition, and called on the state to take the initiative, creating publicly owned popular urban developments (UPIS) which would replace the informal settlements. Neither of these provisions was successful, however.

The ban on new settlements was designed to drive a wedge between the old informals and the new, on the assumption that the recognition and benefits conferred on existing settlements would otherwise become a powerful incentive for increasing the number of invasions. However, it was naïve to assume that a new law could halt a social trend when, to the informals, that law meant that, in the long run, the authorities were prepared to recognize faits accomplis and legalize the informal sector.

The electoral campaigns of 1962 and 1963 soon created new problems. The various political parties promised agrarian reform, provoking a wave of peasant invasions of rural areas. The promises had a similar effect in the cities, where the informals had already learned to interpret favorable political conditions. As Act 13517 had basically been limited to reducing the cost of acquiring property informally and had kept the cost of formal acquisition intact, invasions continued. Many tenants in the inner city, anticipating that the slums might be classified as marginal neighbor-hoods, also began to create disturbances. The military, who had seized power briefly (1962–1963), apparently interpreted this civil disobedience as a drastic radicalization of the urban masses. Forty-seven percent of the invasions that occurred during this brief interim period were followed by evictions.

Many expectations were aroused when Fernando Belaunde came to power in 1963 as part of a movement apparently aimed at liberalizing the state. The new government enforced Act 13517, however, and began an aggressive program of building UPIS, since it was already clear that the problem could not be solved simply by banning further invasions. The UPIS were not as successful as expected, however: over the years, they never accounted for more than 16 percent of the housing in informal settlements. Besides, their physical characteristics never fully met the needs of Lima's new residents: for instance, they provided dwellings of an average area of 18 square meters per person while the other settlements offered 25 square meters.

Perhaps the most important consequence of legal recognition was not that it provided another way of organizing things, but that it created an additional incentive and increased the expectation of gaining secure housing in the cities. By the time President Belaunde was deposed by a military coup in 1968, the informals had gained control of Lima's growth. Of every 100 houses built that year, 57 were informal and only 43 were formal.

Confrontation with the government

The fifth stage was marked by the political victory of the informals in their first massive confrontation with the state.

When the Revolutionary Government of the Armed Forces, headed in its first phase (1968–1975) by General Juan Velasco Alvarado, took power, discontent was widespread. Too many expectations had been left unmet by the previous government. Already established informal settlers who had expected massive government assistance had found that such assistance was minimum, while as yet unestablished informals had had to continue to resort to invasions, with their inevitable sacrifices and violence. Formal property owners who feared the illegal takeover of their land had found that invasions could not be halted by a law. Politicians and public officials had experienced directly the inadequacy of their efforts.

Last, the intellectuals had argued that the problem lay in the absence of "structural reforms" which they were unable to define.

The military decided to take the bull by the horns. Allying themselves with a group of socialist intellectuals, they involved themselves directly in the organization of the settlements as no other government before them had done. They tried to impose another standard model on the informals as a condition for state assistance. This model, called a "neighborhood organization," established a mechanism for controlling the settlement dwellers through direct state intervention, under the guise of providing them with technical assistance.[15]

It was impossible to lock the settlement dwellers into a rigid system, however, because their society was far more complex and dynamic than the government officials realized. To start with, informals were building housing far faster than the rest of civilian society. Most of them were trying to build a second floor onto their homes in order to rent it out, even though this was illegal. Houses in the older settlements were being sold despite the government's ban. People were organizing to build roads and sidewalks and obtain services. Informal trade, manufacturing, and transport were beginning to spring up all over the city. It was a bad time to try to pigeonhole the incipient market economy that was emerging in the face of the many distortions created by the legal system. The government's efforts resulted in additional tension which heralded further confrontations.

Since the UPIS program had failed to take the lead in the capital's urban development, the invasions had gone on. The military government was not prepared to allow this tide to continue, believing itself able to impose a new order on the process, from above. Thus, between 1968 and 1970, the police evicted 79 percent of the new invaders. This harsh repression ended suddenly in 1971, when a violent invasion overthrew the government physically and politically, triggered a ministerial crisis, and led to the adoption of a new state policy.

On April 29, 1971, a massive invasion began at Pamplona, a site bordering the College of the Immaculate Virgin owned by the Society of Jesus, whose congregation included the assistant bishop and later "bishop of the young towns," Luis Bambarén Gastelumendi. The invasion, which was to extend to nearby public and private land and in which several tens of thousands of people took part, is thought to have been the largest in recent history, dwarfing the Ciudad de Dios and Comas invasions.

[15] Directives 01-70 PND and 03-70 PND of May and August 1970.

The military government reacted by ordering a police eviction which left one leader dead and many people injured. The settlers, for their part, captured a police commander and threatened to kill him if the eviction continued. It was the first time that a confrontation of this kind had occurred. The incidents filled the pages of every newspaper and magazine. The invasion was regarded as an eruption of civil disobedience, particularly serious for a dictatorial regime which claimed to represent "the people and the armed forces" and to advocate the creation of a revolutionary order in the country.

The minister of the interior, General Armando Artola Azcárate, who had earned fame in the antisubversive campaign waged by the army against communist guerrillas in 1965, announced that innocent people were being manipulated by the invasion's leaders for seditious purposes. However, he made the mistake of crossing swords with Bambarén, who was present at the scene during the most critical days of the invasion and who held an open-air mass for the soul of settlement leader Salvador Saldívar, killed in the skirmish. The minister viewed the bishop's attitude as a provocation and ordered his arrest and imprisonment. The Catholic Church protested angrily, and Artola counterattacked by organizing a demonstration of "genuine settlers" in support of the government's position. In the meantime, the invasion had been gathering physical and moral strength as a result of Saldívar's death and the Church's intervention, and a further uprising was feared. Bambarén was released on May 13 and Artola was forced to resign four days later.

The invasion was apparently very well planned, for it coincided with a meeting in Lima of the board of governors of the Inter-American Development Bank (IDB), which had earlier provided resources for various housing projects in Peru. The incident attracted international attention and earned the invaders considerable publicity. The invaders were also very skillful at arousing the interest of the remaining independent information media, which took it upon themselves to emphasize the contradiction between the social justice that the "revolutionary government" claimed to be seeking and the drastic repression of the invaders at Pamplona.

For the first time, the residents of an informal settlement had been able to bring down a minister of the interior—moreover, one who wielded considerable power and had a reputation as a strongman. A compromise was reached: the invaders agreed to move to a site chosen and, to some extent, equipped by the government, where they established the Villa El Salvador or Villa Salvador settlement, originally named, it is said, after Salvador Saldívar.

The Pamplona invasion affected the military government's subsequent attitude toward the establishment of new settlements. Although the ban on further invasions imposed by Act 13517 remained in effect, the policy of relocating invaders on government land set aside for that purpose was resumed, although this time in the form of lots with services, rather than in UPIS.

The authorities thus adopted an apparently contradictory position. Invasions were still illegal. But, since the government was a revolutionary one, whenever an invasion occurred it recognized that people wanted a lot on which to build a home and therefore undertook to relocate them. This served the twofold purpose of seeing that justice was done and avoiding the urban problems created by informal settlements. The position apparently encouraged further invasions, for invaders could be sure that the military government would relocate them in one of the established "reception areas."

However, the invasion of Pamplona also increased the military government's desire to gain political control of the settlements. Argentina's and Uruguay's experiences with urban guerrilla movements at that time heightened this concern since, so far as we know, the military high command feared a political radicalization of the people. The dictatorship was determined to compete with the APRA and the left wing for influence and hegemony over the informal settlements, for it was aware that any government which claims to be revolutionary gains "legitimacy" by increasing its base of support.

In its determination to prevent events from eluding its grasp as they had at Pamplona, the military government decided to take the offensive, setting up the National Social Mobilization Support System (SINAMOS), designed to concentrate under its authority all the state's relations with the settlements.[16] The original idea was to use SINAMOS to mobilize, organize, and control the settlement dwellers by transforming the settlements into model villages in which land would be distributed and economic activities would be generated for the inhabitants. Villa El Salvador was chosen as a pilot experiment, probably because of the political impact to be gained from taking the offensive in the very place where invaders had brought down the minister of the interior, and the first Self-Managed Urban Community (CUAVES) was established there.

The CUAVES program represented the government's twofold ambition of creating model human settlements and controlling the population

[16] Legislative decrees 18896 and 19352.

politically. Its structure was to consist of a complex system of affiliations headed by a secretariat which would handle problems ranging from law and order or disputes to education, provision of services, health care, and the production and marketing of goods. SINAMOS, for its part, would centralize decision making. In time, the entire initiative failed. Both SINAMOS and CUAVES gradually lost influence, basically because the state could control settlement dwellers only to the extent that it provided them with such tangible benefits as basic services and did not affect their economic and social activities. Their spontaneous organizations far more effectively represented the residents' interests than the bureaucratized and centralized system proposed by the government.

Although SINAMOS outlived the Velasco regime, it did no more than handle the legal affairs of informal settlements between 1976 and 1977, and in July 1978 it was finally dissolved. CUAVES, for its part, never achieved the viability hoped for by its proponents. It fell into disuse when the government promoted Villa El Salvador to the category of "district" in 1983.

Strictly speaking, the informals defeated the revolutionary government on every front. Despite Velasco's effort to establish a new revolutionary order in which the necessary changes could be made, he was overthrown by the armed forces themselves in 1975. In that year, 62 of every 100 houses built in Lima were informal and only 38 were formal.

The emergence of associations and cooperatives

The sixth stage began when the informals took advantage of the agrarian reform launched by Velasco to convert agricultural land to urban land illegally, thereby creating a second front for the development of informal housing.

Although the state had been trying since 1950 to plan the city's development in the face of an uncontainable wave of migration, it was only when the military government began its agrarian reform in the early 1970s that there was any official attempt to define precisely the city limits beyond which existing cultivated land would be subject to redistribution. As the cities had to keep growing, the planners defined areas of urban growth which contained part of this cultivated land and, as such, would not be affected by agrarian reform.

The rural landholders became very interested in ensuring that their land was incorporated into such growth areas. In so doing, they left no stone unturned, exploiting their political influence to the hilt or resorting to bribes. In no time at all, vast areas of growth were established which, in practice, were exempt from agrarian reform. The military government, growing suspicious, ordered the owners to urbanize their land within five years. The landowners, who could not obtain sufficient financing, clients, and construction within this period, began to deal with associations and cooperatives.

The settlements which had been organized as associations and cooperatives prior to the 1970s had been in urban areas such as Santoyo, Huerta Perdida, Pedregal, or Ancieta, where there were a number of slums. Such settlements were henceforth located primarily on agricultural land. As a result, during the Velasco government, informal land sales of this type joined invasion as a second way the informals could defeat the state.[17]

Urban recognition

The seventh stage occurred when the authorities were forced to allow originally informal settlements to become formal neighborhoods which would not be subject to any exceptional rules if they complied with the prescribed process of legalization.

In its second phase (1975–1980), the military government had been overtaken on all sides when it had proved powerless to prevent or control invasions and when associations and cooperatives had begun to acquire agricultural land illegally as a result of its own agrarian reform. The city's informal growth now seemed irreversible.

It was in this context that Decree-Law 22612 was adopted in 1979. The new law was to be a milestone in the recognition of popular property, for it provided that, as soon as settlements completed the legalization process established by Act 13517, they would become regular city neighborhoods and therefore eligible for reclassification as districts. On the pretext of correcting an administrative error in the 1961 Act, which had failed to establish what status the settlements would ultimately enjoy, the military placed them in the same urban category as the city's traditional neighborhoods. The ruling not only enhanced the security and stability of

[17] Examples are the Daniel A. Carrión, San Pedro, and el Valle cooperatives at San Juan de Lurigancho; the San Miguel, San Carlos, Pachacútec, 27 April, Jardín Azul, DEMSA, and Santa Clara cooperatives, among others, at Ate-Vitarte; and the Tayacaja, los Chancas, Andahuaylas, and los Huancas cooperatives, among others, at El Agustino. Other examples are the Las Flores and Campoy associations "for housing" at San Juan de Lurigancho; and the Fuerzas Policiales, San Roque, San Martín, and 11 October associations "for housing" at Ate-Vitarte.

expectative rights, it also amounted to recognition that informal settlements were, after all, another way of creating neighborhoods in the city. The weight of the evidence had finally convinced the authorities that, contrary to what the legislators had thought in 1961, they were not dealing with some passing urban aberration which could be put right by a bureaucratic procedure, but rather with an alternative form of urbanization which was in fact an expression of the people's desire to own private property.

The recognition marked the end of the central government's attempts to involve itself in the internal functioning of the settlements. When the new Constitution was drawn up that same year, its drafters transferred responsibility for the settlements to municipal governments. By 1979, informality had grown even further: of every 100 houses built in the capital that year, 65 were informal and only 35 were formal.

Recognition of private property and informal organizations

The eighth stage occurred when the authorities stepped up the distribution of titles and recognized informal organizations as the legitimate representatives of the informal settlements.

Since the central government had transferred responsibility for the settlements to them, the municipal governments had no choice but to tailor their actions to the wishes of their voters, in other words to give them the titles they were demanding. A rapid march toward legal ownership of private property began.

Over the years, the attention given to this task had varied. All in all, in some twenty years of work—from 1961 to 1980—valid titles to only about twenty-five percent of all lots had been granted. In the first ten years of the life of Act 13517, approximately eight thousand titles had been issued. In 1971 and 1972, SINAMOS had expedited the issue of another seven thousand or more. The number soon declined, however; between 1979 and 1980 only some one thousand titles were issued.

SINAMOS apparently neglected the technical work essential for granting titles—plans, remodelling, and so forth—so that when the work done by its predecessors came to an end, it was unable to continue the process. It was also more interested in communal property than private property, as one of its confidential documents shows:

The legalization process described above has certain adverse effects for marginal populations because it generally acts as an element of family and community breakdown, drastically undermining the high level of social cohesion achieved by these groups in the invasion's earlier stages through their spontaneous organizations. This process also gives rise to serious disputes among residents, as the considerable amount of litigation in legalized neighborhoods shows.[18]

The advent of a democratic government drastically altered this perception and showed how mistaken the authorities had been. The evidence showed that what people wanted was private property and that their interest in socialized models of community living was more rhetorical than anything else. When Lima's municipal government was elected in 1980, this aspiration for private property finally found political expression. Since the City Council was interested in preserving its popularity and seeking reelection, and since it realized that voters in the informal settlements were particularly concerned about their land, it decided to grant them title instead of trying to impose the ideal community from above. By relaxing the requirements during the mayoralty of Eduardo Orrego (1981–1983), the Lima City Council managed to issue more than twenty-two thousand titles, a record. When the predominantly Marxist left wing headed by Alfonso Barrantes won the 1983 municipal elections, the City Council tried to continue granting titles, in recognition of the people's interest in acquiring private ownership of their land. According to ILD calculations, however, by July 1986 the Marxist municipal government had issued fewer than eleven thousand valid titles.

The Council also recognized that organizational autonomy for the settlements was another expectation that had been repeatedly postponed. To satisfy it, it issued Ordinance 192 creating the "settlers' organization." This ordinance did not establish a uniform model for organizing the settlements, but instead recognized the settlers' right to freedom of association without prior authorization, granting legal status to any of the forms of association envisaged by the law—even to de facto groups. Significantly, the ordinance affirmed the recognition of settlers' organizations formed to carry out invasions and other illegal acts.

Toward a state modeled on the informal sector

The ninth stage was reached when, faced with the unworkability of the legal system, the state resorted to the extralegal system, specifically, to invasion, in order to create a housing project.

[18] "Preliminary Draft of the Two-Year Plan, 1973–1974, 10th SINAMOS Region," October 1972. Mimeo. Restricted circulation.

On July 15, 1984, seven thousand families invaded 640 hectares of land at Km. 18 on the Carretera Central, by the Huaycán ravine. The invasion was planned, organized, and carried out by the Lima City Council itself. Most of the invaders were public employees or belonged to organizations which could hardly be suspected of being informal. According to accounts gathered by the ILD, the first Huaycán invaders were grouped into eleven organizations previously recognized by the City Council.[19] Of these, two belonged to its own employees and those of the Ate-Vitarte district council, one consisted of the employees of the National Cultural Institute, which wanted the land as an archaeological area, and another consisted of the employees of the College of Architects. All the future settlers had some kind of special relationship with the authorities or were closely involved with housing problems, making them an interest group which could easily be mobilized by the state.

The delay in the procedures for adjudicating the land, ownership of which had to be transferred from the ministry of housing to the City Council, finally exasperated the municipal authorities and convinced them to give the go-ahead for the invasion. Mayor Alfonso Barrantes himself, frustrated by the interminable red tape, had raised the matter two months earlier with the then Minister of Housing Javier Velarde Aspíllaga who, by his own admission, acknowledged that, given the impossibility of speeding up the administrative procedure, invading Huaycán was the only solution.

The fact that a mayor and a minister, with all the political weight of their office, were unable to deal with the established procedures and had to resort to invasion made it clear that the legal system was incapable of providing housing to the people. However, unlike informals, public officials are unfamiliar with the extralegal system that governs invasions.

A week after the invasion, four thousand people from the Horacio Zeballos settlement, led by Jaime Zubieta Calderón, tried to enter Huaycán and were thrown out after a violent clash with the original invaders. In August and September, these clashes continued intermit-

---

[19] These were the Andrés Avelino Cáceres Association, José Carlos Mariátegui Association, National Cultural Institute Housing Cooperative, Lima City Council Employees' Housing Cooperative, Ate-Vitarte District Council Housing Association, Colegio Teresa González de Fanning Housing Association, College of Architects of Peru Housing Cooperative, 18 January Association, Asociación Paraíso de Huaycán, Coastal Education Sector, and Las Malvinas Association.

tently, always resulting in victory for the settlers, backed by the council. On October 8, eight thousand settlers engaged in another pitched battle, this time with Molotov cocktails, homemade shotguns, and bombs. Dozens of people sustained injuries or bruises and the civil guard had to intervene to restore order.

The clashes resumed toward the end of October. Frustrated by their repeated defeats, the Horacio Zeballos settlers, numbering some three thousand men, women, and children, this time began to invade privately owned land bordering the righthand end of Huaycán in the early hours of October 27. Here they established a new settlement which would be able to benefit from the various public works and services which the City Council would provide to Huaycán. The violence continued in November and December. Just when the storm appeared to have subsided, Jaime Zubieta, chair of the Horacio Zeballos settlement and leader of the new settlers, was mysteriously murdered.[20]

All this violence occurred because the City Council failed to take the extralegal system into account. When informals plan an invasion, they act by consensus, make a thorough survey of their shared interests, assemble the critical mass needed to cover the area almost completely, and set up a system for incorporating people who later ask to join the settlement, giving preference to local residents. Invasions thus have an operating logic which determines their capacity to coordinate efforts, design a settlement, distribute lots, organize self-defense, administer justice, negotiate with the authorities, and generally make progress. Unfortunately, by replacing the wishes and spontaneous cooperation of the settlers with an ideal order which sought to determine how the settlement should be, the Council robbed the invasion of its efficiency and distorted the inherent logic of the process. The invasion was not agreed upon but approved; because people's shared interests were not properly surveyed, they started to fight among themselves instead of cooperating, and backing was given only to organizations recognized by the Council, ruling out the possibility of incorporating new parties interested in residing in the settlement.

The most significant thing about the Huaycán invasion was that informality not only defeated formality but also infected it.

---

[20] According to statements by Franklin Acosta, mayor of Ate-Vitarte, published in *El Nacional* in May 1985, the Ate-Vitarte district council filed a report of aggravated homicide with the public prosecutor's department in connection with Zubieta's murder.

The unsuccessful prosecution of associations and cooperatives

The tenth stage was marked by the legislative recognition of illegal land sales as a second informal means of access to property for housing.

Associations and cooperatives had flourished since 1975. Sales of agricultural land illegally converted to urban land had given rise to hundreds of new neighborhoods with thousands of homes. In early 1985 alone, forty-five associations and cooperatives managed to sell approximately six hundred thousand square meters of land. To do this, they advertised publicly and widely in the mass media in order to obtain as many members as possible. The resulting tide of informal housing overflowed the valley of the Rímac, reaching that of the Lurín to the south and the Chillón to the north. In these circumstances, the associations' and cooperatives' activities could not continue to go unnoticed by the authorities. They denounced these activities in a massive newspaper campaign and proceeded to penalize offenders for urbanizing agricultural land without a permit, imposing huge fines, demolishing sales offices, and even instituting criminal proceedings against informal brokers.

The authorities found that all this did not do away with the homes which been built by the thousands on the land in question. Demolishing these houses and removing their occupants would have been very unpopular, physically, socially, and politically unacceptable. The authorities had no alternative but to return, less than a year after launching their campaign, to the easier course of legalization. Now defeated, the Council ordered that a census be taken of settlement dwellers in order to "regularize their situation."

On January 12, 1985, Act 24071, requiring housing cooperatives with ongoing programs to issue titles to their members within sixty days, was promulgated. Although this measure was directed only at the cooperatives, perhaps because of the kind of political immunity they seem to enjoy in Peru, Congress was, for the first time, implicitly recognizing illegal land sales as a means of access to property. It was a definite victory for informality.

The growth of informality continues apace. The inability to clamp down on associations and cooperatives, as well as the example set by the municipal government when it tried operating outside the law, has further weakened the legal system and strengthened informal methods of acquiring property. Takeovers of land increased in 1985. As Minister of the Interior

Abel Salinas reported in a statement to Congress, 282 new invasions had occurred by October of that year.

Of every 100 houses built in Lima in 1985, 69 were owned by informals and only 31 by formals.

The Long March toward Private Property

The process of development we have been discussing shows that people are capable of violating a system which does not accept them, not so that they can live in anarchy but so that they can build a different system which respects a minimum of essential rights.

In the case of informal housing, these rights are property rights. The history of the informal settlements is the history of the informals' struggle to own private land.

The people's struggle to acquire private property is reflected clearly in the names used to denote settlements over the years. These names also show how they have gradually enhanced their urban status: from "neighborhood," their first official title, to "young towns," "marginal human settlements," and, finally, "municipal human settlements."

In the process, the state steadily retreated. Its defeat is reflected in the succession of government departments officially entrusted with dealing with the settlements. Between 1957 and 1985, eleven different offices were given this responsibility, for an average of two and a half years each. These offices were, in chronological order: the National Office of Neighborhoods of the Ministry of the Interior and Police in 1957; the Office of Technical Assistance in the same year; the National Housing Institute in 1960; the National Housing Corporation the following year; the National Housing Board in 1963; ONDEPJOV and the Ministry of Housing in 1969; SINAMOS in 1971; the Urban Development Department and the Unregulated Settlements Department in 1978; and the Executive Department for Marginal Human Settlements of the Provincial Council in 1981. Thus, informality, which began as a police problem in 1957, defeated a succession of central government experts and politicians over the years, until responsibility for it was finally turned over to municipal governments.

Similarly, the main function of the prevailing extralegal system and the informal organizations has been to safeguard and enhance the private property thus acquired, rather than to impose a system of collective ownership. There is, of course, considerable and widespread communal activity in the settlements, but this activity springs from the need to make up for the lack of public services and is generally aimed at benefitting private property.

In the period between 1961 and 1981, independently owned housing in Lima increased by 375 percent, while rented housing declined by 34 percent. This means that people abandoned rural areas or rental slum dwellings in formal neighborhoods, to live in their own homes in informal settlements, thereby seeking to lay the essential material basis for participating in the incipient market economy generated by Peru's people. As a result, in districts of Lima with a large proportion of informal settlements, the percentage of owner-occupied dwellings is greater than in formal neighborhoods. For instance, in Villa María del Triunfo, an informal neighborhood, over 99 percent of the homes are owner-occupied; in Breña, where there is virtually no informal housing, only 28 percent of all homes are owner-occupied. The development of informality has brought home ownership to a larger percentage of low-income residents than middle-income residents.

The development of informal settlements has also prevented Lima from becoming one vast slum. The ILD has calculated that, were it not for the settlements, Breña, el Cercado, and Barranco would today have a population 91 percent, 85 percent, and 81 percent, respectively, greater than at present. The Rímac, for its part, would have 45 percent more inhabitants; Magdalena del Mar, 48 percent; Lince, 58 percent; and Surquillo, 59 percent. Similarly, La Victoria would have 32 percent more slums; Miraflores, 25 percent; and Pueblo Libre, 17 percent. Moreover, had the slums prevailed, the $8,319.8 million created by the informal settlements could never have been generated. The additional slums would be worth only $460 million, a mere 5.5 percent of the value generated by the informals.

Informal settlements have proved themselves highly preferable to slums. They have given rise to a system of private, extralegal property rights developed in an environment in which there are no efficient legal mechanisms to express the value which people of humble origin attach to land.

The informal system is neither perfect nor desirable, however. The range of choices open to informals when they decide to acquire land informally is limited. It also involves a tremendous waste of resources because of the high costs of invasion or informal land sales and the uncertainties inherent in illegality. The property rights acquired are diminished by a kind of legal apartheid. And the system is unstable because it does not protect the informals when others try to invade their land. The absence of a legal system of efficient property rights is detrimental to all.

As we shall see in the chapters which follow, these characteristics are common to all informality. We live in a costly society in which the opportunities provided by the law are not available to all Peruvians.

Still, the migrants from the countryside to the city, who have become informals, have over the years staged a long march toward private property, subjugating the state and formal society as they go. Seventy years afterward, and all the laws enacted since 1915 notwithstanding, informal urban development continues in Lima—no longer in San Isidro, Chacra Colorada, or Orrantia, but on river banks and former estates and within the confines of the people's city.

CHAPTER THREE

Informal Trade

As the city filled with people and its space was gradually taken over by informal housing, other economic activities began to undergo a similar evolution. One such activity was trade, which began to be conducted on a massive scale outside and even in defiance of state laws intended to regulate it. This marked the birth of informal trade, carried on essentially in the street—where it is known as "street vending"—and in markets built by vendors in order to move off the streets.

Street vending commenced when people began to invade the public thoroughfare, the use of which is open to everybody, in order to sell goods and services and for commercial transactions—without obtaining permits, giving receipts, or paying taxes. Some of this trade benefitted from a legal exemption granted in exchange for payment of a charge or "excise," which secured it the tolerance of the municipal authorities.

Informal markets, on the other hand, began when vendors who were already operating on the streets sought to end the insecurity of doing so and began to build their own markets without complying with the legal provisions governing invaded land or legally developed lots. Others engaged formal businesses to do so or became their customers, but in either case the markets were built without complying with state regulations.

When the Instituto Libertad y Democracia (ILD) began its research into street vending, it found that no one had a clear idea of the number of vendors in Lima. A census conducted by the National Statistical Institute (INE) in 1976 had come up with a figure of 58,284 street vendors in the capital's twenty-nine main districts. Any projection of these figures to the situation a decade later would have been highly inaccurate. It was widely believed that there were between two and three hundred thousand street vendors, a figure which the authorities, including Mayor Alfonso Barrantes put as high as four or five hundred thousand.

This diversity of estimates convinced the ILD to assemble its own statistics. In January 1985, it conducted a new survey of street vendors in the area covered by the INE in 1976 and found that there were 84,327 vendors in the city. A year later, in January 1986, it repeated the exercise and this time came up with 91,455 vendors. Thus, while the average annual growth had been 4.6 percent between 1976 and 1985, it shot up to 8.5 percent in 1985. The survey further showed that most street vendors were to be found in poor neighborhoods. Eighty percent of all the city's vendors operate in the fifteen districts generally regarded as low-income neighborhoods: the greatest concentrations are in the districts of Lima, 21 percent; and San Martín de Porres and La Victoria, 11.5 percent each. The smallest concentrations are in San Borja, 0.5 percent; and San Isidro and La Molina, 0.1 percent each.

The survey also showed that the 91,455 vendors occupy only 79,020 "pitches," i.e., spaces to hawk their merchandise, on the public thoroughfare, which means that, although vendors usually operate on their own, some work in partnership or as employees, under what is also an informal system of relations. It further established that street vending is a specialized activity. Of the pitches then in existence, 59.5 percent were used for the sale of foodstuffs; 17.5 percent for personal accessories; 13.7 percent for services; and the remaining 9.3 percent for household and office supplies.

Last, the survey showed that 90 percent of street vendors are within the age group traditionally defined as the economically active population (EAP) and 54 percent are women.

All these statistics made it clear that, like the case of informal settlers, the contribution of the street vendors to the country's economy is considerable. According to the ILD's estimates, some 294,000 people are directly dependent on such trade, either as vendors or as their dependent relatives. A further 20,000 people are indirectly dependent on it, as employees of those who supply the street vendors with goods. Thus, for every four vendors on the city's streets, there is an additional job among their suppliers. A total of some 314,000 people are dependent on street vending.

According to a sample obtained in the 1985 survey, gross sales are considerable: $6.2 million a week, or roughly $322.2 million a year. Gross monthly sales per pitch range from a maximum of $431 for the sale of foodstuffs to a minimum of $155 for the provision of services. These gross sales earn the street vendors a considerable income. For every $100 in sales, they net a profit of $18.30. Net income varies according to the line of business, however—from $74 a month for sales of personal accessories to $48 for services. This makes the net per-capita income from street vending $58 a month, 38 percent more than the minimum legal wage at the time of the sample.

The number of informal markets was also unclear when the ILD began its research. They were simply ignored by official researchers and there was no benchmark from which to make an estimate. However, the street vendors interviewed insisted on the existence and the importance of their "projects" and cited the "many" markets established by their colleagues over the years. It seemed important to find out how many such markets existed and what proportion of informal trade they represented. To do so, the ILD conducted exhaustive field work in parallel with the 1985 survey. The researchers found that there were 274 informal markets in the capital city, as compared with 57 built by the state. If we go by these two figures alone, that means that 83 percent of the markets in the capital city are informal.[1]

Like the street vendors, the informal markets are more numerous in informal settlements than in residential areas: 59 percent of such markets are to be found in the nine districts with the highest proportion of informal housing, and this proportion increases to 64 percent if we take the number of stalls in the markets into account.

ILD researchers then assessed these markets, funded principally by street vendors who desired to move off the streets, and estimated their current value at $40.9 million. More detailed research was later conducted, but statistics could be obtained on only 239 of them. There were 38,897 people working at 29,693 stalls in these markets. This means that the former street vendors who are now off the streets also maintain a considerable number of people. The ILD estimates that 125,000 people are directly dependent on this second type of informal trader. Altogether, there are 439,000 people dependent on informal trade carried out on the street and in markets.

That the volume of informal trade is this considerable; that street

---

[1] Lima also has an indeterminate number of shopping centers built formally by the private sector but housing an indeterminate number of former street vendors.

vendors and their markets are to be found in almost all districts of Lima, particularly to sell food to the city's poorest inhabitants; that they provide sustenance and employment to a large number of people and even enable them to earn, on average, 38 percent more than the minimum legal wage means that formal trade must first have declined and that informal trade must have gathered strength until it became a system capable of supporting all this development.

In the following pages, we will attempt to show how this occurred. We shall first consider the various types of informal trade and the phenomena to which it has given rise, trying to identify the prevailing system of extralegal norms and its operating logic. We shall then explain how this activity evolved, thus demonstrating the gradual advance of informality. Last, we shall consider the long march of street vendors toward private enterprise and property as expressed in their aspiration to build their own markets.

Types of Informal Trade

Although informal trade falls into two clearly defined categories—street vending and informal markets—these are not rigidly compartmentalized activities but rather different stages in the same process. The people who start out as street vendors do not do so with the idea of remaining on the street forever, but with the intention of moving at some point to markets away from the public thoroughfare in order to conduct their activities under better conditions. All the traders now working in markets worked on the street at one time or another.

Street vending

Street vending has traditionally been regarded as the sum total of informal trade, but it is only one form of illegal trading on the street.

The term "street vending" brings to mind two definite activities: that of the trader who walks around the city offering goods or services without a fixed place from which to operate, and that of the trader who sells merchandise or provides services from a fixed point on the public thoroughfare.

This is not a recent distinction: as early as colonial times, the former were called "peddlers" because of their retail function and their skill in negotiating contracts, and the latter "stallholders" because they set up wooden stalls on the public thoroughfare. We can thus talk of two kinds of street vending: itinerant vending and vending from a fixed point on the public thoroughfare. These are generally stages in street vending through which traders pass as they gradually come to operate with greater security.

Itinerant vending

Itinerant vending is carried out by people who purchase small quantities of trinkets, delicacies, or nonperishable foodstuffs and walk around the streets trying to sell them to passersby. They have no fixed location and operate on a fairly small scale. Their income depends entirely on the skill with which they move about in search of customers, since it is highly unlikely that customers will go in search of them. They are not organized because they operate on their own and have no fixed location to defend. They have no great physical capital or access to credit, with the result that they must finance themselves and generally operate with cash.

When they start to work, these street vendors are not only providing a service, but also investing in their human capital. While they walk around the streets in search of customers, they observe what goods are being sold. They see other, apparently more prosperous, vendors working from barrows in the same location each day. Various suppliers offer them goods at different prices and on different terms. They learn from more experienced friends and relatives and swap experiences with others who are also just starting out. In so doing, they discover that the street is the school where one learns what goods are needed and the value attached to this need.

As time passes and they acquire more know-how, street vendors begin to establish routes for their daily itinerary. At the same time, they replace their hands, or the small cases they used for carrying wares, with a barrow which makes them more mobile, is a more efficient means of storage, and increases the scale of their operations.

By repeating the same sales circuit over and over again, vendors begin to identify with their customers and with other vendors operating near that circuit. This gradual process of identification generates a reputation which will earn the vendor not only the trust of customers but also the credit from suppliers.

At this point a new process begins: as repeated trading in the street helps to identify locations that are commercially attractive, the vendor begins to aspire to setting up a fixed location. The advantages of operating in a known and specific place, where merchandise can be stored and displayed, and where a reputation can be established, become clear. The street vendor aspires to stability.

Vending from a fixed location on the public thoroughfare

When the street vendor gives up itinerant trading, identifies a location, and conducts business there, an invasion of the street occurs.

The ILD found that, like the informal settlers, street vendors do not invade the streets arbitrarily or haphazardly, but only after a complex economic calculation.

The first thing a vendor does when trying to invade a fixed place on the public thoroughfare is assess the value of the location. This requires estimating the number of customers who may frequent the pitch daily, which will determine whether the location can be operated economically. The assessment thus reflects the potential customers' preference for buying here rather than elsewhere. This also enables the vendor to determine by how much the anticipated net income will exceed the wage or profit the vendor wants, including any agreed upon with an assistant, or partner. That income will result from the price that customers would be prepared to pay to buy merchandise in the new location.

The vendor also evaluates other factors, such as resistance from vendors already established in that location, residents who may be harmed by the new activity, and the authorities. The first question is generally resolved by making prior contacts: if there is a particularly high level of resistance from established vendors, the vendor may decide to look for another location. The ILD did not find evidence of much contact between the vendor and the residents, however: since the vendor is invading public property, such as roadways or sidewalks over which no one has clearly defined interests, the possibility of a popular reaction is somewhat remote. Similarly, the vendor evaluates the possibility of an agreement with other people also operating on the street, particularly transport operators, since large numbers of people gather at the intersections of their routes and also at their first and last stops. Street vendors offer to look after their passengers while they wait, and even provide transport operators with other services, such as preparing their food. Once the vendor has invaded the location and established a pitch, these agreements can develop into a strong alliance of interests when affected residents and the authorities must be dealt with. This has occurred on more than one occasion.

Street Invasions When invading a street, the vendor generally acts alone. Moreover, the invasion does not occur all at once, but little by little, as if preliminary calculations and the possible consequences are being tested. As a result, the invasion contract which the ILD found in the formation of informal settlements does not exist here. Instead, neighboring vendors conclude partnership agreements after the street has been invaded, in order to set up informal organizations for their own defense or promote the construction of a market into which they might move. Although still a street vendor, the informal trader has now ceased to be itinerant and has a fixed location on the public thoroughfare. Although the establishment— generally a barrow—has wheels, the vendor no longer moves around in order to sell. Instead, wheels are used to move the merchandise to a safe storage place at the end of the day.

An individual vendor who occupies a permanent location is inevitably surrounded by other vendors. If the site is a new one, the success of the original vendor will determine whether others will follow suit, setting up nearby. If, on the other hand, the site is already occupied by other vendors, a new arrival will consolidate their presence. In both cases, however, the critical mass essential for defining the location is being assembled. The vendors realize that the safety, cleanliness, quality, and variety of the goods available, and the volume of customers affect the flow of buyers and that they have a shared interest in maximizing this flow. In this way, vendors gradually develop different types of locations on the public thoroughfare which ILD researchers have classified as "belts" and "minimarkets."

Belts arise when vendors set up their barrows around markets. The belts around the Central Market or the Ciudad de Dios Cooperative Market, the city's two main markets, are examples. Here we observe a tendency for vendors to supplement the markets by expanding the range of both products and prices. Lines of business unavailable in the nucleus are offered in the belt. Similarly, when price controls cause a shortage of goods in the nucleus, these are offered in the belt at higher prices. In belts like the one around the Central Market, the competition from informal trade has moved buyers to the outside, to the point that many merchants use their stalls inside the market only to store goods and conduct their transactions on the public thoroughfare. There has been such a widespread trend toward the informalization of sales that it is difficult to determine whether the market or the belt is the real nucleus.

The second kind of location is the minimarket, a group of vendors which, unlike the belt, forms a new nucleus of commercial activity. In its 1986 survey, the ILD found 829 such minimarkets throughout the city. These markets, sufficiently large and complex to be self-supporting, offer every conceivable kind of goods and services. They may be located in the traditional city, as the Tacora and Avenida Aviación markets are. In informal settlements, which generally lack other markets, they cover all basic needs.

Special Rights of Ownership When the ILD observed vending from fixed locations on the public thoroughfare, especially from fixed sites, it found, just as in informal settlements, an extralegal system that ordered and regulated the informal activities in question. There is a special relationship between the vendor and the location occupied, in that the location remains the same and the vendor may exercise certain rights over it. This relationship does not correspond to an equivalent right in the formal legal system, however, because it governs a piece of street which is open to public use. Instead, it constitutes an informal relationship which we have called the "special right of ownership."

The importance of this right is that, from the standpoint of the vendor and the customer, it permits the economic use of public thoroughfares which in normal circumstances would serve only for traffic, decoration, or public safety. It also helps to increase the scale of the operation and enables vendors to specialize, since the larger space inherent in a fixed location allows efficient storage of goods. The mere fact of remaining stationary also shows that the vendor wants to be identified; it is thus a sign of dependability. By developing a right over this location, the vendor can establish a commercial reputation among buyers and suppliers far more easily than by remaining itinerant. This growing reputation also facilitates credit, mostly informal credit, so that the vendor can increase the economies of the commercial operation a little further.[2]

The special right of ownership is not perfect, however, because it is transitory and extralegal. Thus, it cannot be compared with formal ownership. It is even weaker than the expectative right of ownership existing in informal settlements, simply because the sidewalks and roadways must remain open to the public. As a result, the threat of eviction always hangs over street vendors, especially when there is traffic

---

[2] Although this is an extralegal concept, a vendor's fixed location is also accepted by many formal merchants in their mutual transactions.

congestion or growing pressure from residents. Practically speaking, this rules out any long-term investment in improving the location, forcing street vendors to keep selling from barrows rather than from stalls made with proper building materials and equipped with running water, electricity, refrigeration, storage, display space, or any of the other facilities that permit the supply of a steady volume of merchandise. The installation of such improvements as toilets, parking lots, or gardens would be impracticable.

The deficiencies of the special right of ownership are also reflected in the ways in which vendors can make exclusive use of or sell their sites on the public thoroughfare. Exclusive use of the pitch is the result of a long process resulting from repeated occupation of the same location. As more and more vendors establish themselves, this exclusive use is reinforced by the ties of proximity and shared interests.

Although exclusive use has to be won by remaining in the location, it is often limited by a system of shifts whereby each pitch may be used by different people in the course of the working day. It is not unusual, for instance, to see the pitch occupied by the breakfast seller in the early morning hours who then, around 9 or 10 in the morning, makes way for the juice seller who, at midday, makes way for the lunch seller who, after four in the afternoon, is followed by the vendor of herbal remedies, who later gives way to the vendor of Chinese food, who stays until the end of the day. These shifts enable a single barrow to operate like a large store, maximizing its commercial value. On their own, the different vendors offer only a small range of goods and services. When proximity does not operate satisfactorily, they try to improve it by establishing shifts, adapting the barrow's use to the different demands of consumers as they arise in the course of the day, thus exploiting the location's commercial value around the clock.

The power to sell a pitch is also limited by the imperfection of special rights of ownership, the main problem being the lack of security inherent in selling a piece of public thoroughfare to another street vendor. Strictly speaking, the street belongs to the community, which will never relinquish it; in fact, the transaction concerns the right to exploit it economically. As a result, it takes more than a written document to secure this transaction: the interested party must obtain the recognition of the other vendors occupying the pitch. The ILD found that, to do this, the person selling the pitch usually introduces the buyer to the other vendors as a relative or friend, or as someone from the same region.

Vendors' organizations help to consolidate this process, since the recognition which vendors give each other is replaced by membership in the organization and, as time passes, by the payment of dues and adherence to its agreements.

All of this makes up the extralegal system which enables street vendors to offset their lack of legal property rights. To test the commercial value of these rights over the public thoroughfare, the ILD assessed a small sample of the more important vendors' sites in January 1985. According to this sample, the average price per square meter of the special right of ownership over the public thoroughfare is $164. An average pitch of 4.3 square meters, then, sells for an average of $705. The ILD researchers found that, in the vicinity of the Plaza Dos de Mayo, some pitches of 3 square meters were selling for as much as $1,000.

The mere fact that a pitch on the street has a price shows that the original street vendor correctly anticipated that his customers would value the site for the convenience it offered. Thus, when a vendor acquires a pitch, even though it has already been assessed, its price conveys information about the value which customers attach to it.

Such operations can be based only on the extralegal system developed by the vendors themselves. However, this system, which is in open violation of the formal legal system, does not make the vendors' activity as secure as it needs to be. As a result, vendors try to obtain some kind of additional recognition of their special rights of ownership from the authorities. The most important way to do this is to pay an "excise" tax to the municipal authorities.[3] In 1985, all districts in Lima except El Cercado, La Molina, and San Isidro levied this tax, on the understanding that it did not confer any right to the roadways and sidewalks thus occupied, but only a permit to trade on them within the limits of municipal jurisdiction. The effect is quite the opposite, however, since the vendors obtain an extremely valuable element of security and stability for their special rights of ownership. That is why they are so interested in paying the tax and show their receipts for such payment. Their understanding is that this constitutes recognition of their rights—a situation accepted, strangely enough, by residents and even the authorities.

[3] The "excise" was a tax of French origin imposed on consumer goods in the Middle Ages. The earliest reference to it in the laws of the Peruvian Republic is to be found in the 1892 Municipalities Act, but no one knows how it evolved from a tax on cows, sheep, and goats to a tax levied on street vendors for occupying the public thoroughfare for commercial purposes.

The authorities are also keenly interested in the excise tax because street vendors pay more per square meter than formal merchants. In February 1985, for instance, excise rates ranged from a penny to 18 cents a day, the average being a little less than 5 cents. In San Juan de Miraflores, a district consisting entirely of informal settlements, street vendors paid an average of between $1.42 and $4.26 per square meter a year. That same year, formally established shops in the district paid only 72 cents a year for the same amount of space. Vendors were, in fact, paying between 98 percent and 495 percent more per square meter than formal merchants.

Income from the excise tax is thus not insignificant to the municipal authorities and, according to the ILD's calculations, is actually one of their main sources of income. In aggregate terms, it came to 70 percent more in 1984 than the income levied from formal traders for municipal operating permits, and to 29 percent of the total amount levied in property taxes from traders, industrialists, financiers, and formal property owners. The excise tax, therefore, is the preferred means of consolidating special rights of ownership because it benefits both the street vendors and the municipal authorities. The vendors pay it because it gives them a measure of stability and security, and the authorities levy it because they obtain more income per square meter than they would if the same vendors were formally established.

The revenue from the excise tax helps to explain why district municipal authorities, impoverished by the concentration of tax revenues in the hands of the central government, have surrendered to the advance of informal trading.

Self-defense Organizations As street vendors begin to realize they have been building up economically valuable pitches, their incentives for organizing to protect them increase, since their special rights of ownership do not offer them sufficient security. They therefore form essentially democratic self-defense organizations whose main aim is to protect the site they occupy from further invasion, from resistance by residents harmed by their activities, and from repression by the authorities. If necessary, they are prepared to use force, but they have developed the ability to forestall confrontation by negotiating politically.

They have been known to use the civil guard or the municipal police to defend their sites from further invasion. Luis Paredes Pinillos, leader of the Plaza Dos de Mayo and one of the vendors' most important leaders, is thought to have been the first to use such means to defend special rights of ownership. It is said that the first time Paredes used this method, he himself was affected: when police evicted the invading vendors, a mistake in the agreed system of signals resulted in Paredes being evicted and beaten by civil guards, prompting his friends to nickname him "Guillotine" after the inventor of the guillotine, who they presumed had suffered the consequences of his own invention.

The fact that a pitch is already economically valuable also induces these organizations to try to maintain order and take steps to improve cleanliness, thereby enhancing its reputation as a location that can be trusted for the quality of the goods and services it offers. Some have developed means of settling disputes among informal traders and of organizing or supervising the shift system that permits increased diversification of the pitches.

With the passage of time, as state authorities have paid greater attention to the problem, have engaged in dialogue, and have even co-opted organization leaders, these organizations have expanded their functions. They have attempted to mobilize street vendors in order to show they have political backing, have organized massive cleanups to please a succession of mayors, have participated in fairs, and have joined political movements or parties.

Even the most sophisticated of these self-defense organizations has little internal cohesion, however. The ILD saw that the extent to which vendors participate in them is directly proportional to the risk to their special rights of ownership, so that they tend to prefer the benefits they can obtain individually to the collective benefits of organizing. As a result, the individual vendors bypass their organizations when this is to their advantage. Moreover, their loyalty to their leaders is somewhat pragmatic. Since their main concern is to further secure their special rights of ownership, vendors choose their leaders for their political and bureaucratic contacts. As soon as a new authority takes over, they have no qualms about replacing their leaders with others who have the necessary access.

These organizations exist at basically two levels: the trade union or associative level and the federative level. At the first level, the organization is small-scale, generally consisting of the vendors on one block or, at most, in one neighborhood; it is an essentially democratic body that calls itself an association or trade union.[4] Decisions are adopted

---

[4] Informals use the term "trade union" even though their members are in fact small business owners because formal businessmen's organizations have traditionally opposed them while left-wing parties

at general meetings and an elected executive body is responsible for carrying them out.

Since their aim is to defend their territory and define their special rights of ownership, however, the institutional life and social relevance of such organizations are somewhat intermittent. Attacks, whether by the state, formal traders, or other vendors, occur in specific places, and only the vendors established in those places have an incentive to organize. We can therefore say that these organizations exist only when they have a function to fulfill. Like the special right of ownership, they are also limited, mainly by a lack of coercive authority which prevents the leaders from forcing recalcitrant vendors to pay their dues for installing sanitation, storage areas, and other facilities—making it difficult to improve conditions on the sites and reduce their adverse effects on third parties.

At the federative level, the organization generally covers more than one neighborhood. It thus operates on a larger scale, although it is never numerically large. The lack of numbers weakens it and, like the vendors' trade unions and associations, it responds basically to attacks or invitations from the state authorities rather than establishing a permanent institutional life. Despite some leaders' ambitions, such organizations are unable to interfere in their members' trading activities and must limit themselves essentially to bringing together neighborhood or block organizations to coordinate the vendors' different defenses against external threats. To do this, they identify common problems, resist the authorities, and negotiate with them.

Two organizations have achieved importance in the capital city over the years: the Federation of Street Vendors in the Central Market and Adjacent Streets (FEVACEL) and the Federation of Lima and Callao Street Vendors (FEDEVAL). These organizations represent two clearly defined tendencies. The former is a professional, politically independent union, while the latter's leadership is Marxist. Both have played an important role in the historical evolution of informal trade.

Informal markets

The second type of informal trade is conducted from markets built informally by or for vendors who want to leave the streets. Basically, vendors try to leave the public thoroughfare because of its inherent

have welcomed their demands and made them part of their political platforms. As a result, these organizations use a more proletarian terminology and their members have joined left-wing parties.

limitations. Long-term investment to improve their property is not rational. Their productivity is very low because the range of goods and services offered by each is extremely limited. They rarely give credit and do not offer repairs or guarantees. They have no special facilities for testing products and cannot give their customers specialized information. They suffer from the absence of proper storage areas and safety systems. All of this prevents them from selling sophisticated goods which require offering the customer-related services.

The street vendors thus have a very strong incentive to move off the street and replace their barrows with the market, in the search to bolster their "special rights of ownership" with more secure "property rights."

Markets and fairgrounds

As the ILD's research continued, it found 274 informal markets in Lima. Of these, 63 percent were built by street vendors themselves, through their organizations, and 28 percent by formal businesses under contract to informals or for sale to them. We have no information on the remaining 9 percent. In general, these markets are establishments built away from the public thoroughfare, with proper building materials and equipped with the necessary cold stores, warehouses, individual stalls, and sanitation.

The greatest concentration of such markets was in San Juan de Lurigancho, which housed 17.2 percent of all the city's informal markets. The districts of Lima, Comas, and San Martín de Porres followed, with 11.3 percent, 9.2 percent and 8.4 percent, respectively. At the other extreme were Magdalena del Mar, Miraflores, and San Borja, with only one market each, and San Isidro, Jesús María, and La Molina, with none. The proportions are roughly the same if we consider the number of stalls: San Juan de Lurigancho comes first, with 16.3 percent, followed by Comas with 11.9 percent, San Juan de Miraflores with 8.8 percent, and San Martín de Porres with 8.5 percent. Informal markets, thus, serve the least well-off, for more than half the markets now in existence—152, to be exact—are in informal settlements.

The state has also tried to intervene—albeit unsuccessfully—in this process, through the central or municipal governments. It has managed to build only 57 formal markets, one for every five built by informals. The difference is even greater if we consider only the twenty years from 1965 to 1985: for each market built by the state, twelve were built by informals. The informal markets are also better distributed than the state markets to serve the poor: 36 percent in "formal" Lima, 28 percent in the

Cono Norte, 20 percent in the Cono Este, and 16 percent in the Cono Sur, as against 86 percent of state markets in "formal" Lima, 9 percent in the Cono Norte, 5 percent in the Cono Este, and none in the Cono Sur.[5]

In view of the state's limited success in building markets, municipal governments began to develop fairgrounds in 1981 to relocate street vendors away from the public thoroughfare. The Polvos Azules, Amazonas, Miguel Grau, Virgen de Lourdes, Plaza Gastañeta, Polvos Rosados, Naranjal, and Las Malvinas fairgrounds were all developed in this way. Such fairgrounds do not consist of properly equipped buildings, but of small, precarious stalls built with wood and rush matting on the actual street. Moreover, the state has tried to interfere directly in the traders' business activities on these fairgrounds through a number of restrictions on the use and transfer of stalls. Such transactions have gone on behind the authorities' backs, however.

The fairgrounds are of relatively small importance in informal trade despite the authorities' political interest in sponsoring them. While 38,897 former street vendors operate in informal markets, only 7,150 vendors are to be found on the fairgrounds. If we compare the value of informal markets with the investment made in fairgrounds, the informal markets come off better: $40.9 million has been invested in the infrastructure of informal markets, but municipal governments have invested a mere $85,000 in fairgrounds. Even if we add the $405,000 contributed by the vendors to improve their fairground stalls, the difference is still tremendous.

Promotional organizations

As informal trade away from the public thoroughfare has developed, so too have other forms of vendors' organizations, now devoted less to defending their rights than to promoting their interests. To do this, a group of block or neighborhood organizations will form an association or cooperative to raise the funds to build a market. Such associations have a clearly defined financial and managerial role which is absent when the main concern is to protect members from, or negotiate with, the authorities. Their institutional life is more constant than in self-defense organizations, the

[5] By Cono Norte, we mean a group of informal settlements made up of the districts of San Martín de Porres, Independencia, Comas, Carabayllo, and Puente Piedra; by the Cono Este, a group of informal settlements made up of the districts of San Juan de Lurigancho and Ate; and by the Cono Sur, a group of informal settlements made up of the districts of San Juan de Miraflores, Villa María del Triunfo, and Villa El Salvador.

essentially democratic structure is maintained, and their membership is larger.

Promotional organizations are devoted solely to promoting the building of the market and do not interfere in the actual trading of each member. As in informal settlements, the organizations tend to be cooperatives. This is because, since the 1960s and especially under the Revolutionary Government of the Armed Forces (1968–1980), the state, and politicians in general, have given cooperatives special treatment; informals have therefore used this structure to hide and protect themselves from the authorities.

In trying to build markets, promotional organizations have encountered numerous difficulties, primarily because of the kind of property rights acquired. There were no major problems when a market was to be located on land within the traditional city, because the land acquired was already equipped with the services required by law. If the land was located in an informal settlement, on the other hand, vendors obtained only an expectative property right, equivalent to that enjoyed by the other residents of such areas. But the mere fact that vendors have built most of their markets in precisely these settlements means that they have had to add to their own problems the costs of acquiring property informally.

Difficulty in obtaining the credit necessary to build markets has been another problem. Uncertainties about title decrease the land's value as collateral. The rigidity and inaccessibility of capital markets increase these costs still further. This has forced vendors to build only as much as their membership can contribute; in more than one case, building has come to a complete standstill because of the lack of money. There have also been organizational problems. Because their activities are private and informal and they lack coercive authority, the organizations cannot compel the vendors to cooperate. Contributions have not been paid on time, and there has been considerable delay in decision making. These difficulties have been compounded in the cooperatives, because differences in the size of contributions are not reflected in the management and administration; members have no incentive to make larger contributions when their ownership of the additional amount is not recognized. There have been numerous disputes about this: organization leaders have been taken to court, premises seized, and there have been brawls and other disturbances. And, as we shall see in chapter 5, "The Costs and Importance of the Law," compliance with the legal requirements for building markets is the biggest obstacle to the vendors' access to formal trade. These organizations have also had to devote tremendous resources to defending the new market from subsequent invasion by other vendors.

All these difficulties have created tremendous expense for vendors determined to move off the streets. An empirical study conducted by the ILD on the basis of the history of five such markets shows that, as a result of such costs, vendors have had to wait an average of seventeen years before being able to actually occupy them.[6]

The Historical Evolution of Informal Trade

The historical evolution of informal trade, like that of housing, is one of changing circumstances, mass movements, conflicting interests, disputes, and even violent confrontations.

This section is organized into thirteen different historical stages, each of which is part of the steady advance of informal over formal society and the latter's corresponding retreat.

Recognition as part of the city's mores

It was actually the formals who gave informality its first chance centuries ago, to move ahead in trade, by recognizing street vending as part of the city's cultural identity and mores. Informal trade has a long history in Peru. In Andean and colonial cities, and later in the capital of the Republic, a myriad of such traders walked, or set up pitches on, their streets. Inca Túpac Yupanqui, according to historian Miguel Cabello de Valboa, ordered that it be proclaimed, throughout his empire, that anyone wishing to be a merchant could roam freely throughout the land and that anyone harassing such merchants would be subject to serious penalties.[7] The first colonial ban on street vendors was issued in 1594 by Viceroy García Hurtado de Mendoza, Marquis of Cañete. The accounts of nineteenth-century travelers provide further evidence of trading carried on outside the law and parallel to the growth of cities.

[6] The markets were Libertad, in San Miguel, Colonial, in El Cercado, Miguel Grau, in Independencia, APECOLIC, in Comas, and Ciudad de Dios, in San Juan de Miraflores.

[7] Miguel Cabello de Valboa, *Miscelánea Antártica* (Lima: Ethnology Institute, Universidad Nacional Mayor de San Marcos, 1951), p. 349.

The early street vendors were either impoverished Spaniards or Creoles, generally soldiers with little booty or sailors without fortune, whose racial status earned them special tolerance from the viceroy's caste-conscious authorities. Other racial groups, such as mestizos, Negroes, and mulattos, later took advantage of the space created by this tolerance and, in the seventeenth century, they were joined by Indians. In response to the fluctuating situation, the colonial authorities adopted attitudes fluctuating between permissiveness and repression which have endured over the centuries. The permissive approach was, basically, to levy an excise tax for occupation of the public thoroughfare. With few interruptions, this tax has been in force since 1553, when letters patent from the king of Spain authorized the city of Lima to keep the revenue from taxes on street vendor trade. The permissive attitude reached its zenith in colonial times: in 1778, colonial inspector Areche recognized street vendors as one of Lima's guilds, along with porters, shopkeepers, and messengers.[8]

Repression was also frequent. In colonial times, street vendors were expelled or banned in at least the following years: 1557, 1560, 1580, 1594, 1603, 1614, 1617, 1620, 1622, 1630, 1639, 1670, 1671, 1673, 1690, 1770, 1796, 1798, 1800, and 1804. This also occurred in the Republic. In 1850, President Ramón Castilla ordered the eviction of street vendors from the Plaza de Armas, by force if necessary. During the war with Chile, the forces occupying Lima, led by Patricio Lynch, tried desperately to control them by imposing fines and drastic penalties. After 1884, the municipal government issued increasing numbers of ordinances against the vendors.

During the Republic's first hundred years, however, street vendors were also gaining recognition as a part of the city's life. Contemporary painters such as Pancho Fierro, writers such as Ricardo Palma or Manuel Asencio Segura, and photographers such as Eugene Courret used them as models for their work. Manuel Atanasio Fuentes wrote that one of them, Na Aguedita, was more famous for his cold drinks and sweetmeats than the inventor of the telegraph.[9] Formal society regarded informal trade as part of the city's mores and cultural identity and did not feel that such trade might one day pose a threat to formal trade and transform the face of the

[8] General Archive of the Indies: Board of 7 December 1778 and General Archive of the Nation, City Guilds No. 3. From Fernando Iwasaki: "Ambulantes y Comercio Colonial: Iniciativas Mercantiles en el Virreynato Peruano," in *Jahrbuch für Geschichte von Staat: Wirtschaft und Gesellschaft Lateinamerikas*, no. 24 (Cologne: Federal Republic of Germany).

[9] Manuel Atanasio Fuentes: *Lima, Apuntes Históricos, Descriptivos y de Costumbres* (Lima, 1925), p. 140, cited by Iwasaki, ibid.

city, for at that time the number of street vendors was very small. This acceptance enabled migrants arriving in the city to identify street vending, like informal settlements, as one of the loopholes in the system through which they could begin to infiltrate it.

Recognition by municipal regulation

The second advance in informal trade occurred when street vendors managed to add to their cultural recognition the recognition of the municipal authorities implicit in the adoption of detailed regulations governing their activities.

Legal restrictions on street vending had been fairly isolated and specific. On September 14, 1915, however, an ordinance was issued which can be regarded as the first set of actual regulations of street vending. In addition to requiring vendors to buy a permit and be registered, it prohibited the sale of foodstuffs, prescribed the design of barrows and other structures for the carriage of vendors' goods, and instituted health controls.

The ordinance did not give the vendors any right to the public thoroughfare, however. The City Council's definition of a street vendor was a person who walked the streets and stopped only long enough to make a sale. The implication is that there already were others who set themselves up on the public thoroughfare and developed special rights of ownership over it.

The ordinance achieved the exact opposite of what was intended, for by issuing a set of regulations to govern the vendors' activities the authorities simply made room for them within the legal system. The number of vendors therefore increased, as did their determination to stop peddling from street to street and begin to acquire special rights of ownership over the public thoroughfare. In January 1916, the City Council adopted a second ordinance which reiterated the provisions of the previous ordinance almost verbatim and added financial penalties for noncompliance.

The basis for special rights of ownership

During the third historical stage, the street vendors gradually developed special rights of ownership in the face of considerable state resistance, a process that took almost three decades.

As their numbers increased and their activities became more complex, it became inevitable that street vendors would attempt to remain on the different pitches they had established on the public thoroughfare. The state's reaction was not consistent. The 1915 and 1916 ordinances established that vendors must, in fact, walk around and stop only to make sales, but the authorities used the excise tax to compel them to do so and, if possible, prevent them from setting up permanently on the public thoroughfare, by varying the tax inordinately.[10]

This method could be used, however, only as long as the number of vendors remained limited and stable. As soon as their numbers began to increase, the central government tried to intervene by limiting their growth and decided to suspend the excise tax in order to prevent them from gaining rights over the public thoroughfare. The decision deprived the municipal government of so much income that in 1936, it decided to go on levying the tax illegally. In so doing, however, the municipal government encouraged the street vendors. They began concentrating in various areas of the city which were henceforth incorporated into the city's commercial life, forcing even the central government to yield in 1944.[11]

Thus, in the end, the state was always forced to accept the bargain, the excise tax in return for occupation of the public thoroughfare. Some time later, in 1946, the APRA's parliamentary group in the Senate introduced an unsuccessful bill which sought to establish the excise levied on vendors as a permanent source of municipal revenue.[12] On December 11, 1947, such a decision was actually taken. The City Council adopted a new ordinance allowing vendors to stop temporarily in places where they did not disrupt traffic or compete with formal traders engaged in the same line of business.

Competition with formal trade

The fourth stage was marked by the transition from traditional street vending—devoted mainly to selling local food and cold or hot drinks—to the provision of goods and services which competed openly with formal business.

[10] In the first decade of this century, itinerant vendors were charged an excise tax of 50 centavos a day, while those who established themselves on the public thoroughfare by building stalls were charged the enormous sum of 5 soles a day per square meter occupied. In Iwasaki, "Ambulantes y Comercio Colonial."

[11] Legislative Resolution 556 of the Regional Congress of the Central Region, Supreme Resolution of 5 February 1927, and Supreme Decree of 17 July 1936; ordinance of 29 September 1936; supreme Resolution of 15 November 1944.

[12] The proposal was signed by Manuel Secane, Alcides Spelucín, Ramiro Prialé, and Edmundo Haya de la Torre, among others. Article 139, paragraph 6, subparagraph 11.

In the first decade of this century, the municipal government had clashed basically with vendors of prepared foods, unsuccessfully imposing bans and penalties against them or, later, attempting to regulate them. But some vendors began to tie in their activities with others being carried out in the city, and an increasing number gave up peddling to become retail outlets for smugglers or for formal and informal industrialists. *Chicha* and water sellers and greengrocers were thus joined by garment, perfume, and cosmetic vendors and even by itinerant plumbers. The growing competition from street vending aroused increasing concern among formal business people, and they demanded state action.

The government of Augusto B. Leguía, for instance, enacted legislation, in 1927, requiring vendors to register in the patent or industrial tax register, declare their working capital and place of residence, provide such documentary evidence as shipment orders or invoices to prove where they had got their merchandise, and present updated inventories. None of these provisions prevented informal activity from continuing to compete with formal trade, however, and nine years later the government banned all street vending other than foodstuffs and trinkets.[13] This also proved unsuccessful. Vendors continued to trade in goods or provide services of a growing aggregate value, which enabled them to increase their incomes.

The emergence of the first informal markets

The building of the first informal markets in Lima was a definite setback to the municipal authorities' attempts to deal with the street vendors. The recognition they had gained for their special rights of ownership enabled them to increase their turnover of merchandise, obtain credit from their suppliers, organize, and save in order to move away from the public thoroughfare into markets built specially for them. In 1950, the first two such markets were built—a small minority, since at that time there were eight state markets for each informal one.

At the same time, the state continued to lose authority over the streets, so much so that it was forced to publish warnings in the larger newspapers "reminding" vendors that there were laws regulating their activities. These laws continued to be broken, however, and to reverse the trend it was necessary to discard the attitude taken since 1936 and return to a policy of regulating the problem as a whole. On November 24, 1959, the City Council, headed by Mayor Héctor García Ribeyro, adopted a new

[13] Supreme resolution of 5 February 1927; supreme decree of 17 July 1936.

ordinance which was to remain in effect, at least formally, until 1981.

This ordinance defined vendors as individuals who, using light means of transport, could trade in authorized places in the city but could stop on the street for only the time needed to conduct their sales. The difference in language proved significant. In 1936, vendors were allowed to stop on the street only long enough "to make a sale." In 1947, they were allowed to stop temporarily. This latest order used the expression "to conduct their sales," and it could be interpreted as permission to occupy the public thoroughfare throughout the working day. As a result, the ordinance was a victory for the vendors, allowing them to increase the volume of goods carried on their carts and therefore the scale of their commercial operations, and to sell not only food and trinkets but also toys, perfumes, toiletries, lace and bead work, and tools and hardware.

However, the ordinance also tried to protect formal traders from competition from vendors through three specific provisions. First, it prohibited the informal traders from trading in goods of greater aggregate value. Second, it limited their capital to a maximum of U.S. $72 in order to restrict their growth. Third, it authorized formal traders who sold fancy goods and printed cards to put their display cases and racks on the public thoroughfare—in other words, it authorized formal traders to become informal so that they could compete with the informals on an equal footing.

None of these measures worked. In 1962, Mayor García Ribeyro declared street vending beyond his control because it could be attributed to "an agrarian problem of national dimensions" which had forced unemployed people from the countryside to engage in the activity in the cities. Meanwhile, the vendors were unwavering in their determination to move off the streets. By that year, for every three state markets in Lima the informals had built two more.

Markets as a solution to street vending

The sixth stage was marked by vigorous municipal action to combat the effects, rather than the causes, of informal trade. But it irreversibly distorted the existing incentives: by encouraging the building of informal markets, it increased the politicization of a group of vendors.

The new municipal government headed by Luis Bedoya Reyes, which won the 1963 elections, tried to take a practical approach to a practical problem. The vendors were in the streets, were retailing a wide variety of goods, and could not be replaced without creating a vacuum in the city. Still, it was undesirable to let them remain on the public thoroughfare, because they obstructed traffic, threatened public health, and were an eyesore. They also competed unfairly with formal traders. To accommodate the vendors removed from the public thoroughfare, markets had to be built.

From the outset, the municipal government committed itself to the project and began building the San Ildefonso market to relocate many of the vendors then in the streets. Expansion of the market to accommodate new vendors was also envisaged.

The municipal government did not try to monopolize the building of markets. On the contrary, with the agreement of the central government, it exempted anyone interested in building such markets from paying taxes and even fees for building permits, and it even established more favorable rules for vendors' organizations. (These remained in force for a number of years.)[14] This was the first time that the authorities, perhaps inadvertently, took steps to facilitate the transformation of precarious special rights of ownership into formally established property rights. The result was that, between 1964 and 1970 when Bedoya left office, informals built four markets for each market built by the state.

The San Ildefonso market complete, the City Council put its plan into effect. On September 20, 1964, it issued a mayoral decree ordering the removal of street vendors from the Avenida Abancay, then one of the main vendors' belts, prefacing it with the argument that the decree was designed to restore the city of Lima to the excellence and decorum befitting its status as capital city of the Republic, although it also recognized the legitimate needs of humble people who sought employment through such trading systems.

The result was not peaceful. There were clashes between vendors and the municipal police, backed by the civil guard, in which vendors took refuge in parking lots or in businesses licensed for the storage of barrows. The City Council then prohibited parking lots from accepting barrows, tricycles, and the street vendors' other equipment. The authorities' use of force also encouraged the vendors to organize to protect themselves. As early as 1963, the first steps had been taken in this direction, when the Union of Small Traders and Street Vendors, the first such union organized in the city, was formed in the Sebastián Barranca, Pisagua, and 3 February areas. It was later joined by the Federation of Street Vendors in the Central Market and Adjacent Streets (FEVACEL), the first large organization

[14] Supreme Decree 028 of 5 September 1964; Mayoral Decree of 20 September 1964.

formed to protect the vendors who had set up around the Central Market as a result of the 1964 fire.

FEVACEL was a self-defense organization serving a limited number of people, but the vendors' ability to mobilize interested some politicians. The vendors had ceased to be a handful of marginalized, picturesque figures on the city's landscape and were becoming a definite group, a potential political protagonist in Peruvian society.

During this stage, those vendors who were determined to build markets were also strengthened. By the time Bedoya left the mayoralty, they had taken the lead in this activity: by 1970, for every market built by the state, there were two built by the informal sector.

Political recognition

The seventh stage occurred when a group of vendors, determined to stay on the streets, won political support for their activities.

The military government headed by General Juan Velasco Alvarado appointed Eduardo Dibós Chappuis to succeed Bedoya in 1970. At first, the new mayor pursued the idea of building markets to relocate the street vendors, but without any use of force because of the change of political regime brought about by the 1968 coup. A new market was built, along the lines of the San Ildefonso market, on Ayacucho street. But the municipal government's own limitations prevented it from continuing to build, and a new policy was required. The municipal government again declared street vending a structural problem, in an attempt not only to justify its limited response but also to toe the dictatorship's more liberal ideological line.

As a result, the municipal authorities suspended all action in 1971, limiting themselves to ordering the civil guard and the municipal police to keep the Avenida Emancipación and La Unión Street free of vendors. The City Council, realizing that the excise tax amounted to tacit recognition of the street vendors, eliminated it and, thus, the corresponding revenue as well.[15] The decision affected only El Cercado, which was under the direct supervision of the Provincial Council: the tax continued to be levied in other districts.

The vendors had to find other ways to operate. One ingenious solution was to operate wherever there were parking meters on the public thoroughfare (since 1967, there had been parking meters in different areas

[15] Ricardo Talavera Campos, *Consideraciones Generales en Relación con el Fenómeno Urbano Denominado Comercio Ambulatorio* (Lima: Meca, 1983), p. III-2.

of the city center, administered by private concessions such as TAXIMAC and COMACO) and to pay the parking fee throughout the day. Previously, the vendors had kept away from these areas because the tax was lower than the parking fee, but now they began to occupy spaces with parking meters en masse. This solution benefitted only a small number of traders, especially those around the Central Market. The others had to begin to negotiate politically for the legal recognition they needed. In Mayor Dibós they discovered a potential ally. His main problem was that, after six years of elections, he was the first mayor to be appointed de facto to the job, and he needed to surround himself with an aura of legitimacy which could come only from a strong base of popular support. The dialogue with the vendors' organizations offered him a natural opportunity for doing so.

Dibós invited the vendors' leaders to maintain a permanent dialogue with the municipal authorities, giving them a new role and winning for himself a popularity which he retained until his death in mid-1974. The vendors' leaders responded with massive support, giving the mayor the popular base he needed and at the same time achieving a political presence which self-defense activities alone would never have given them. The vendors also benefitted by winning a temporary reprieve from the loss of their special rights of ownership even though they were no longer being charged excise tax. After this, it became customary for municipal laws affecting street vendors to be negotiated with them before being enacted. When Dibós died, Lizardo Alzamora Porras took over as acting mayor and followed the policy established by his predecessor. Since then, it has never been possible for the authorities to ignore the vendors completely.

The vendors' incentives were also altered. When they realized they could affect the mayor's legitimacy, they discovered the political value of their organizations. This gave them an unaccustomed measure of security on the public thoroughfare. But soon they split into two clearly defined groups: those who, because of their contacts, preferred to remain on the street and rely on the mediation of leaders specialized in political bargaining; and those who, because they lacked political connections or were more successful in business, pursued their aim of building or moving to their own markets.

A sociological interpretation and the creation of free zones

The informal traders' eighth historic stage occurred when the authorities, realizing that they had been left behind politically, gave them even more room to operate by recognizing street vending as a structural problem which could be solved only by structural changes which were never defined. Instead, the municipal government declared the areas occupied by street vendors "free zones."

In 1976, during the second phase of the Revolutionary Government of the Armed Forces (1975–1980), retired General Arturo Cavero Calixto was appointed mayor of Lima. That year, he called for the creation of a multisectoral commission to study the street vending trade and, on the basis of its conclusions, propose alternative solutions. He enlisted the support of the then–prime minister, General Jorge Fernández Maldonado, who called on representatives of the Provincial Council, the Ministries of Food, Industry, Labor, the Interior and Trade, and the National Statistical Institute to join the commission.[16] The commission conducted the city's first census of street vendors.

The mere fact that the state, through some of its most important departments, was for the first time studying the problem as a whole, was an important victory for the vendors, for it amounted to a confirmation of their problem as structural and thus safeguarded them from purely administrative measures. And, for as long as the commission's work continued, the municipal government undertook to respect the vendors' right to trade in certain areas of the city (Avenida Alfonso Ugarte, Avenida Grau, Plaza Unión, among others) by declaring such places free zones. This was a major step toward consolidating their special rights of ownership. To confirm the establishment of free zones, a written commitment was signed by the municipal authorities and by the vendors, led by Victor Alcántara, who had just founded the National Association of Street Vendors of Peru and was their most prominent leader. Never before had such a commitment been obtained.

The multisectoral commission began its work amid fairly widespread enthusiasm. It was expected to usher in a new era in street vending and open the way to a final solution of the problem. The vendors' leaders were invited to participate and did so. They helped plan the census and offered all kinds of suggestions. However, when the vendors came to realize that the commission could only make proposals, they gradually lost interest. The establishment of free zones had given them the minimum security they wanted anyway. The commission's early meetings had attracted more than two thousand leaders, but their numbers gradually dwindled to two or three and they finally stopped attending altogether.

When its work was completed in March 1977, the commission

[16] Ministerial decision 0031-76-PM-ONAS.

submitted a written report which concluded that street vending was a structural problem that could be solved only in the long term, and that for the time being it must be regulated and controlled in order to reduce its adverse effects. The commission proposed a set of regulations which would recognize street vending as a temporary form of trade, establish a national register of vendors, require vendors to submit invoices and pay excise tax, establish strictly defined areas, and impose limits on the scale of business conducted—principally on turnover of merchandise and equipment—and impose various penalties for noncompliance. It also suggested setting up a fund to finance marketing infrastructure, relocation, and activities related to street vending, and recommended, inter alia, that a national employment plan be formulated, markets built, action taken to limit migration, and vendors' business organizations promoted. Mayor Cavero endorsed the proposals and presented them to the Ministry of Trade which in turn presented them to the Council of Ministers for consideration. The Council, invoking its current political difficulties, referred them to the different departments concerned for appropriate action. The executive branch thus virtually washed its hands of the problem.

When the multisectoral commisson presented its findings in 1977, for each market built by the state there were three built by the informals.

The strengthening of the vendors' organizations

In the ninth stage, the vendors resisted the most determined repression ever unleashed against them, a process which strengthened and radicalized their self-defense organizations.

In April 1978, the municipal government headed by General Enrique Falconí Mejía, former military chief of staff to President Francisco Morales Bermúdez, abandoned its passive approach and launched one of the most vigorous offensives against street vending in living memory. The change of attitude might be explained by the fact that the new mayor was trying to put his own—military—stamp on his administration, taking advantage of the annoyance felt by certain sectors of the public at the disorder on the streets. However, some observers believe that Falconí's real intention was to undermine the Marxist-led vendors' organizations. Whatever the reason, he organized, with the cooperation of the police, the "Operation Sombrilla," which was designed to seal off the area bordered by the Tacna and Nicolás de Piérola avenues, Ayacucho Street, and the Rímac embankment, evict street vendors from the sealed-off area, and prevent them from returning.

On the date set for the operation, a police detachment cordoned off the entire area, trapping any vendors who happened to be in it. At the same time, another detachment began to clear the area, hunting down vendors, street by street. A pitched battle broke out between the vendors and the police in which antiriot vehicles (Rocha buses) and tear gas were used and barrows and goods were seized. Once the area was cleared, the municipal authorities ordered the police to surround it, to prevent the vendors from reentering. Since the police could not keep up their siege all day, however, their commanding officers ordered them to take up position only in the morning, when it was assumed vendors would try to enter the area to work. The vendors countered by altering their working hours: as long as the police maintained their siege, they kept a safe distance. As soon as the police withdrew, they reinvaded the area. Falconí retaliated by maintaining a permanent guard until 7:00 in the evening, but the vendors soon returned. The authorities ordered the guard to remain until 9:00 P.M.

What had begun as a determined police operation gradually degenerated into a ridiculous game of "cops and robbers," which ultimately undermined the authority of the municipal government. After a number of weeks, it became clear that the police could not continue to assign a large force to besiege the city's center. Police pressure declined considerably and the vendors emerged triumphant from their clash with the municipal government. The entire episode made it clear that a mass eviction of the vendors was impractical. Most of the night-time sales of prepared foods, which today characterize such important vending locations as the Plaza Dos de Mayo and the Plaza Unión, were begun during the siege.

Instead of collapsing, the vendors' organizations (principally FEVA-CEL and FEDEVAL) gathered strength because they were formed to defend their members every way they could. Since the operation mainly affected vendors in Lima Cuadrada and not those around the Central Market, however, the organization which emerged the strongest was the Marxist-led FEDEVAL. Thus, not only did they fail to achieve what they had set out to do, but the authorities had to resign themselves to dealing henceforth with organizations which were not only highly politicized and capable of confronting the forces of law and order, but also led by communists who had gained prestige from an alleged class confrontation with the military. And here, as in other sectors, incipient business owners were forced to hide under the cloak of organizations whose leaders professed an antibusiness ideology.

The apportionment of the streets

The tenth stage occurred when vendors painted on the public thoroughfare the boundaries of their special rights of ownership.

When Roberto Carrión Pollit became mayor in January 1979, he tried to regain the ground lost by his predecessor by co-opting the informals and getting them to share the authorities' responsibilities. As a result, everyone had to compromise: Carrión offered tolerance and participation, the leaders offered representation, and the vendors promised order.

To the public's surprise, the results became apparent almost immediately. Vendors altered the appearance of their pitches, stopped obstructing access to shops, and organized cleanups. The vendors on Andahuaylas Street, who sold fish and were viewed by reporters as the city's dirtiest, donned dark brick-red uniforms to give the neighborhood a better image. This had an immediate effect on vendors in the areas surrounding the Central Market and the Avenida Abancay. They not only cleaned up or embellished their pitches but also took a further step toward confirming their special rights of ownership. Leaders in both places painted the sidewalks in order to demarcate the pitches occupied by each of their members. Formal traders, represented by the National Confederation of Traders (CONACO), as well as the media, interpreted this as an audacious attempt to apportion the streets, but it was simply a painted confirmation of a situation that had existed for some time.

The incident also showed how mistaken incentives can alter behavior: politicization made the vendors apportion the public streets instead of the private property in the markets.

From street vendors to legislators?

The eleventh advance occurred when politicized vendors made their first attempt to become lawmakers.

During the administration of Piero Pierantoni Cámpora, the last mayor to be appointed by the military government, vendors had the feeling that, given the proximity of the 1980 general elections, there was no point in continuing negotiations until the municipal authorities had been elected, and that the best course of action was to take the initiative and present legislative proposals themselves. On July 25, three days before Fernando Belaunde became president of the Republic, a group of vendors informed the public that they had engaged a team of experts to prepare a street vending bill for presentation to Congress. The vendors thus demonstrated not only that they were beginning to grasp the importance of the law to their own interests but also the extent of their politicization. Since the municipal authorities were not in a position to solve the problem, the vendors would try to show the legislators the best way to do so.

The proposal did not become law at that time, and in some information media and sectors of the public it was viewed as the height of audacity on the part of people who were occupying the streets against the law.

The illusion of municipal control

The twelfth stage occurred when the municipal government realized that it was impossible to remove the vendors from the entire city and decided to confine its efforts.

The advent of the democratic government marked the end of mayoral appointments and a return to municipal elections. Eduardo Orrego, running on the government party's ticket, won in November 1980. When he took office, the new mayor found that the vendors had taken over almost the entire city. Streets in the city center were completely covered, especially La Unión Street, the area surrounding the Central Market, the Plaza Dos de Mayo, and the Plaza Unión. In outlying districts, the vendors' invasion was even more massive. They had formed compact belts around markets, and minimarkets were the population's main suppliers, especially in informal settlements.

The public was far from happy about it. The information media, recently restored to their owners, were ridiculing the situation. Formal traders were complaining bitterly. The city's residents wanted the municipal government to take a stand against the street vendors, who were regarded as one of the most deplorable social legacies of the military government. All of this created a particularly difficult situation which prompted the new municipal government not to try to solve the problem, because it had lost before it even started, but instead to try to achieve limited political objectives. It decided that the battle for Lima was a battle for the city's center, thereby disguising what was essentially a surrender: Lima Cuadrada, the area to which the City Council was to limit its action, is only 0.3 percent of Lima's entire urban area. In the remaining 99.7 percent, the street vendors were to be left alone.

In late March 1981, the city government announced that street traders would shortly leave Lima Cuadrada for good and would be relocated on the new fairgrounds at Polvos Azules, behind the Palace of

Government, and the Avenida Argentina, which would later be changed for the Amazonas fairground. But the strategy of taking action only against vendors in the city's traditional center and leaving untouched those established around the Central Market and in adjoining areas—by far the most important concentration of vendors in the city—brought the municipal government into conflict with the vendors protected by FEDEVAL.

On April 24, the fuse was lit. A FEDEVAL march led by parliamentarians Rolando Breña (Maoist) and Hugo Blanco (Trotskyite) set out from the area around the Central Market headed for the Plaza de Armas. On the way, it was violently broken up by police. (The two parliamentarians later leveled charges of abuse against their office.) The clashes delayed a final decision for some time until, on June 7, Mayoral Decree 110, irreversibly evicting vendors from Lima Cuadrada and ordering their relocation on the fairgrounds, was unexpectedly published in the capital city's daily papers.

The clashes resumed. There were meetings, marches, and protest demonstrations, vehicles were stoned, and Molotov cocktails were thrown at the Amazonas fairground. By August, Mayor Orrego had won: most of the vendors had finally been relocated on the Polvos Azules and Amazonas fairgrounds, they had generally built up a satisfactory clientele, and everyone had calmed down.

Orrego, a hard-working and realistic mayor, achieved his objective of removing vendors from a number of central thoroughfares and relocating them in other areas. Like many other municipal victories over disorder, however, his triumph was an illusion: the disorder on the streets had simply been transferred from the commercial avenues of the city's center to the vicinity of the Palace of Government, to a fairground which, because it was built by the City Council, to this day enjoys a tacit immunity which has turned it into Lima's main center for the marketing of smuggled goods. And the repression so strengthened the position of Guillermo Nolasco, the Marxist leader of FEDEVAL, that in the next municipal elections he was catapulted to membership of the City Council, with responsibility for the street vending problem.

Politicized street vendors in the municipal government

The final stage was marked by the ascension of politicized street vendors to executive positions in the municipal government.

In November 1983, Lima's mayoral elections were won by Alfonso

Barrantes Lingán, heading a coalition of predominantly Marxist parties, into which he drew Nolasco and therefore FEDEVAL. At the beginning, the new administration continued to support the fairgrounds and opened new ones at Plaza Gastañeta and Virgen de Lourdes. It was not long, however, before the politicized street vendors within the municipal government tried to increase their influence over this activity, ignoring its entrepreneurial nature and trying to transform it into a bureaucratic partisan organization.

This occurred in April 1985, when Lima's Provincial Council promulgated Ordinance 002 defining the Council's new policy toward street vending. Briefly, it stipulated that vendors must obtain a permit for their activities, must not prepare food on the streets, must submit invoices and proof of the origin of their goods, wear white aprons and standardize their working equipment, obtain a health card, limit their capital to two tax units, neither own nor rent other businesses, abide by preestablished working hours, and join a professional organization. The ordinance also set up a Vendors' Assistance Fund.[17]

Very little of this was new. Five of every six of the provisions contained in the ordinance had already been tried unsuccessfully. Vendors had been required to obtain a permit in 1617, 1670, 1936, 1947, and 1959. Limits had been imposed on their capital in 1947 and 1959. They had been prohibited from preparing food on the streets in 1789, 1916, 1936, 1947, and 1959. They had been ordered to wear white aprons in 1915, 1916, 1936, 1947, and 1959. Attempts had been made to standardize their equipment in 1915, 1916, and 1959, and they had been required to obtain a health card in 1936, 1947, and 1959. And the Vendors' Assistance Fund was unmistakably based on one of the conclusions of the 1976 multisectoral commission. The only really new element was the obligation to join a vendors' organization in order to operate legally, and to adhere strictly to a preestablished timetable. It was clear that the left-wingers viewed street vendor trade no differently than did their predecessors.

The ordinance had at least two significant aims. The fact that the only new element was the vendors' obligation to join an organization suggested that the intention was to politicize and proletarianize professional unions. The requirement that vendors limit their capital, neither open nor rent other businesses, obtain a permit before working, and comply with a number of unrealistic esthetic and ornamental requirements suggested that the municipal government also intended to deny them entrepreneurial

[17] A tax unit in 1985 was equal to 4,500 intis, or $409.80.

status by increasing their costs inordinately and preventing them from saving enough money to move off the street and into markets.

The ILD publicized the adverse effects of the ordinance in newspaper announcements, receiving the support of some one hundred vendors' organizations, and hastened the demise of the ordinance when it proved unworkable. None of this disturbed the vendors who were trying to move off the street by their own efforts, however. In 1985, when the ordinance was promulgated, for every state market there were five informal ones.

The March toward Markets

The history of informal trade is the history of a long march, slowed by overpoliticization, toward markets which represent the people's aspiration to obtain secure private property in order to conduct business in a favorable environment. The vendors' efforts to achieve this goal have contrasted with the inconsistency of the state. The fluctuation between persecution and cooperation, which began in colonial times, has shown—century after century—that the authorities do not understand what is happening. For more than fifty years, both the central and the municipal governments have been exchanging responsibilities without ever arriving at a coherent policy which would enable them to act independently of their political interests. This has completely distorted incentives, politicizing a group of vendors and delaying the majority's march toward formal business activity.

We have seen how the vendors have, over the years, waged major campaigns to make their businesses legally secure. The first such battle was for special rights of ownership. The second was the battle for markets; it brought the majority of vendors, who were prepared to save sufficient money to start building them, into conflict with the state which, allied with a minority of these vendors, was prepared to politicize the system in order to avoid losing influence as vendors became private owners. In both battles we see the confrontation between an insurgent, informal Peru and the status quo in one or another of its political manifestations.

From the vendors' standpoint, both of these major battles were rational ones: property rights make it possible to use and preserve resources, stimulate production, and guarantee the inviolability of investments and savings. They make it possible to reap the benefits of a fixed location and even to use that location as collateral. As a result, they reduce uncertainty, provide security, and are essential for pursuing any economic activity efficiently. This is why informal traders do everything they can to obtain them, basing themselves first on their own extralegal system which, for all

its ingenuity, is an imperfect system for guaranteeing such rights, and later
recognizing the need for political negotiation and even confrontation in
order to safeguard them.

Such a waste of resources could, however, create the impression that
the vendors' efforts to move off the streets are in vain and that the state
must intervene directly. If we take this view, the ILD estimates that the
national treasury would have to invest over $108 million to transfer the
91,455 street vendors currently operating in the city to even the most
modest of markets. An additional $5.4 million a year would also have to
be budgeted to house new vendors in such markets.

If we consider that this initial investment of $108 million in Lima
would, on its own, come to 7.6 percent of total public investments in 1984
for the entire country, the possibility that the state might be able to remove
the vendors directly and effectively becomes extremely remote. What
would make sense would be to see how vendors might be helped instead of
hindered, since they are already the main builders of markets. The 274
markets they have built, as compared with the 57 markets and 8
ramshackle fairgrounds built by the state, show that, in spite of everything,
an overwhelming informal movement is already under way.

The ideal solution would be to remove the obstacles and convert
political incentives into legal facilities in order to free and increase the
vendors' entrepreneurial energies and to allow them, within the competitive process in which they are immersed, to use their talents to the full and
serve the community more effectively.

CHAPTER FOUR

Informal Transport

As informal housing and trade evolved, so too did mass transit in the city. Over fifty years ago, thousands of informal transport operators began to link up poor neighborhoods with the rest of the city.

In informal transport, which like informal housing and trade is carried on outside and even in defiance of the law, the vehicles used to provide transport services are sedans, station wagons, Volkswagen buses and other types of vans, and D-300 minibuses and other kinds of buses.

According to studies made by the Instituto Libertad y Democracia (ILD) in 1984, 91 percent of the 16,228 vehicles used for mass transit were being operated informally. If we add taxis and rental vehicles, the percentage is even higher, informality accounting for 95 percent of Lima's total public transport vehicle fleet that year. Formal transport accounts for the remaining 9 percent of mass transit. Of this, the state-owned National Urban Transport Corporation of Peru (ENATRU) provides 4 percent, and former cooperatives, worker-owned corporations, and the Lima Metropolitan Transport Corporation (TLMEPS) account for the remaining 5 percent.

The ILD estimates the replacement value of the informal fleet to be $620 million in 1984 money. Leaders of informal transport operators estimate the additional investment in infrastructure—gas pumps, repair shops, and other installations—at at least $400 million.

Informals perform a very important social function by meeting the transport needs of dwellers in informal settlements. To do this, they have established a corridor between the Túpac Amaru, Abancay, Tacna, Alfonso Ugarte, Paseo de la República, Tomás Marsano, and Pachacútec avenues which connects the Cono Norte, the Cono Este, and the Cono

Sur with the rest of the city. Informal transport operators concentrate their services in popular areas, while the state corporation and other formal companies mostly serve traditional neighborhoods.

The fact that informality accounts for such a large proportion of mass transit means that, as in informal settlements and informal trade, a complex system of economic and legal relations must first have developed to permit the subsequent evolution. In the pages that follow, we will attempt to explain how this phenomenon occurred, describing the various modes of informal transport, the extralegal norms governing them, their historical evolution, and the many problems informal transportation has encountered as a result of its political relationship with the state.

Types of Informal Transport

The use of different vehicles in informal mass transit prefigures the existence of at least two basic modes of transport. The first is known popularly as the "collective," or public taxi, and consists mainly of sedans with room for 5 passengers and station wagons which carry 8 or 9. The second is the minibus, including Volkswagen or similar vans holding between 8 and 11 passengers; the D-300 minibus with 16 or 18 seats and room for 43 passengers; the D-500, BB-57, and Mercedes Benz buses, with room for 71, 77, and 90 passengers, respectively; and Scania Vabis, GMC, and International buses with a capacity of more than 80. The difference between public taxis and minibus transport is basically the size of the vehicles used and, therefore, the scale of their operation. There are no qualitative differences.

Like types of informal trade, these modes of transport do not fall into strict compartments but are successive stages in the same process. Over the years, many of the informal transport operators who began with public taxis have gradually acquired minibuses.

Not all public taxis or minibus operators are equally informal, however, for some enjoy a special kind of administrative recognition in the form of a concession. Those who have no such recognition are called "pirates" because of their total illegality. The public taxi or minibus operators with concessions are not formal, however, for the recognition they enjoy does not give them access to any of the benefits of formality, for instance, protection of the contractual system and property, or limited liability, so they can obtain insurance and credit, among other things. Their bureaucratic recognition affords them only a special status, a measure of stability and security in conducting their operations. It is this state of affairs that makes transport operators' activities informal. In consequence, like other informal activities, public taxi and minibus transport are governed by a common extralegal system which regulates, inter alia, rights of ownership and organization.

We can see the importance of this extralegal system from the fact that 91 out of every 100 vehicles engaged in mass transit in Lima comply with it, while only 9 observe state regulations. It is the extralegal system that is socially relevant.

The invasion of routes

Just as informal settlers invade land and street vendors occupy the public thoroughfare, informal transport operators invade routes. Routes are not physical assets like land or the street, however, but intangible assets defined by the population's movements and travel needs. A route is a unit consisting of different journeys between a first and last point. But like street vendors, transport operators generally invade routes individually, following a prior process of research and selection which the ILD has tried to identify.

The process is an economic calculation in which, primarily, informal transport operators try to evaluate different possible routes in order to decide which one to take over. To do this they must identify, at minimum, where there is potential demand, for which journeys there is inadequate service, and which new neighborhoods or settlements lack transportation. They must also determine the population's need for travel and the actual possibilities of serving them. The evaluation of different routes thus involves the technical characteristics of the routes and the preferences of potential users. These elements identified, the informal transport operator can define the route which seems most attractive and go ahead with the invasion plan. In the process, informals become entrepreneurs since, in looking for the best way to earn money and identify and satisfy demand, they learn to adjust the resources available to them to the circumstances.

The informal transport operator then has to consider the likely reactions of other people, since the invasion of a route always affects third parties. First, are there other informal transport operators who are also trying to take over the route? If so, there may be a competition to see who will serve the route, in which case the person who is able to operate the route most profitably will generally win. That is also the person who is prepared to invest more resources in acquiring it.

Second, the would-be transport operator must evaluate the probable attitude of the authorities, whether the police or the bureaucracy. If they resist, the operator must be prepared to negotiate, by producing sheets of signatures of users to show that the service is needed or already successful, or else resort to outright corruption, which normally also wins some kind of protection against aggression by other transport operators.

Last, the informal transport operator must determine the likely reaction of other citizens, some of whom will be interested in seeing the service continue and will become customers, and others who will oppose it because of the risks created by increased traffic and congestion in their neighborhoods. When all these calculations have been made, the informal transport operator is in a position to decide whether to invade a chosen route.

Invasion is used not only to discover and appropriate original routes. It is also used by established informal transport operators to extend or modify the routes they already use. Such invasions are carried out not by individuals but by groups, since an informal organization or committee must approve the invasion at a general meeting, following an evaluation fairly similar to the one described above. In the course of its research among various committees, the ILD managed to contact one which was in the process of extending its route through an invasion. The committee was a pretty small group, operating a marginally profitable route inherited from the public taxi committee that preceded it, and was trying to invade other routes in order to increase its profits.

The ILD was thus able to witness the various steps taken by the informal transport operators in question. First, they evaluated the potential length of the route they were to invade, bearing in mind the possibility of attracting a greater number of passengers. Then, since they were planning to invade a small stretch of route and were unlikely to encounter major resistance from third parties, they contacted a junior official they knew in the Ministry of Transport and Communications and forewarned him, paying him approximately $60 to use his good offices to secure them subsequent official recognition. Later, this same official, acting on the informals' behalf, arranged for the police to be paid a monthly bribe of around $10, popularly called a *bolsa*, in order to avoid trouble in the future.

These preparations made, the informal transport operators invaded the route they had chosen and, at the same time, applied to the ministry for recognition in order to obtain a document, which they could show in case of need, certifying that their application was being processed. They then tried to maintain a regular service in order to create demand among the people, and even collected signatures to show the authorities that there was a market for the service and that it satisfied a need. After a year of providing the service, when not only passengers but also the police, public officials, and the neighborhood in general were used to their presence, the informals managed to obtain exceptional official recognition in the form of a new concession.

However, while many transport operators have gone through this process and now enjoy bureaucratic recognition and even route concessions, their rights actually stem from the original invasion. The ILD estimates that almost all the mass transit routes now in existence were established, extended, and modified at some point in their history through invasions, some of which were later recognized by the authorities on the invariable pretext that such recognition was a temporary exception.

Invasion is not desirable, however. Tremendous resources are wasted before a right that is in any case insecure is finally obtained. Moreover, since transport does not only involve the people using it, society in general ultimately suffers from the resulting corruption of public officials and the disorder, danger, and lack of safety on the streets.

The right to appropriate routes

Conducting a successful invasion enables informals to operate routes before the state has conferred any recognition on them. This possibility presupposes the existence of an extralegal relationship which the ILD has called the "right to appropriate routes."

A transport service can be operated economically only because this right enables informals to operate routes on an exclusive and inalienable basis, exclusive in that they can use them as they wish and enjoy the resulting income, and inalienable in that they can sell that right freely. However, since the right to appropriate routes originates in invasion and is based on extralegal norms, it is not perfect. Informal transport operators have to negotiate with the state for recognition in the form of a concession.

The right to appropriate routes is thus subject to a lengthy process of improvement, in the course of which attempts are made to give it greater security and stability so that it more closely resembles formally recognized rights of ownership. The exclusiveness of the right of appropriation gradually increases so that, while some sections may be shared or intersect, no two routes are completely identical in any service. The inalienability of the right, for its part, becomes more secure as more complex systems are developed for exercising it. The ILD has been able to identify two such systems. The first is a free system, in which a committee member can sell his share in that right at will, without having to obtain prior authorization or being forced to offer it to the other transport operators in the committee. In such cases, the sale is not significantly different from the sale of a share in a formal business, and the registers kept by the committee have to be changed to include the new member. In some cases, the purchaser pays the entire committee an additional premium, commonly referred to as the "admission fee," in recognition of the investments, contributions, improvements, and common funds provided by the other members over the years, as we shall see later.

The second system is fairly restrictive. The member who sells the share must observe an order of preference established in favor of transport operators belonging to the committee. This system either favors drivers and fare collectors who do not own their vehicles or stipulates that the committee alone can buy the share and then auction it off to interested parties.

These procedures do not preclude other practices. In some older committees whose routes have very few passengers, the sale of shares is banned and new members are admitted only if they inherit them. The ILD found that some of these committees are already in their third generation. The extralegal system also regulates what happens when informals withdraw or retire from a committee. Using a concept known as a "communal right," the committee pays the member withdrawing from the activity a percentage equivalent to the individual's investments, improvements, and contributions to the common funds. The authorities are usually totally unaware of such transactions. Since they lead to changes in the official registers, however, the authorities simply accept the communications sent them by transport operators indicating changes in membership.

Informal transport operators' organizations

As the invaded route and the rights to it gradually increase in value, the informal operators begin to have an incentive to organize, negotiate, and deal with legal institutions. This requires them to set up organizations at basically two levels: first, committees of informal transport operators operating the same route; and second, different committees grouped together into unions and, later, federations.

The committee

In informal transport, there is generally no contract prior to the invasion. There is an initial stage in which, after invading a route independently, each informal transport operator runs a separate service, manages its hours and timetables, and decides what fares to charge. The operator cannot remain independent indefinitely, however, and will have to organize with other transport operators covering the same route, for a route well chosen for its length and number of passengers increases in value and tempts an increasing number of invaders.

Organizing has a number of advantages. Operating a route in an orderly manner helps to reduce operating costs and ensures a regular service, which keeps passengers happy. Organizing also brings together a sufficient number of transport operators to negotiate with the authorities and preserve the route they have established. Third, it keeps out new invaders once there are sufficient vehicles to meet demand.

At the initiative of the more enterprising members of their group, invaders begin by holding closed meetings at which they elect their leaders and try to agree on the operation of the route. They take a census of members, establish an essentially democratic mechanism for the periodic election of leaders, and decide to set up common funds with compulsory contributions and to establish a body, which they call a "committee," with specific responsibility for achieving the members' aims. This set of agreements can be regarded as an "informal partnership agreement."

The committee is the institutional organ actually formed after the invasion to achieve the goals of the informal partnership agreement. Its nature is therefore twofold: it is an informal business in that it organizes the economic operation of the route, and it is an interest group in that it negotiates with the authorities for the security of the extralegal rights acquired. This duality also leads to a specialization of functions within the leadership of the committee. There is a general secretary who runs both the informal business and the interest group, and there are other secretaries who have different functions. The administration of the business is entrusted to the organizational secretary, responsible for its general administration; the financial secretary is responsible for administering the common funds; the technical or maintenance secretary is responsible for organizing repair shops, the supply of spare parts, and gas pumps; the welfare secretary is responsible for industrial relations; and the secretary for culture or education and sports is responsible for organizing libraries and soccer matches. The interest group is entrusted to the defense secretary, who is responsible for negotiating with the authorities and paying bribes, and to the press and publicity secretary, who publishes circulars and bulletins.

The committee's entrepreneurial tasks are fairly complex. The leadership must improve the section of route created by the invasion by constantly reviewing market conditions, setting up terminals in the middle of the public thoroughfare marking the beginning and end of the route—which is expressly prohibited by law—and evaluating the fares to be charged. If the committee has already agreed to state control of fares in exchange for bureaucratic recognition, it simply evaluates whether the ceiling imposed meets its expectations and decides what privileges it might demand to make up for any profits it has sacrificed. Pirate committees, which do not accept state controls, establish their own fares, imposing either one fare for the entire route or different fares, according to distance, if the route is a long one.

The business leadership also decides on the frequency and dispatch of vehicles in order to distribute the trips. The general meeting, which establishes frequencies, also appoints dispatchers who monitor compliance with those frequencies at the beginning and end of the route. They have the power to penalize drivers who deliberately lengthen or shorten the frequency. When the ILD conducted its research, both violations were punished by only token penalties: never more than 50 cents per violation.

The business leadership also decides which drivers who do not own vehicles—popularly called *palancas*—will drive members' vehicles when the owners are resting, and establish the rules governing fare collectors on each vehicle. Normally, the general meeting authorizes drivers who have some connection with a member, or are recommended by someone, to become *palancas*, and they are usually paid a percentage of the net income brought in by the vehicle they drive. This percentage varies from one committee to another, but averages around 25 percent. The recruitment of fare collectors, on the other hand, is left to individual transport operators, because they act as a kind of foreman for the service and are responsible for filling up the vehicle, dealing directly with customers, and supervising the *palancas* to make sure they do not pocket the fares. The business leadership also keeps the register of members and vehicles up to date, mainly to authenticate sales and provide the authorities with the information they need.

As an informal business, the committee also tries to fund its own members' activities because it is difficult for informal transport operators to obtain credit from traditional financial bodies. Three types of funding are used. The first is a common fund, made up of the members' periodic, voluntary contributions. Their contributions go into a communal fund deposited in a joint bank account and administered by the finance secretary. This fund is generally used to buy spare parts and oil wholesale, to improve the fleet, and, in general, for any committee expenditure, for instance, a building or a special party.

The second type of funding could be called a "common credit fund." It is very similar to the common fund but is also used for loans to transport operators so they can maintain their operations. In computing the interest to be charged on such loans, the committee uses, as a standard, not the bank rates established by the state but those charged by money lenders on the informal free market. This obviously benefits the transport operators who deposit their savings in such funds, for it yields them higher interest than they would obtain from a bank; it also benefits the borrowers, who are generally unable to obtain formal credit. The third type of financing is provided by "cooperatives," which also lend money to their members and, except for the fact that they are legal entities, do not differ significantly from the common credit fund.

Last, as an informal business, the committee tries to set up a mutual insurance fund for its members to cover accidents to their vehicles since, in general, they do not have access to formal insurance policies. The risks to be covered are established at a general meeting and usually include only personal injury or material damage sustained by members as a result of an accident, not third-party liability. These mutual insurance funds exist only in the wealthier and more sophisticated committees. In other committees, when an accident leaves a member without his means of livelihood it is an unwritten extralegal rule to allow him to drive the committee's best cars as a *palanca* until his financial situation improves.

The committee's functions are no less complex when it operates as an interest group. Its first such function is to negotiate with the authorities. Since the committees are informal, they try to negotiate with the authorities for recognition of their right to appropriate routes and, once this recognition has been won, to obtain such additional benefits as unauthorized extension of routes and the establishment of terminals and stops along the route. Basically, such negotiations involve mutual concessions. When the authorities' interests are political, they sometimes grant certain privileges in exchange for public pledges of support or for an agreement not to join in a strike against them.

Transport operators often use additional forms of pressure to speed up the outcome of negotiations. Because they are informal, lack full state recognition, and have no access to formal channels for presenting demands, this pressure is mostly confrontational—threats, strikes, marches, work stoppages, protests—and also other means, such as collecting signatures, used especially when they are trying to win recognition of a route.[1] In these ways, whether by offering political support or provoking disturbances, informal transport operators have sought to preserve their extralegal rights at the cost of politicizing themselves and investing a growing proportion of their resources.

The second function performed by the committees as interest groups is corruption. In general, corruption is used to obtain two types of benefits from the government bureaucracy: speeding up of bureaucratic procedures and recognition or protection of the right to appropriate routes.

In seeking recognition or protection of their rights to appropriate routes, committees follow certain procedures. When bureaucrats solicit bribes, one of their representatives visits the committees periodically to solicit a bribe or, if the bribe has already been agreed to, to collect it and share it among his accomplices. When the informals offer bribes, the defense secretaries of the committees concerned go around to the police station or government departments to offer a bribe in exchange for the desired service, which may range from turning a blind eye to the extension of a route by invasion to protecting the committee from pirates who are trying to invade their routes.

Unions and federations

While committees may be relatively effective in securing recognition of their rights to appropriate routes, they encounter tremendous difficulties in gaining access to higher authorities.

These difficulties soon increase since, in exchange for bureaucratic recognition, the state normally imposes a number of obligations on transport operators—in particular, fare controls. At this point, the informals become interested not only in gaining security and stability for their rights but also in trying to obtain other benefits which will enable them to offset their new obligations. Since committees, on their own, cannot mobilize sufficient transport operators and vehicles to make an impression on the authorities and public opinion, they join forces in larger organizations which enable them to benefit from the state's redistributive powers. They join together to form unions, which in turn join federations, and between them they supplement the informal transport operators' political organization.

While committees are part of the informal partnership agreement,

[1] A typical example would be Committee 74M, which extended its route by means of an invasion and worked with the leadership of the Huáscar settlement to collect signatures and stage a march to put pressure on the Ministry of Transport and Communications.

unions and federations are the result of subsequent political agreements reached in an attempt to formalize rights and offset controlled fares and other burdens imposed by the state in exchange for bureaucratic recognition. They negotiate, explicitly or implicitly, for a mutual exchange of favors, just as the committees do, and they resort to very similar means of pressure, such as the collection of signatures, threats, work stoppages, marches, and strikes. Likewise, when the need arises, they bribe the authorities.

It is the absence of legal means of protecting themselves individually that forces informal transport operators to resort to this kind of political organization. The parties who become involved in this process have reason for doing so. Controlled fares illustrate this. If the government is a democratic one, it tries to prevent fares from going up in order to protect its image and preserve its popularity. If it is a dictatorship, it does so in order to win legitimacy. Organizations, for their part, hope to increase their membership, gain strength, and maintain influence, and informal transport operators in general want to win privileges to offset fare controls.

This set of clearly defined interests gives rise to a "mercantilist" exchange in which the parties try to use the redistributive power of the state. This, in turn, makes the survival or leadership of the different unions and federations basically dependent on the quantity or quality of the benefits they offer to committees interested in joining them. The committees, for their part, serve the interests of the informal transport operators pragmatically and have no ideological qualms whatsoever about moving from one organization to another according to the benefits offered. Over the years, this has given rise to an openly competitive atmosphere among the different organizations, based on their ability to establish connections, or negotiate, with the state.

The two institutions that have vied with one another to become the transport operators' most representative bodies are the Federation of Drivers of Peru (FED) and the Federation of Drivers and Related Workers of Peru (ANEXOS). The FED, which is politically independent, has the larger number of transport operators, its base in Lima being the Union of Minibus Drivers, which represents 95 percent of the committees. The ANEXOS is connected to the Peruvian APRA and does not have a large membership. Its base in Lima is the Union of Public Service Taxi, Public Taxi, and Minibus Drivers of Lima, representing only 5 percent of the committees. As we shall see later, the influence of these two organizations has varied with successive governments; still, as a result of this competition, informal transport operators in general have managed to win a truly surprising set of privileges over the years.

In tax matters, the unions and federations have managed to win, inter alia, cancellation of their tax debts in 1968 and 1970; exemption from stamp tax, payroll tax, social security contributions, and contributions to SENATI in 1968, 1970, and 1971; exemption from taxes on the purchase of secondhand vehicles, sales tax and additional sales taxes in 1968, 1970, 1971, 1978, 1981, and 1983; exemption from the vehicle tax in 1970 and 1971; and exemption from the employers' share of income tax and the revaluation of assets and capitalization of the revaluation surplus in 1983.[2] In tariff matters, the unions and federations have won informal transport operators the right to import vehicles and spare parts completely tax-free in 1955, 1956, 1957, 1958, 1959, 1960, 1961, and 1964; twice in 1968, 1970, 1971, 1972, 1973, 1976, and 1977; and twice in 1980, 1981, 1982, and 1983.[3] In the area of penalties, the unions and federations have secured reduced penalties for traffic violations on at least four different occasions. In 1972, operators were ordered to pay only 10 percent of the fines for minor violations. That same year, the authorities first defined which violations were minor, but then said that, with only a few exceptions, all violations were minor. Finally, in 1981, it was established that urban transport vehicles would not be impounded in official vehicle pounds when violations occurred, because that would leave Lima without transport services.[4]

Turning to participation in government mechanisms, the unions and federations won the privilege of participating in the bodies responsible for price controls in 1969 and 1981, in those responsible for regulating transport services in 1970 and 1981,[5] in those responsible for resolving disputes over routes in 1979, and in the administrations of the Land Transport Finance Fund in 1983. The unions and

[2] SD 260–68 HC and DL 18387; SD 260–68 HC, SD 269–68 HC, and DL 19256; DL 22344, Legislative Decree 17, and Legislative Decree 273.

[3] SR of 11 May 1955, SR of 9 February 1956, SD of 20 September 1957, SR of January 1958, SD of 10 June 1959, SD 16 and MR of 3 March 1961, SD of 3 January 1964, SD of 27 October 1964, SD 260–68 HC, SD 269–68, DL 18387, DL 19256, DL 19282, DL 19398, DL 21413, DL 21805, DL 22943 and DL 23171, Legislative Decree 9, SD 017–81 TC, Legislative Decree 18, SD 006–82 EFC, SD 183–82 EFC, SD 380–82, MR 0084–72 TC/DNT, and SD 423–83 EFC.

[4] DL 19282; MR 012-72 PC/CSB; MR 016-72 PC/CSB; SD 055-81 PC.

[5] DL 17948, SD 009-81 TC and Legislative Decree 166; established unofficially and by SD 009-81 TC, respectively; Official note 0047-TC and Legislative Decree 267; Code of Civil Proceedings, Article 617, para. 12, amended by Legislative Decree 329.

federations have also managed to use commercial operating norms to enable informal transport operators to avoid seizure of their vehicles if they fail to pay their debts, thereby diminishing their commercial liability. Last, through the creation of the Land Transport Promotion Fund in 1980 and the Land Transport Finance Fund in 1981, they won informal transport operators the privilege of obtaining subsidized credit on easy terms.[6]

Despite these privileges, however, informal transport operators have not benefitted from the process. As we shall see in the following section and in chapter 5, the state has in return imposed many requirements on them which we shall call the "costs of formality" and which include controlled fares and bureaucratic recognition different from that given to formal businessmen in other areas. This situation has provoked periodic crises in the transport system.

The Historical Evolution of Informal Transport

As in earlier chapters, we have organized our account of the historical evolution of informal transport into stages, this time seventeen, which trace the history of the service, the development of informality, its effect on formal society, and the way the state has tackled the problem over the years.

The birth of mass transit

The birth of mass transit in the last century was made possible by technological advances which enabled railroads to be used for passenger transport. This situation restricted the mass transit market, however, since, by their very nature, the routes of railroads are difficult to take over. The first mass transit service in Lima was established in 1851 when the locomotive *Chalaquito* set out from the vicinity of what is now the Plaza San Martín, headed for the main port, thereby opening the Lima-Callao railroad.

While this interurban railroad developed, Lima itself maintained its age-old rental carriage service, a precursor of the modern taxi, which sufficed for the needs of a small city with a relatively limited population. When the population increased toward the end of the century, however, these carriages began to proliferate, and more or less clearly defined routes developed. In response to this transformation, the state, in 1874, enacted

[6] DL 23171; Legislative Decree 155, 059-81, EFC, and Legislative Decree 267.

the first regulations of vehicular traffic in the history of the Republic and authorized the authorities to set fares.[7]

The development of fixed routes facilitated the transition from carriages to animal-drawn trams, which were, strictly speaking, the city's first mass passenger vehicles. Hitherto, isolated carriages had not given rise to property rights other than those over the carriage itself. The emergence of routes and trams with rails, however, required the establishment of property rights to routes. This resulted in a system of concessions negotiated by the state with each person interested in operating a tram. It included the route to be taken, the characteristics of the service, and the amount of the fare. The earliest corporations established their fares by agreement and these fares were contractually binding on the parties: they could not be changed as the market fluctuated, but only as the parties chose. If a change were to be made, one of the parties proposed it and the other accepted or rejected the proposal. The state, for political reasons, usually preferred to keep fares as they were and the corporations generally proposed increases.

Technological improvements accelerated the development of this service and, on the eve of the twentieth century, the first steps were taken to replace the animal-drawn trams by electric trams. In 1895, Lima's municipal government was authorized to engage firms to set up this system, but it was only in 1903 that it granted the first concessions to different groups of formal businessmen: in January, to operate the route between Lima and Chorrillos and in March to operate the route between Lima and El Callao.[8]

As the administration of this new service became increasingly complex, it became easier for the state to deal with a single concessionaire. Accordingly, in 1905 it gave to a single corporation, the Lima Urban Railroad Company, Ltd., the power to serve more than one route, initiating a trend toward monopoly which was confirmed in 1913 and 1920 when the Lima Light and Power Company took control of both the urban and interurban tram systems. The state thus established a preference for dealing with as few contractors as possible, forcing private business owners to acquire political influence if they were to enter and remain in the transport business.

It was into this restrictive context that, first, formal entrepreneurs, who would try to provide the service in buses and, later, informal

---

[7] Rules Governing Public and Private Carriages and Coaches, 5 June 1874.

[8] SR of 12 January 1903; SR of 13 March 1903.

operators, who would try to provide it in public taxis, entered. Both found the state unwilling to negotiate with more applicants than necessary.

The emergence of motor transport and the end of the transport monopoly

The emergence of bus transport services provided by formal operators and the first transformation of vehicles used to transport goods into passenger vehicles ended the railroad's and tramway's monopoly of mass transit and prevented the state from restricting the market.

In May 1921, Luis Tirado was authorized to establish the first bus line on the route between Lima, Miraflores, Barranco, and Magdalena del Mar.[9] Like those that followed, his was a relatively small business with no more than ten buses. These small owners of bus lines joined forces with a local industry of vehicle repair shops and other small businesses which they put in charge of maintaining and repairing their vehicles. That same year, the first workshops for adapting imported chassis to the capital's transport regulations were established. The first of these belonged to Vito Pavone, a mechanic of Italian origin nicknamed "Thomas A. Edison" Pavone, who that year assembled the first national transit vehicles on a Fiat truck chassis. These vehicles, with 22 seats and entry and exit doors, combined the flexibility of motor cars with the capacity of buses. Known popularly as "gondolas," doubtless because of the manufacturer's Italian origin, they came into service immediately and can be regarded as the precursors of today's minibuses. The gondolas first operated between La Victoria and the Parque Universitario, then throughout the city's center, and later between Magdalena and the center. According to Margarita Petrera, Pavone received financing from the Italian Bank, today the Credit Bank, to set up these first bus lines.[10]

By 1926, bus transportation had become so popular that at least eight new companies sprang up to serve routes between Lima, Miraflores, Barranco, and Magdalena del Mar. This growth was encouraged, to some extent, by the public road building program of the government of Augusto B. Leguía. Tram companies had to bear the cost of laying their own rails, but the bus companies were able to take advantage of the state's investment in streets and avenues.

[9] SR of 7 May 1921.

[10] Margarita Petrera, "La Experiencia de la Propiedad Social en el Transporte Terrestre" (Master's thesis, Pontificia Universidad Católica del Perú, Lima, 1977), p. 19.

During this period, residential areas outside the city also began to expand and land along routes connecting outlying communities with the city center became gradually occupied. Buses were able to adapt more easily than trams to such changes in the use of urban land, establishing a precedent which was later imitated by the informals.

The emergence of the informal "colectivo," or public taxi

The first advance of informality began in the period described above and consisted in the emergence of the first sedans used as colectivos, or public taxis. The vehicles used, sedans, were inefficient because they occupied a very large area of the thoroughfare in relation to the number of passengers carried.[11] However, this basic defect was offset by a number of advantages.

First of all, the fares agreed upon between the formal bus operators and the state were so high that they made it possible to operate sedans profitably, even though they offered fewer economies of scale than buses. Second, the cheap gasoline policy which characterized all Peru's governments until the second half of the 1970s made sedans inexpensive to run. Third, the relatively small population and the distances traveled in those days prevented the increase in congestion that was then occurring from being noticed immediately.

Thus, the informal operators were initially able to use sedans without worrying about economies of scale. Besides, sedans were the only vehicles available to informal operators: they required only a small investment and it was easier to avoid detection by the authorities and by formals in a motor car than in a larger vehicle.

The emergence of transport operators' organizations

The first informal transport operators' organization was the committee, whose origin probably dates back to the end of the second decade of this century. At first, the committees were small groups formed by informal taxi owners who had invaded such popular routes as La Victoria–Viterbo and Cocharcas–Avenida Bolivia. In order to resist the formal bus companies operating the same routes, who called out the police against them, the operators needed strong committees and had strong incentives for negotiating with the authorities and organizing the rational operation of their services.

[11] Approximately 12 square meters of public thoroughfare per 5 passengers, i.e., 2.4 square meters per person.

As more and more committees emerged, they found unity and political expression in unions and federations. Many joined the Union of Lima Public Taxi Drivers which, together with the Bus Workers' Union consisting of bus drivers from traditional bus companies, later joined the Central Drivers' Union. The Central Union, in turn, joined with other drivers' groups to found the Federation of Drivers of Peru (FED) on 16 April 1921.

Like any entity whose main objective is to protect itself from the state, the FED soon fell into the hands of politicians. At the outset it was dominated by anarchist groups, most of whom later joined the APRA. In 1925, the communist presence in the FED began to grow, so much so that, years later, it was among the groups which founded the General Confederation of Workers of Peru (CGTP).[12] The anarchist leadership managed to regain power almost immediately, withdrawing the FED from the CGTP for the first time in order to defend its members itself.

All these events overlay a more complex situation, however: the informal transport operators found that their only allies were political organizations specialized in the defense of proletarian interests. This has posed a dilemma for them throughout their history because their interests has not always coincided with the interests of these organizations. As a result, they are always joining and withdrawing from these organizations—according to whether or not their interests coincided—adopting an increasingly proletarian political consciousness when they failed to generate, among formal business owners, an attitude which would permit their assimilation. In fact, in 1926, the formal transport operators formed their own organization, the Association of Urban and Inter-urban Bus Owners (APOUI), which was to play an important role in the years to come.

The great strike of 1930

The informals' third stage began when, allying themselves with the formal operators, they managed to open up the market and end a monopoly created by the Leguía regime.

In 1930, the government granted a monopoly contract to the Metropolitan Company, a joint association of the Lima Light and Power

---

[12] According to Margarita Petrera ("La Experiencia . . .," pp. 43–44), in 1929 the FED was one of the seven main organizations which launched the *Manifesto of the Workers of the Republic*, which criticized the failures of the anarchosyndicalist organization and proposed the formation of the National Confederation, established on the principle of the "union of the proletariat."

Company, which held the tram monopoly, and United States investors, for the operation of all routes in Lima. The formal and informal bus operators responded by joining forces, winning the support of the gas pump owners, who were also harmed by the monopoly, and calling a massive transit strike in Lima. The strike coincided with a wave of protests which ended in the overthrow of the Leguía regime after it had governed for eleven years.

The conflict intensified in April 1931, when a massive soup kitchen was organized by the FED, CGTP, and other striking organizations. Shows of solidarity and street demonstrations increased and there were clashes with the police. The drivers rejoined the CGTP to strengthen their position.

Even after the junta presided over by David Samanez Ocampo was installed, the strike continued. At first, the junta showed no signs of wanting to terminate the agreement with the Metropolitan Company. This radicalized the strikes. The Metropolitan's vehicles were stoned and set on fire and the government felt compelled to set up an arbitration tribunal to settle the dispute. It called on such eminent personalities as J. A. Encinas, A. F. Pérez Araníbar, C. A. Doig y Lora, A. Wiese, C. A. Ugarte, L. Villacorta del Campo, and J. I. Barreda Bustamante to serve on this tribunal, demonstrating the importance it attached to the problem. The tribunal's ruling was conclusive: it annulled the monopoly awarded to the Metropolitan Company, opened the vehicle register to all transport operators, and granted administrative recognition to the service provided by informals as of May 1931. This decision favored both private and informal transport operators because it gave them room to operate. It also demonstrated to the informals that they could use political action to impose their demands on the state.

An understanding between the formal operators and the state

The fourth stage was marked by the transformation of formal operators into the state's new interlocutors and the gradual imposition on them of a number of legal obligations which ultimately reduced their flexibility and permitted the growth of informality.

Formal business owners belonging to APOUI seemed to have been the main winners in the battle against the Metropolitan Company's monopoly and, because they brought together groups of relatively wealthy investors with access to the main channels of government, they rapidly became the decisive group in the transport sector.[13] The result was that the state, although it had been unable to impose a monopoly in order to control the transport sector more easily, could still reduce the number of its interlocutors by dealing with a single, oligopolistic organization. The advantage to the formal operators was that it reduced competition. The stage was set for the development of an exchange of favors between the state and the formal transport operators.

In 1931, they persuaded the state to confirm their oligopoly by prohibiting the free access to the operation of transport services granted by the arbitration tribunal, and in 1936 they won even greater protection when the tribunal established the principle of nonduplication of routes, according to which operating licenses were denied to new concessionaires if the routes they proposed duplicated existing ones. The state's position was also strengthened. As early as 1931, it required the formal operators to pay a tax equivalent to 6 percent of the fares collected, to issue 100 free passes for public officials, and to reduce fares by 50 percent for members of the military, who were then in power. The following year, the state gave itself the power to control mass transit fares, which had hitherto been established by agreement with transport operators along the lines of the original concessions.[14]

During the Second World War, when formal transport underwent a crisis because of restrictions on the supply of rolling stock, spare parts, and other necessities, the state, rather than strengthen its allies, the formal operators, intervened directly. In 1942, it set up the first public urban transport corporation, the Government Transport Commission, which became the Municipal Transport Corporation in 1946 and the Municipal Transport Service in 1948.[15] At the same time, the formal operators were facing other serious problems. As a result, in 1944, they were authorized to increase fares for the first time in twenty years, although they were also required to charge primary school children less than 50 percent of the new fare.[16] The increase was inadequate: three bus companies were bankrupted. The municipal government took over their services because it could not leave the city without transport.

---

[13] See Hans de Wit, *El Transporte Público en Lima Metropolitana* (Lima: Centro de Investigaciones de la Universidad del Pacífico, 1981), p. 38.

[14] SR of January 1932 and SR of 8 November 1932.

[15] SD of 13 November 1942; Act 10601 and SD of 10 September 1946; SD of 2 June 1948.

[16] SR of 29 December 1944. Ten years later, the reduced fare was extended to secondary school students (SR of 10 August 1954) and in 1960 to university students (Act 13406 of 4 March 1960).

The decline of formal transport left more room for informal operation to grow in the years to come.

The strengthening of unions

In the fifth stage, the informal transport operators managed to win sufficient political recognition to develop their activities. This was the result of a clash between the different groups vying for control of their organizations.

While the formal operators ultimately suffered from their understanding with the state, the informal ones gradually strengthened their organizations to take advantage of the space created for them and to obtain sufficient recognition to conduct their activities in peace. They approached this task with considerable pragmatism: they elected their leaders or changed unions according to the benefits to be obtained from their relationship with the state, without letting themselves be influenced by ideological preferences. They took advantage of the rivalry between communists and APRA members, who had gradually replaced anarchists in the unions, making them compete to obtain the greatest possible benefits.

The communists won the first victory in this process. In 1939, their party had supported Manuel Prado, a conservative presidential candidate (whom they nicknamed the Peruvian Stalin) on condition that, among other things, he would include Juan P. Luna, FED leader and general secretary of the Communist Party, in his parliamentary lists. When Luna was elected a member of Parliament, his position within Prado's regime enabled him to increase the communists' influence in the unions, giving informal transport operators, at least temporarily, the security they needed to conduct their activities.

In 1945, when a change of political regime brought José Luis Bustamante y Rivero, who was supported by the APRA, to power, it was members of the APRA who gained the upper hand and, with it, control of the FED, which then became a member of the Confederation of Workers of Peru (CTP), run by its trade-union cells. Luna not only lost control of the organization but was expelled from the Communist Party in 1947.

The APRA's success was short-lived, however. As its position in Bustamante's government gradually weakened, especially after the 1948 military coup which brought General Manuel A. Odría to power, the drivers' leadership, members of the APRA, gradually fell out of favor with the authorities and, therefore, with the transport operators. At this point,

Juan P. Luna, now Odría's ally, embarked on the reconquest of the FED, promoting, along with other leaders, an anti-APRA trade-union organization called the Peruvian Workers' Political Action Committee. In 1950, the FED left the CTP. In that year's manipulated general elections, Luna ran as an Odría candidate, winning a Senate seat, which strengthened his negotiating power. Members of the APRA, for their part, founded a new organization called the Federation of Drivers and Related Workers of Peru (ANEXOS) in an attempt to maintain some kind of political presence so as to compete for control at some later point.

Thus, after the Second World War, instead of becoming fully integrated into the business world, the informal transport operators' organizations acquired the political presence they needed to defend their interests. Just as the political parties had learned to use them, they had learned to use political parties.

The public taxi crisis and the introduction of station wagons

The next stage in the history of informal transportation occurred in the 1950s, when public taxi operators began to increase the size of their vehicles, replacing their sedans with station wagons. Their vehicles thus began to approach formal transport vehicles in size and to threaten them with renewed competition.

This development was necessitated by economies of scale. As we saw earlier, public taxis were not very efficient because, among other reasons, the sedans occupied an excessively large area per passenger. This ratio could not be maintained as demand grew and routes became increasingly complex. Station wagons could hold up to nine, instead of five, passengers.

In 1950, however, not long after station wagons came into service, they were expressly prohibited by the authorities. The formal transport operators, still powerful at that time, viewed the new competition with concern. The increase in scale, by itself, posed a greater threat than the sedans. Nevertheless, since the informals were filling the vacuum which the formals, overwhelmed by the state and their own oligopoly, could not fill, the number of station wagons continued to grow.

The first redistributive privileges

The next advance occurred when the informals persuaded the state to grant them periodic exemptions from import duties on vehicles and spare parts as a privilege to which they were entitled in return for backing the government.

The first such exemption was negotiated between Luna's group and the Odría regime in 1955. Basically, it granted permission to import tax-free sedans, which the FED would then make available to informal transport operators who could prove that they had not been members of the APRA party. This marked the birth of a long tradition of tax exemptions and lent a clearly political cast, which persisted in years to come, to such exemptions.

In 1956, Odría's government was superseded by Manuel Prado, who became president a second time. He needed the APRA's votes to win, and in return he promised its members a system of "coexistence." The APRA thus regained influence in the government and was able to reconstitute its trade-union presence, heavily damaged by Odría's persecution, and revitalize ANEXOS. The informals again behaved rationally: they abandoned the FED and joined ANEXOS in the expectation of obtaining useful privileges. Indeed, ANEXOS pursued the course adopted by the previous regime, negotiating and winning tax exemptions in 1957 and 1959. To emphasize its renewed status, it persuaded the state to establish, in the 1959 law, that it was essential to obtain a favorable ruling from the APRA in order to benefit from the exemption. This was clearly a retaliation for the FED's attitude in 1955.

Luna's group did not simply sit back and let such things happen. It accused the APRA of countless shady dealings, although it could do nothing to prevent the exemptions from ultimately being legitimized as privileges to which informals were entitled in return for obeying the state, and also because they became a way for their organizations to increase their influence within the industry.

The crisis of formal transportation

The eighth advance occurred when the crisis and final bankruptcy of formal transport businesses considerably expanded the space to be occupied by informals.

By the late 1950s, traditional transport, as represented by APOUI, had ceased to be profitable. In 1959, when the El Sol Transport Company closed its doors, an unexpected succession of bankruptcies left Lima almost without formal transport services. By 1960, 32 of the 42 private bus companies then in existence had ceased to be operated by their owners.

At least three factors underlay this situation. Declining profits, a result

Informality in Photos

From the countryside to the city. Arrival at Desamparados, 1969.
Photo: Carlos Domínguez

Birth of an informal settlement. Invasion at Pamplona, 1971.
Photo: El Comercio *archive*

Igloos on invaded farmland at Km.15, Carretera al Norte, 1986.
Photo: El Comercio *archive*

Urban definition and provision of services in an informal settlement, Mi Peru.
Photo: El Comercio *archive*

All the available land has been used at El Agustino settlement, 1986.
Photo: Carlos Domínguez

Houses and buildings in the San Martín de Porres informal settlement,
thirty years after its formation.
Photos: Caretas *archive*

Private roads. They pass only in front of houses whose owners contribute to road building in La Balanza, Comas, 1986.
Photo: Carlos Domínguez

Pickets defending invaded property at Huaycán settlement, 1984.
Photo: La República *archive*

Violent eviction. Police intervention at Garagay, 1985.
Photos: El Comercio *archive* (*top*)
La República *archive* (*bottom*)

Repression of invaders. Buckshot wounds in Garagay, 1985.
Photo: La República *archive*

Invaders strip evicting magistrate of his belongings at Jicamarca, 1986.
Photo: El Comercio *archive*

When formal justice is absent. Lynching of Jorge Yanama Quispe, accused of theft in an informal settlement to the south of Lima, 1984.
Photo: La República *archive*

Itinerant street vendors on La Unión Street.
Photo: El Comercio *archive*

Progress. Vendor with cart.
Photo: Luis Peirano

Special rights of ownership. Street vendor staking out a "pitch" on the public thoroughfare.
Photo: La República *archive*

Gaining economy of scale. A street vendor's truck.
Photo: Caretas *archive*

Street vendors' belt around the Central Market.
Photos: El Comercio *archive*

Eviction of street vendors. Operation Sombrilla, launched by Mayor Falconi, 1978.
Photo: Carlos Domínguez

Los Inkas informal market, Independencia.
Photo: José Casals

Miguel Grau informal market, Independencia.
Photo: José Casals

PECOLIC informal market in Comas, interior view.
Photo: José Casals

Interior view, second floor, of Ciudad de Dios informal market in San Juan de Miraflores
Photo: José Casals

Polvos Azules municipal fairground in El Cercado.
Photo: José Casals

Old informal "colectivos."
Photo: Caretas *archive*

The first minibuses.
Photo: Caretas *archive*

The first minibuses.
Photo: Caretas *archive*

The classic D-300.
Photo: Caretas *archive*

A Mercedes Benz bus.
Photo: Caretas *archive*

Pirates in Volkswagen buses.
Photo: Caretas *archive*

Clandestine shoe factory, Rímac.
Photo: Carlos Domínguez

Open for business. Tailor shop in an informal settlement.
Photo: Luis Peirano

Ernesto Sánchez Silva, also known as "Poncho Negro," organizer of invasions, 1964.
Photo: Caretas *archive*

Ananías Balbín Contreras, also known as El Rey,
who organized fifty invasions, 1986.
Photo: La República *archive*

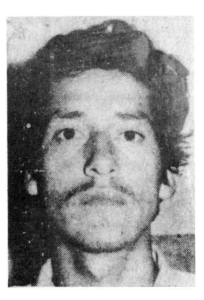

Charles Lastra Domínguez, also known as
Tulín, leader of the Huaycán informal
settlement. Detained as a terrorist, 1986.
Photo: El Comercio *archive*

Roberto Araujo Espinosa, leader of the Federation of Street Vendors of the Central Market and Adjacent Streets (FEVACEL).
Photo: Carlos Domínguez

Guillermo Nolasco Ayasta, Marxist leader of the Federation of Lima Street Vendors (FEDEVAL).
Photo: Caretas archive

Luis Paredes Pinillos, also known as Guillotín, leader of the Plaza Dos de Mayo Street Vendors.
Photo: Carlos Domínguez

Hernán Chang Lofock, leader of the Federation of Drivers of Peru (FED).
Photo: La República *archive*

Juan P. Luna, leader for sixty years of the Federation of Drivers of Peru (FED), 1978.
Photo: Carlos Domínguez

Informal water distribution service, Villa El Salvador, 1985.
Photo: Carlos Domínguez

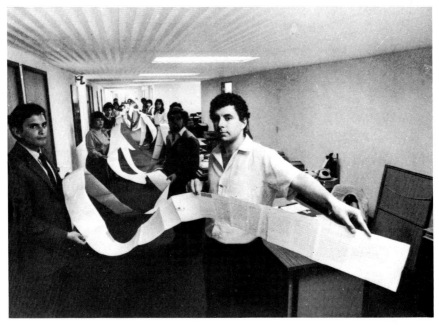
Researchers from the Instituto Libertad y Democracia (ILD) with a printout 30 meters long: procedures needed to set up a small industry.
Photo: Caretas *archive*

of strict fare controls, forced formal companies to postpone dealing with the depreciation of their vehicles, with the result that their fleets became ramshackle and obsolete. Second, informal transport, since it was not subject to state control, was better able to adapt to the growing demand created by Lima's urban growth. Last, the increasing reserves which the formal companies were required to maintain to pay their workers' social benefits ultimately condemned them to insolvency.

The formal operators, in consequence, withdrew from the market, declared their companies bankrupt and, claiming that they were unable to pay the social benefits due them, transferred ownership of their companies to the workers. Some writers suggest that there was a shady side to these bankruptcies. Sanchez León, Calderón, and Guerrero, citing another study, claim that many owners systematically decapitalized their companies, arranging fraudulent bankruptcies either to avoid paying their workers' social benefits or to transfer capital to other, more profitable, activities.[17]

Two methods were used for the transfer of ownership: setting up cooperatives in which all workers received an equal share, and worker-owned companies in which each worker's share varied according to the amount owed him by the owners. The new formal businesses were not very successful, however. In 1970, some tried to form themselves into the National Federation of Transport Cooperatives (FENACOOT) which, in 1973, at the urging of the military government, became the Metropolitan Lima Transport Cooperative and the publicly owned Metropolitan Lima Transport Corporation (TLMEPS). By the end of 1982, the TLMEPS had received subsidies totalling $12.9 million, yet its fleet had declined from 285 to 189 vehicles.

The ground left free by the bankruptcy of the formal companies was not to be occupied by the businesses formed by their own employees, but by informals.

The recognition of minibuses

In the ninth stage, minibuses were recognized by the state as the main vehicles for mass transportation.

As the formal businesses collapsed, the informal transport operators began to replace their sedans and station wagons with Volkswagen, OM, or Ford vans. They ceased to be taxi operators and became minibus operators,

---

[17] Abelardo Sánchez León, Julio Calderón Cockburn, and Paúl Guerrero de los Ríos, *Paradero Final? El Transporte Público en Lima Metropolitina* (Lima: DESCO, 1978), p. 76.

almost doubling the number of passengers they could carry. The change-over was gradual. In 1963, minibus operators were a minority. After 1963, their numbers began to grow, but it was in 1965 that the changeover really speeded up, forcing public taxis out of even the smallest lines.

The momentum was apparently created by the government's decision to encourage the formation of a national industry of vehicle assembly. As a result, thirteen factories began to produce bodies for the new minibuses. They needed a market, and the state had little choice but to cooperate with them. In 1965, it recognized the minibus operators. The following year, it granted a concession to the first minibus committee, formed from a former public taxi committee. This recognition did not give informals the legality which the formal bus companies had enjoyed; it was a bureaucratic procedure which gave the committee neither legal personality nor definitive ownership of the routes. The state continued to grant this kind of recognition to minibus operators on a relatively liberal basis, however, until 1968, when it approved tax exemptions and benefits for mass transit but decided to stop granting new concessions.[18]

Even so, the government forced the informals to accept fare controls in exchange for the recognition given. At the same time, since it apparently viewed such operations as a passing phenomenon, the state decided to increase its direct business involvement in the transport sector: on October 26, 1965, the Provincial Council established the Lima Paramunicipal Transport Administration (APTL). Like the cooperatives and worker-controlled companies which followed the formals, the APTL was not very successful. After periodic decapitalizations, the state replaced it with the National Urban Transport Corporation of Peru (ENATRU-PERU) in 1976. Neither corporation ever posed a serious threat to the informals. According to the ILD's calculations, between 1965 and 1982 the state had to subsidize its creatures, either directly or indirectly to the tune of $87.5 million in order to keep them in operation.

The informals, for their part, retained the committee as their basic business and political unit, and the public taxi committees became minibus committees. Higher-level organizations had to compete for the privilege of representing a sector which was acquiring ever-greater economic influence. The FED was more successful at this than ANEXOS, for by setting up the Lima Minibus Drivers' Union in January 1967, it managed to attract 95 percent of the committees, leaving ANEXOS the

[18] SD 009-68 DGT of 26 April 1965, SD 260-69 HC of 26 June 1968.

remaining tiny percentage to form the Lima Union of Public Service Taxis, Public Taxis and Minibuses in May of the same year.

The incorporation of the informals into the bureaucracy

The informals' tenth advance took place when their union representatives were incorporated into the state offices responsible for controlling fares and regulating transport. First, not long after it had imposed fare controls on the informals, the state incorporated them into the government office established for that purpose, the Transit Fares Regulating Agency (ORETT).[19]

The ORETT was established to prevent a further transportation crisis by creating a price administration mechanism which included the state, the transport operators, representatives of most ministries, the armed forces, and university students. Prices thus became the result of institutionalized negotiation among the different groups in society; the result was that, instead of indicating the economic consensus reached in the market, prices became indicators of the political strength of the parties involved. This hampered the state's own objectives, since negotiation was never able to result in terms on which transport services could be operated at a profit. The need for some of the parties to strengthen their position in the ORETT also prompted them to take a number of steps to exert political pressure—for instance, strikes or protest marches—which disrupted the peace even further.

The incorporation of informals into the government's mechanism for controlling fares was followed in 1970 by their incorporation into the state offices responsible for designing overall transport policy when the Technical-Labor Commission was unofficially established as a consultative body to the Department of Traffic and Road Safety. Politics was thus extended to virtually all transport-related decisions.

In the meantime, informality continued to grow. By 1971, six years after their recognition as minibus operators, the informals controlled 70 of every 100 mass-transit vehicles, leaving only 30 for the formals.

Big business: the D-300's

The informals' next advance took place when, legal prohibitions notwithstanding, they replaced their vans with D-300 minibuses.

[19] DL 17848 of 14 October 1969.

Until the 1970s, informals were unable to bring into service vehicles with a capacity of more than 12 seats because this was expressly prohibited by the 1965 regulations. However, increasing demand—this was the decade of the greatest growth of population in Lima's history, as well as of the highest migration rate on record—and the inadequate economies of scale offered by minibuses made it difficult to provide adequate services without using larger vehicles. The José Granda Transport Operators' Association and the 37-M Committee, veritable pioneers in the history of informal transport, took the initiative.

The minibus operators' union had learned, by experience, that if they were to increase the scale of their operations they must pool their political resources rather than their technical resources. Since they knew that they could not easily ignore the existing ban, they sought an alliance with formal interests which were sufficiently strong to overcome the legal barriers.

Accordingly, they approached Chrysler, offering to buy more than a hundred chassis of its D-300 model for assembly in Peru. From a technical standpoint, the D-300 was an obsolete three-ton, gasoline-powered Dodge truck, manufactured in Brazil and designed to carry goods, not passengers. The informals then approached MORAVECO, a national industry, offering it the contract to manufacture the bodies needed for the conversion. They even gave it a model designed especially for them by a U.S. firm, Wayne—a 43-passenger vehicle, almost four times the capacity authorized by the 1965 regulations. [20]

The scale of the operation required the assistance of a financial institution. For this, informals from the José Granda Association and the 37-M Committee turned to a foreign institution, the Deltec Banking Corporation. They concluded a funds-in-trust contract under which Deltec acquired the vehicles on the informals' behalf and the latter undertook to pay off the debt periodically. In the contracts signed, the José Granda Association gave its place of residence as Condevilla, an informal settlement which at that time had no deeds of title. That its formal partners raised no objections is evidence of the recognition of the extralegal system.

Once the informals had allied themselves with Chrysler, MORAVECO, and Deltec, they still had to bring the D-300 into service, bearing in mind that, having more than 12 seats, it was actually prohibited. To do so, they resorted to a very clever ploy; they convinced the

[20] Once it owned the design, MORAVECO used it repeatedly for other work, which is why most of the D-300s in Lima look the same.

government that it was gaining a political victory, rather than that they were breaking the law. They approached the minister of transport and communications, General Aníbal Meza Cuadra, and invited him to preside over the launching of the new fleet, hinting that, since these were the first large vehicles to serve the public, this was an historic occasion which a representative of the "Peruvian revolution" could not afford to miss.

The accomplishment was significant for a number of reasons. It demonstated the informals' entrepreneurial skill. It showed that the incentives in our society have been so distorted that, instead of using technical criteria for the vehicle, the informals were forced to use political criteria. It also demonstrated that the informals, like the formals before them, could reach an agreement with the state to ignore the law.

Privileges, but not property rights

In the twelfth stage, there were active negotiations between the state and the informals which ended in 1976 with an open confrontation. As a result, the informal transport operators lost their official recognition and were henceforth forced to work solely within their extralegal system.

The FED, which had joined the Communist Party–dominated CGTP in 1969 because it had the approval of the military government, withdrew from it in 1973 in order to establish even closer ties with the government, joining the newly established Confederation of Workers of the Peruvian Revolution (CTRP), the dictatorship's trade-union arm. The FED thereby so increased its negotiating strength that any committee that wanted anything had to join it. In July 1976, Juan P. Luna was able to claim that transport operators "were in with the government in office."[21]

The FED was trying to strengthen the informals' extralegal rights to appropriated routes in order to make the transport services more stable and secure. It never succeeded, however. Instead, the close political ties between the informal transport operators and the military government aroused the latter's interest in maintaining and expanding its control of the industry by limiting their rights in order to keep them dependent. Accordingly, each year from 1970 to 1975, a ban was imposed on new routes, although, as an exception, existing routes were regularized.[22] The state offset this negative attitude by granting the informals, through the

[21] Margarita Petrera, "La Experienca . . .," p. 49.

[22] DL 18383, SD 032-70 TC, SD 008-71 TC, DL 19282, DL 19966, and DL 21329.

FED, all manner of privileges such as tax exemptions, exemption from import duties on vehicles and spare parts, and exemption from certain regulations.

None of these privileges made up for the lack of security and stability, however, and informal transport operators became so exasperated that they decided to go on strike in July 1976, amid violent protest demonstrations. In retaliation for this betrayal by its former allies, the military government canceled the concessions it had made. From then until 1981, informal transport was operated without any government recognition and was completely informal, sustained only by the power of its own extralegal system. This so strengthened it that, in 1979, while still refusing to recognize the informals' right to appropriate new routes, the state declared that the informal transport operators' organizations were the organizations responsible for arbitrating disputes arising in the service.[23]

At the same time, the FED changed hands. Around 1978, it withdrew from the CTRP, became an independent union, and Juan P. Luna lost its leadership to Hernán Chang Lofock. None of this prevented the informals from increasing their influence in the transport service, however. By 1976, 81 of every 100 mass transit vehicles belonged to them, while only 19 belonged to the formals.

The search for yet larger vehicles

The next advance occurred when the minibus operators again found international trading partners. In an attempt to meet the ever-growing demand, they tried to introduce into the service vehicles with room for 80 passengers.

After the 1973 oil crisis and the fall of General Velasco in 1975, the military government decided to put an end to the cheap gasoline policy. The gas-guzzling D-300s became extremely expensive, especially as the government was not prepared to raise fares. The informals countered by trying to acquire larger vehicles. The first was the D-500, a truck also made by Chrysler. This vehicle has a longer chassis than the D-300 and is also designed for carrying goods. MORAVECO and Thomas designed for it a body with an average capacity of 71 passengers. Since it also ran on gasoline, it was not very attractive to transport operators, although some of them replaced the engine with a Perkins diesel engine.

The introduction of the D-500 precipitated the appearance of other,

[23] MR 39-76 TC/TC of 4 July 1976; official communication 47-79 TC/TE of 27 March 1979.

larger vehicles. First came the Chrysler D-800, which also had a truck chassis and a Peruvian-built body but could run on either gasoline or diesel fuel. This was followed by the Volvo BB-57, a bus in every sense of the word: designed for passenger transport, it had a diesel turbo engine and an average capacity of 60 people.

These acquisitions were not sufficient to meet the requirements of the service; moreover, the informal transport operators encountered numerous difficulties in concluding contracts and obtaining credit. The unions and federations therefore decided to become directly involved. The FED promoted the formation of a corporation called Transportes S.A. (TRANSA) to purchase vehicles on behalf of the informals. To do this, the FED took advantage of the tariff exemptions granted in the final years of the military dictatorship and contacted representatives of Mercedes Benz in Argentina, who expressed an interest in doing business. It thus acquired buses designed specifically for the service, with Argentinian bodies, diesel engines, and a capacity of 80 passengers.

Scania Vabis of Peru also became interested and contacted groups of minibus operators who did not belong to TRANSA, offering them Marco Polo buses manufactured in Brazil. These were state-of-the-art vehicles designed specifically for the service, with diesel turbo engines, an average capacity of 80 passengers, and a price of approximately $72,000 each. In this instance, however, the main problem was financial, because purchases were to be made individually. Scania asked its headquarters in Brazil to approach that country's export credit insurance system to accept the minibus operators as the final purchasers of the vehicles, and the insurance managers agreed.

As many as four different methods were used to establish guarantees. First, Scania's representatives in Peru assessed the value of the route. Then they brought together interested transport operators in groups of five, combining people with greater and lesser assets to vouch for each other. Next, the operators were asked to mortgage their homes for up to 50 percent of the value of the vehicles. Since most of the operators lived in informal settlements and had no title to their homes, Scania verified that these people actually owned homes, and valued them by appraising the building and the land. The appraisal made, a pledge was signed, committing the minibus operators to turn their titles over to Scania when they were received. Last, the new vehicle was also pledged to Scania as collateral.

Informal property and routes thus became acceptable guarantees for commercial transactions. It was implicitly recognized that the extralegal system was strong enough to permit such transactions even though the state had canceled all its concessions to the informals.

Formality kills

In the fourteenth stage, the informals were incorporated into a sui generis legal regime which, by formalizing them, paved the way for their subsequent decline.

The change of political regime in 1980 offered the informals the possibility of increasing their contacts with the state and exerting pressure on it again. In January of the following year, they organized a massive strike which ended with the signing of a compromise between their leaders and the authorities.[24] The outcome was that the state again recognized their rights to appropriate new routes and included their leaders in a body called the Joint Technical Commission, which was to regulate transport activities during the next four years.[25] In exchange, the state wanted the informals' backing or political neutrality, as well as their continued readiness to accept political control of fares and the service in general.

As a result of these controls, however, fares declined by 15 percent in real terms between 1980 and 1984 and the debts incurred in dollars to purchase larger vehicles were inflated by a devaluation of 1,676.5 percent. At the same time, the government introduced a tax on gasoline which, combined with inflation, increased the price of gasoline 1,727.3 percent.[26] In this situation, instead of authorizing realistic fares, competitive terms for

[24] A confidential memorandum of 17 January 1981 summarizes the agreements reached as follows:

1. Rationalization of the service: general norms for minibus drivers, study of transport in Lima, and reorganization of all ministerial units, among others.

2. Renewal of the vehicle fleet: evaluation of the condition and legal conformity of vehicles to determine the state and age of the motor vehicle fleet.

3. Reimbursement: each month, transport operators will give a sworn statement which will serve as a basis for calculating the reimbursements granted by the State to offset fare controls.

4. Import facilities: the government undertakes to grant facilities for purchasing new or secondhand vehicles and spare parts abroad for use in the service. It also undertakes to obtain exemptions from sales tax and additional taxes, and the tax on used vehicle sales. Lastly, it undertakes to arrange for lines of credit and to make it easier to obtain insurance policies.

5. Recomposition of the fare controls agency: transport operators' leaders are guaranteed participation in the fare controls agency and it is agreed that sufficient information will be gathered on operating costs before fares are established.

[25] SD 009-81 TC of 11 March 1981.

[26] The state does not try to adjust fares to the marketplace but instead determines the cost structure of the service by means of a complex computation which includes such fixed costs as manpower, overhead, administration, depreciation, and financing; such variable costs as fuel, lubricants, tires, spare parts, and repairs; and, last, the drivers' "reasonable" margin of profit.

the purchase and import of vehicles and spare parts, entry to the formal capital market, and so forth, the state chose the traditional policy of negotiating the alternatives in detail, bureaucratizing and further complicating the situation.

Thus, in January 1984, it set up the Land Transport Finance Fund to subsidize minibus operators and finance their purchases, agreed to allow them to pay their tax debts in installments, exempted them from such taxes as sales tax, wage taxes, and tax on the capitalization of the revaluation surplus, and halted all coercive proceedings instituted against them. Two months later, it established a special import regime which institutionalized tax exemptions for vehicles, provided that they were assembled by national corporations. In 1985, in a last ditch attempt to save the operators, it promulgated the Public Service Land Transport Act to "promote a system which balances the value of fares with the real cost of operating the service, in order to enable public service transport operators to recover financially" and "to penalize unfair competition, particularly fare competition."[27]

All these measures simply prolonged the agony. None was able to offset the reduction in fares, the increase in taxes and fuel costs, the weight of state controls, and the need to comply with interminable red tape. Minibus operators had to cannibalize vehicles if they were to continue to operate, prompting one leader to exclaim, "We are eating our own vehicles." When their income declined and they began to operate at a loss, they neglected the maintenance of their vehicles. The informal operators began to lose capital on a massive scale.

A new generation of informals

The final stage in this history is marked by the invasion of the pirates, informals who took advantage of the minibus operators' deepening crisis to seize control of the service. While the minibus operators were using obsolete vehicles, were up to their necks in debt and were spending most of their time on red tape and negotiations with the state, they were invaded by a new generation of informals in almost the same way as they had invaded the formals before 1965.

Recognizable by their modern versions of the same vans that the minibus operators had driven twenty years earlier and by the stickers with the pirate flag on their windshields, these new informals proliferated rapidly. The ILD estimates that by 1984 they numbered some 6,800, as

[27] Legislative Decree 267, Legislative Decree 275, Legislative Decree 329.

compared with the 7,969 informal transport operators whose routes they were invading.

Like the APOUI operators before them, the informal minibus operators had become unable to meet the growing demand for transport services and were invaded by others who, because they did not have to assume the costs of dealing with the state, could charge more and provide a better quality service. The declining service and the newly emerging one repeated the past, but this time the victims were the earlier murderers.[28] The same can still happen to the pirates. The state soon began to absorb them, giving their activity much sought after bureaucratic recognition in return for their acceptance of government controls.[29]

Informal mass transit has nonetheless continued to grow. By 1984, the old minibus operators and the new pirates owned 91 of every 100 vehicles in service. Only 9 were formal.

The Mystery of Cyclical Bankruptcies

The operating logic and evolution of transport services suggests an ironic conclusion: each time a group of formal or informal businessmen has managed to establish a relatively complete service, it has gone bankrupt within a few years.

The formal operators belonging to the APOUI removed the Metropolitan Company from the market and were displaced in 1965 by the minibus operators, who began to lose ground to the new pirates twenty years later. The history of transport services has thus become a vicious circle of bankruptcies for which the legal system produced by the state is largely responsible.

The legal system has never been seen as the problem, however. People have preferred to blame the informals, the bureaucracy, or the government. As a result, between 1926 and 1984 the responsibility for transport was transferred fifteen times: the executive branch, which took responsibility for transport services in 1921, was followed by the Municipal Traffic Department in 1926, the Public Works Department in 1927, the Government Traffic and Vehicles Department in 1929, the Omnibus Section of the Traffic and Vehicles Department in 1934, the Transport Coordinating Board in 1942, the Transit and Vehicles

[28] The fares charged by pirates are on average 63 percent higher than those set by the state.

[29] SD 026-84 TC.

Department in 1946, the Transit Department in 1963, the Land Transport Department and the Urban Transit and Transport Department in 1969, the Transit Department in 1972, which was reorganized the following year, the Land Transport Executive Committee and the Land Traffic Department in 1981, and the provincial government as of 1984.

The fact is that, over the years, the legal system has not allowed the tremendous business energies and entrepreneurial talents of formals and informals alike to be tapped. On the contrary, it seems to be designed to deal politically with only a very small number of interest groups, not with a widespread entrepreneurial class. Legal recognition of transport operators is not considered a right, but an agreement to be negotiated in exchange for the acceptance of political interference and the imposition of numerous burdens, including the control of fares.

This situation has completely altered the behavior of the transport operators and has shifted the competition in transit services from prices and quality to safety. Instead of competing by lowering fares or improving quality, the transport operators have been forced, over the years, to compete by reducing safety and paying the bribes requested by the authorities. One of the many privileges which transport operators have received in exchange for accepting government controls is, in fact, the relaxation of safety requirements by the authorities. When the government ruled that the minibus operators would have to pay only 10 percent of the fines imposed by the police or when it conferred on them exemption from impoundment of their vehicles for most traffic violations, it was actually reducing the incentives for maintaining a safe service.

Attempts by magistrates to punish the lack of safety indirectly through civil liability suits have been thwarted by the same process. Clear-cut laws govern contractual liability, namely the transport operator's liability to his passengers, as well as noncontractual liability, the operator's liability to the rest of society. But judicial proceedings are so tortuous, and the damages awarded have tended to be so ludicrous, that the cost of taking a transport operator to court far outweighs the benefit. In other words, the system has prompted the state to prefer detailed control of the transport business to the creation of a proper infrastructure both for passengers and for others traveling on the public thoroughfare.

All of this has made Peru's transit system one of the most dangerous in the world, far worse than in the large European countries. There are eleven times as many traffic fatalities in Peru as in West Germany and nineteen times as many as in England.[30] This appalling rate also represents a very high cost to society in terms of material losses, which in 1984 were estimated at $9.15 million. This then is the price which Peruvian society has to pay because the authorities' resources are devoted, above all, to controlling the transport operators politically rather than to controlling transport technically. The situation has also engendered tremendous frustration and discouragement among the thousands of individuals who, with nothing but their own labor and savings, have managed to provide 91 percent of mass transit.

Such problems might prompt some people to think that informal transport should be completely abolished and replaced by a publicly owned transport corporation which complies fully with safety and quality standards. Such a decision would also have tremendous costs, however. The ILD calculates that if the state were to eliminate or prohibit informal mass transit, only 9 of every 100 public-service vehicles would be able to keep operating and they could serve only 21 percent of those who currently use the service daily. The sharp reduction in urban transit would hit the poorest people hardest. In the informal settlements of the Cono Norte, Cono Centro, and Cono Sur, it would completely immobilize the population.

The state would have to replace the informal fleet, requiring $620 million—in 1984, 41.2 percent of all public investment in the country. The state would also have to invest an average of $49 million more a year to meet the growth in demand. And, if it maintained fares at their current levels, the state would incur an annual loss of $93 million. In short, replacing the informals would require an investment of state resources which would increase the already tremendous budget deficit by 7.2 percent. Nor have we taken into account the corresponding infrastructure (gas pumps, repair shops, and such), which the FED values at $400 million more.

In light of the above, some questions remain. Why have the informal operators been unable to acquire or approach legality through channels which do not involve breaking the law? Why do they win only de facto recognition even though they serve a precise objective of the state, and never the permanent recognition which would finally make them inde-

---

[30] In 1984, it was estimated that there were 390,487 motor vehicles in Lima, 55,058 traffic accidents annually, and approximately 1,502 fatalities, i.e., one fatality for every 260 vehicles. That same year, in West Germany there were 25,300,000 vehicles and 11,600 deaths, i.e., one death for every 2,183 vehicles. In England, with 18 million motor vehicles, there were 4,800 deaths, or one for every 3,729 vehicles.

pendent? Why, when they finally win some kind of formal acceptance, does this bankrupt them? Why cannot Peruvian society identify the tangible causes of the chaos in its transport system instead of just blaming the unpopular transport operators? We believe that these problems are caused by Peru's legal system, to which we devote the chapters that follow.

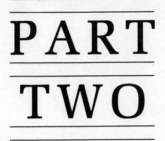

PART TWO

CHAPTER FIVE

The Costs and Importance of the Law

In earlier chapters we examined in detail how informal activities emerged and developed in three specific areas. Thus far, in our account, which is based on empirical research, we have sought to describe the fundamental characteristics of the system of extralegal norms identified by the researchers of the Instituto Libertad y Democracia (ILD) and to trace their historical evolution in order to establish their underlying logic.

All of this has shown that we are living in a costly society in which formals and informals alike waste tremendous resources. We have seen how invasions occur, traffic congestion and accidents increase, and permanent legal instability diverts resources, effort, and ingenuity from productive to political action to avoid legal penalties and win recognition of acquired extralegal rights.

Such problems have generally been thought to have many causes—migration, maldistribution of income, unemployment, even climate. As the ILD pursued its research, however, it became clear that none of these could explain the magnitude and complexity of these problems. Migration may explain the increase in the number of people living in the capital city. Maldistribution of income may explain why such migration occurs. Unemployment may explain why labor is so available. Climate may explain why a certain type of urban development is possible in a given geographical context. None of these, however, can explain why people choose to invade land to build their homes, occupy streets to conduct trade, or appropriate routes to provide transport services. In short, no one can explain why some people prefer formality and others informality, nor can they determine what the outcome of such a process will be.

This was why we decided to talk to the informals themselves. That is how we found that their main complaint is with the law and why they try to win recognition from the legal system. Accordingly, we set about to examine the legal context in order to determine its influence on individual decisions to operate formally or informally and on the outcome of such choices. The ILD then decided to conduct a number of field studies and analyses to identify and quantify this influence.

In the pages that follow, we present the results of this research. They show, in detail, first the costs of formality—these influence the decision to join or remain in formal activity or outside it—and then the costs of informality—the costs of the lack of protection and facilities that arise when one operates outside of legal institutions. We also show the costs to Peruvian society as a whole. Last, we consider the importance of the law in the entire process and in development in general.

The ILD's research confirmed the role of the law in determining the efficiency of the economic activities it regulates. It is in this sense that we shall refer to "good laws" and "bad laws": a law is "good" if it guarantees and promotes economic efficiency and "bad" if it impedes or disrupts it. The *unnecessary* costs of formality derive fundamentally from a bad law; the costs of informality result from the absence of a good law.

The Costs of Formality

In an economic activity, there are essentially two moments at which people evaluate their relationship with formal activity: when they enter it and when they decide to remain in it.

To define these two moments in time, the ILD coined two corresponding concepts, "the costs of access" to the activity and "the costs of remaining" in it, so as to examine all the requirements which citizens must meet in order to obtain the right to engage in a specific economic activity legally, and later all the requirements they must meet in order to preserve that legality. We wished to determine whether these costs influence individual choices.

We must make it clear that while our research identified the different costs of obtaining legal access to, and remaining in, an activity, this is not the approach taken by the average person. People who defy the legal system or make use of it make only an overall assessment, generally based on prices, of what it might cost them to comply with legal requirements and what they can obtain in return for such compliance. Their choice is based not on a precise evaluation but on a vague notion, as if the forest were far more frightening than the individual trees. Our research shows that Peruvians' decisions to conduct their activities informally are in large measure the result of a rational, though less detailed, evaluation of the costs of formality.

The Costs of Access

None of the economic activities investigated by the ILD can be exercised legally unless a whole variety of requirements has first been met. In order to identify these requirements and the costs they entail, the ILD examined four specific areas in which informality is a major social problem: industry, housing, trade, and transport.

The costs of access to industry

The ILD was forced to resort to a simulation to measure the costs of access to industry because, when we began the research that gave rise to this book, we kept hearing conflicting accounts about the difficulty of establishing an industry. The formal business people we interviewed said these procedures were very cumbersome, and the informal business people shuddered at the mere mention of them, but the lawyers maintained that the procedures were very simple and took little time. We decided to find out for ourselves.

In the summer of 1983, a team of ILD researchers set up a small garment factory in an industrial area of the Carretera Central in Ate district on the outskirts of Lima, and decided to comply with all the bureaucratic procedures required to establish it in accordance with the law. They simulated a business with a single proprietor, without incorporating it, since this would provide an extra measurement of the costs of access to the industry itself and would be easier to dismantle.

To do this, they rented the premises of an established factory, installed sewing machines, knitting machines, and other necessary implements, and recruited four university students to undertake the various bureaucratic procedures under the supervision of a lawyer experienced in administrative law. In addition to being very widespread in Peru and thus culturally significant, the activity chosen for the simulation was highly representative. It required approximately 60 percent of the bureaucratic procedures common to all industrial activities and 90 percent of those required of nonincorporated individuals.

The team also decided to handle all the necessary red tape without go-betweens, as a person of humble origin would do, and to pay bribes only when, despite fulfilling all the necessary legal requirements, it was the only way to complete a procedure and continue with the experiment. In the months that the simulation lasted, ILD simulators were asked for a bribe on ten occasions in return for speeding up the procedure. On two of these occasions, they were forced to agree because there was no other way to continue. In the other eight, they were able to avoid having to pay a bribe, although it was far from easy. The simulation was organized as if the ILD researchers were leaving the informal settlement of Villa El Salvador, to the south of Lima, every day to visit the different administrative centers where the procedures were carried out. They went from office to office, took detailed notes, timed the various procedures, and collected the multitude of required documents.

The results showed that a person of modest means must spend 289 days on bureaucratic procedures to fulfill the eleven requirements for setting up a small industry. Graph 1 shows the various procedures, the order in which they had to be complied with, the time they took, and the places where they were carried out.

After the simulation, the ILD calculated the cost of complying with all these procedures. According to these calculations, the cost per procedure was equivalent to $194.40. The almost ten-month wait to begin business would result in a loss of net profits equivalent to $1,036.60. The total cost of an individual's access to small formal industry is thus $1,231—thirty-two times the monthly minimum living wage.

In addition to showing how severely restricted access to industry is, particularly for lower-income people, these initial results confirmed that it was absurd to claim that the law creates no problems. It also demonstrated the utter pointlessness of the entire exercise: despite the 289 days and 11 permits needed, at no point did the authorities realize they were dealing with a simulation.

The costs of access to housing

The next step was to examine the problem of access to housing.

It was not feasible to use a simulation because it would have been necessary to set up an association or cooperative and commit several hundred people to the experiment for a long period of time. It was possible, however, to use two indirect sources. By examining laws, we could determine the characteristics of the various procedures; and by studying

Graph 1. Procedures to Set Up a Formal Industry

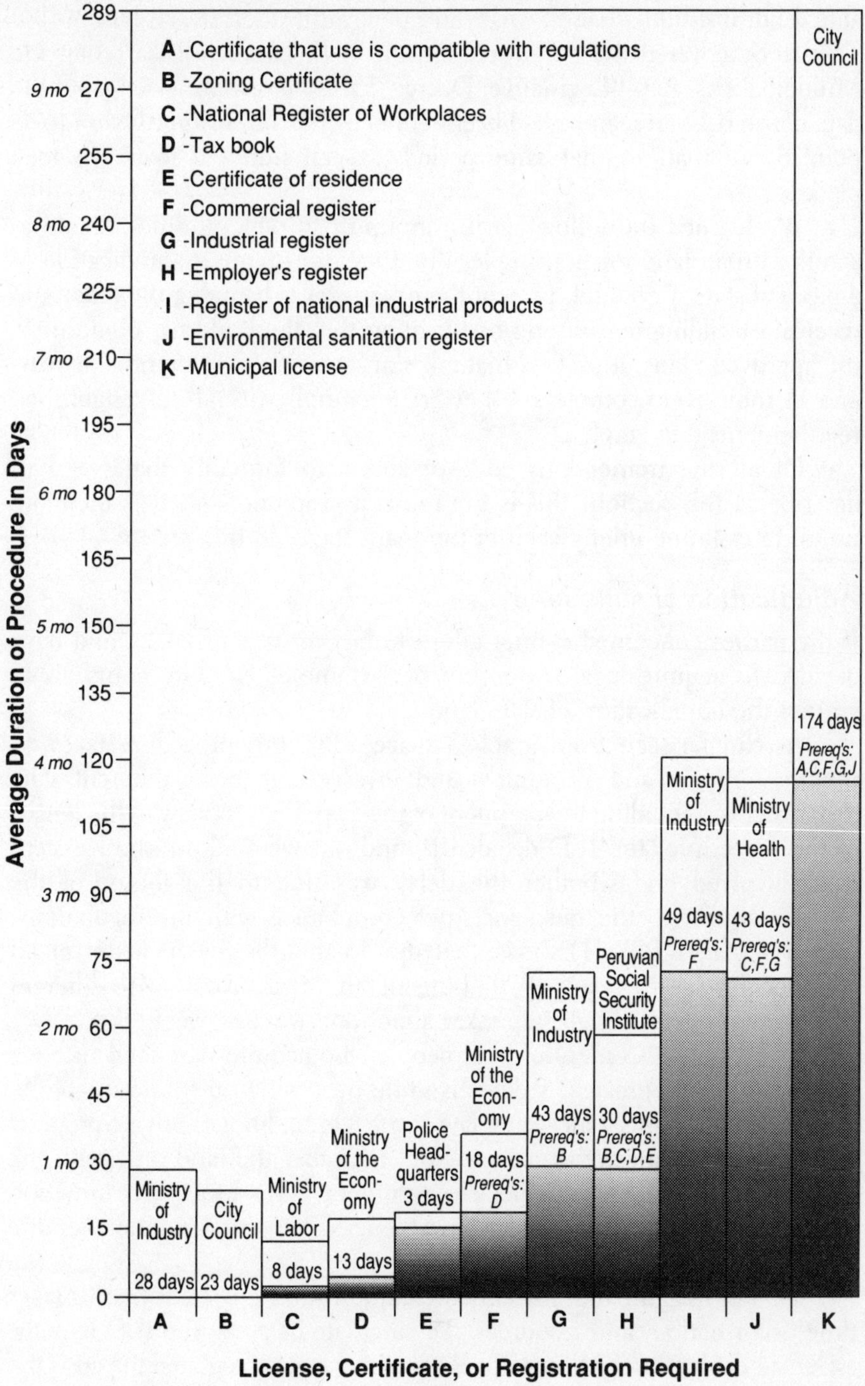

A -Certificate that use is compatible with regulations
B -Zoning Certificate
C -National Register of Workplaces
D -Tax book
E -Certificate of residence
F -Commercial register
G -Industrial register
H -Employer's register
I -Register of national industrial products
J -Environmental sanitation register
K -Municipal license

Average Duration of Procedure in Days

Letter	Authority	Days	Prereq's
A	Ministry of Industry	28 days	
B	City Council	23 days	
C	Ministry of Labor	8 days	
D	Ministry of the Economy	13 days	
E	Police Headquarters	3 days	
F	Ministry of the Economy	18 days	Prereq's: D
G	Ministry of Industry	43 days	Prereq's: B
H	Peruvian Social Security Institute	30 days	Prereq's: B,C,D,E
I	Ministry of Industry	49 days	Prereq's: F
J	Ministry of Health	43 days	Prereq's: C,F,G
K	City Council	174 days	Prereq's: A,C,F,G,J

License, Certificate, or Registration Required

Vertical axis markings:
289
9 mo 270
255
8 mo 240
225
7 mo 210
195
6 mo 180
165
5 mo 150
135
4 mo 120
105
3 mo 90
75
2 mo 60
45
1 mo 30
15
0

actual administrative cases, we could determine their average duration. This study covered the *only* three cases which, between 1981 when the Municipalities Act—Legislative Decree 51—was promulgated and the date of the ILD's research, had been settled by the authorities. It should be pointed out that, in that same period, several hundred invasions took place.

We learned the following: if a group of humble families decide to acquire urban land for housing legally, they must request adjudication of a piece of state wasteland, present their plans for urbanizing the land, and receive a building permit and certification that the buildings conform to the approved plans, a process that takes an average of 83 months (6 years and 11 months) to complete if they are to comply with all the established requirements (see graph 2).

Of all the tremendous costs of access to formality that we shall describe in this section, this is the most disproportionate. It is therefore useful to examine briefly each of the main stages in this process.

Adjudication of state land

If the parties concerned cannot afford to buy an urbanized lot and have decided to acquire legal ownership of a home, their only course is to request the adjudication of state land.

As can be seen from graph 3 (page 138), this procedure takes 43 months (3 years and 7 months) and involves up to six different state departments, including the president of the Republic. In view of the length of the procedure, the ILD decided to find out what administrative steps were involved and whether the delay was due to the torpor of the bureaucracy or to the need for strict compliance with the regulations. Graph 4 (pages 140–41) shows that the 43 months that it takes for an adjudication are the result of 207 bureaucratic steps involving 48 different government offices. Each step takes about one working week.

We should also mention that people who acquire state land receive, at the end of the process, a defective title over which they are unable to exercise all the rights which civil law accords to traditional private property owners. For instance, they can sell or encumber the land only with the express consent of the provincial government. This legal discrimination hurts precisely those people who have the least resources and most require the adjudication of state land for their homes.

Do not imagine that this obscure adjudication process is free. It takes time, information, and resources. To calculate its costs, the ILD hypothesized a housing association with 244 members and calculated the costs the

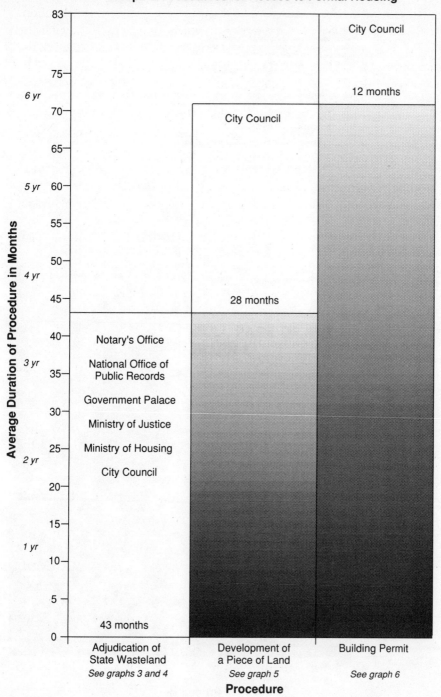

Graph 2. Procedures for Access to Formal Housing

Graph 3. Procedures for Adjudication of a Piece of State Wasteland

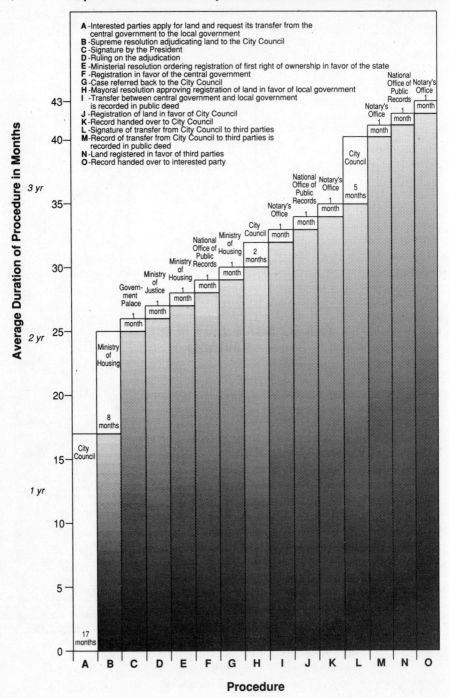

A -Interested parties apply for land and request its transfer from the central government to the local government
B -Supreme resolution adjudicating land to the City Council
C -Signature by the President
D -Ruling on the adjudication
E -Ministerial resolution ordering registration of first right of ownership in favor of the state
F -Registration in favor of the central government
G -Case referred back to the City Council
H -Mayoral resolution approving registration of land in favor of local government
I -Transfer between central government and local government is recorded in public deed
J -Registration of land in favor of City Council
K -Record handed over to City Council
L -Signature of transfer from City Council to third parties
M -Record of transfer from City Council to third parties is recorded in public deed
N -Land registered in favor of third parties
O -Record handed over to interested party

Average Duration of Procedure in Months

Procedure

members would have to bear to obtain by honest, formal means a piece of state land on which to live.

According to our estimates, the association must invest $526,019 in the adjudication procedure. Each member would have to pay $2,156: in other words, someone who at the time was earning the monthly minimum living wage would have to pay out his or her entire income for four years and eight months.

Approval for development of the land

Once land has been acquired by state adjudication, it must be developed, a "process involving a change of use of rural or waste land and requiring the provision of public utilities."[1]

The land cannot be developed freely, according to the preferences or requirements of the owners or as their finances permit. Any development plan must first take into account the land uses indicated in the zoning regulations and the minimum quality standards and maximum permissible density for basic services. Only when the plan complies with criteria can development begin. As can be seen from graph 5 (page 142), this takes an average of 28 months and involves at least three different stages, all of which must be processed with the Lima City Council: approval of preliminary studies, approval of plans, and authorization of the improvements.

Building permits

Finally, once the land has been acquired and developed, it must be built on. For this, building permits must be obtained prior to construction and, once construction is complete, certification that it conforms to the earlier approved plans. The ILD found that it usually takes about 12 months to obtain these two documents from the City Council. Graph 6 (page 143) illustrates the process.

Obviously, one reason people invade land and build their homes outside the law is that the legal channel established for gaining access to land for housing is severely restricted.

The inefficiency of the restrictions becomes particularly painful if we bear in mind that 5 percent, at most, of the national territory is currently being used for economic purposes. The remaining 95 percent has economic significance only in terms of the value added to it by people. One popular way to add value is to build on it, and it is precisely this course that is restricted by the law.

[1] National Building Regulations II.1.

Graph 4. Sequence of Administrative Requirements for Adjudication of Undeveloped, State-Owned Land

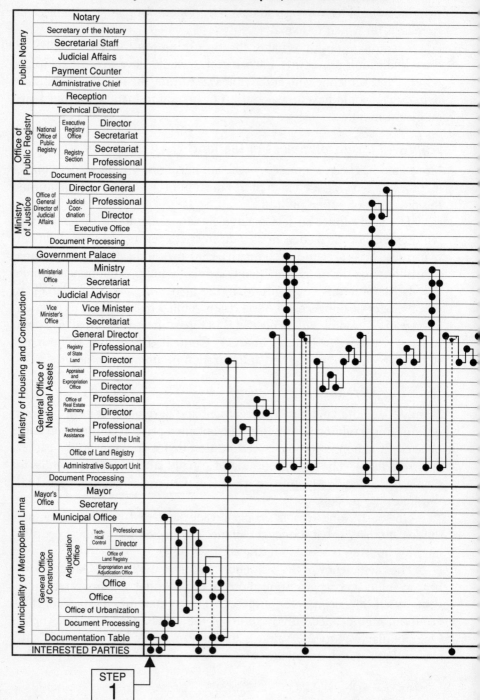

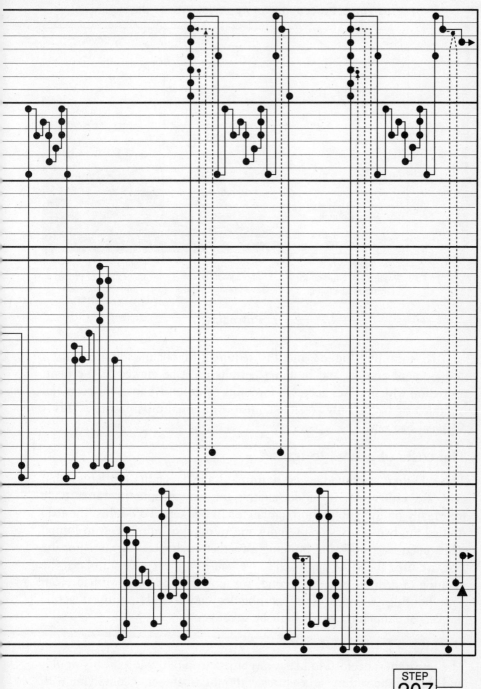

STEP
207

Graph 5. Procedures for Approval of Land Development

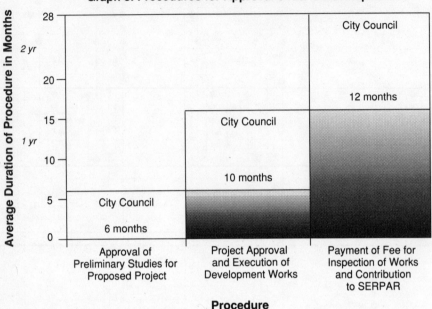

To sum up, the 83 months required to obtain adjudication, a development permit, and building permits must be viewed as the main restriction which makes access to formality so expensive that, for people of humble origin, the only possible course is informal urbanization. This is a typical bad law.

The costs of access to trade

The ILD then examined access to formal trade, since the restrictions that exist are crucial to an understanding of why people in Lima trade informally on the public thoroughfare or in markets. To do this, the ILD studied the two courses open to anyone wanting to gain access to formal trade: opening a store and building a market or shopping center. For the first, we used the same approach as we had in industry: we simulated the opening of a store. For the second, we took the approach we had taken with housing: we went over existing legislation and examined actual markets or shopping centers built by street vendors.

Opening a formal store

The researchers decided to behave as any person of modest means would, undertaking the various procedures without go-betweens, complying with

Graph 6. Procedures for Obtaining Building Permit

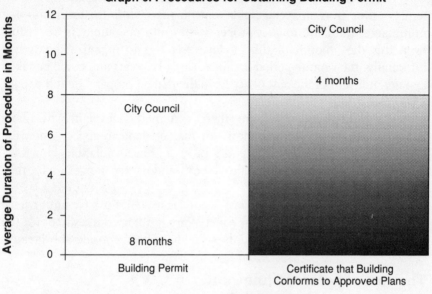

Average Duration of Procedure in Months

City Council
4 months

City Council

8 months

Building Permit

Certificate that Building
Conforms to Approved Plans

Procedure

all requirements, and trying to avoid paying bribes. The San Juan de Miraflores district was chosen because it is a new, prosperous commercial area with popular roots that go back many years. Suitable premises were rented and fitted out, and the process was initiated.

The simulation showed that a person wishing to open a small store legally must comply with bureaucratic procedures involving three different government departments. This takes 43 days and costs $590.56, 15 times the monthly minimum living wage in effect on the date on which the simulation was completed. Graph 7 (page 145) shows the results.

These findings show how the regulations create the incentives for choosing informality.

Building a market

The ILD studied five actual cases in which vendors had organized to build their own markets. The sample covered the city's various main commercial locations and areas.[2]

---

[2] Studied were Libertad market in San Miguel, Colonial market in El Cercado, Miguel Grau market in Independencia, the APECOLIC market in Comas, and Ciudad de Dios market in San Juan de Miraflores.

The exercise showed that the cost of access to formal markets, in terms of time, was an average of seventeen years, from the formation of a minimarket until the market proper comes into operation. If we deduct from this the amount of time it takes vendors to organize themselves informally, the waiting period is still at least 14½ years and could be taken as a net indicator of the cost of access to the market proper.[3] Graph 8 (page 147) gives details of this process.

The difficulties of building their own markets explain why many people decide to be street vendors, for markets tend to appear when the vendors have organized and begun a process of accumulation. However, they explain why many remain street vendors far longer than they otherwise would.

Despite everything, in the last twenty years vendors have built twelve markets for each one built by the state. Were it not for the restrictions, the number of markets built by vendors would have been considerably greater.

The cost of access to transport

Last, we come to the costs of access to transport. Here, things are far simpler than in industry, housing, and trade, but also more dramatic. There simply is no legal access to this activity.[4]

As a result, the ILD did not make a simulation or consider actual cases—since none existed—but turned to the law itself to determine what obstacles existed. The present procedure for obtaining access to formal transport is as follows.

First, only the state has the power to award rights. No group of transport operators can, of its own initiative, establish itself and request a route. This completely eliminates freedom of access to transport activities. Second, only the authorities can decide what routes have inadequate transport services that must be increased. These needs established, no one has the right to apply to operate a service, because the authorities are obliged to offer the new route to the existing committees or the companies nearest it. In the latter case, they acquire new rights and the process takes the form of an extension of the route. Only if authorized transport

[3] According to a large formal business which specializes in building markets, it takes formals approximately 100 days to complete the same procedures.

[4] The procedure used was the one provided by the 1981 regulations. Responsibility for this sector was transferred from the Ministry of Transport and Communications to the City Council in 1984, and a change in the procedure for awarding concessions has been pending. As of the time of writing, the new procedure had not been announced.

Graph 7. Procedures for Setting Up a Formal Store

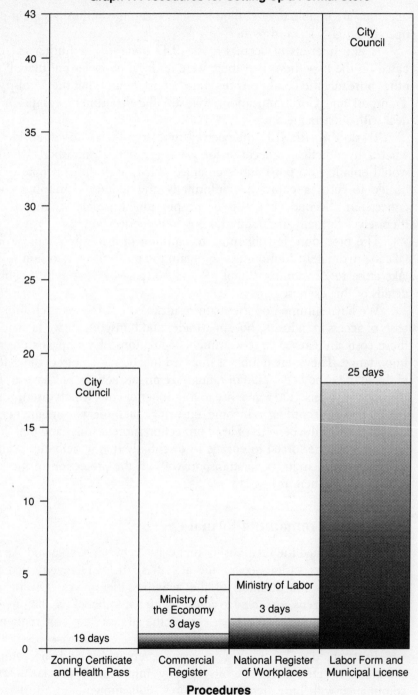

operators are unable to offer their assistance can the authorities grant new operating rights to third parties.

In the interests of accuracy, the ILD undertook a further exercise based on the hypothesis that there were no legal obstacles but that all the other bureaucratic conditions remained constant and that the Ministry of Transport and Communications was still the department competent to deal with such matters.

To do this, the ILD interviewed ministry officials to get an idea of what a hypothetical procedure for gaining access to transport activities would entail. Two possibilities emerged. First, a group of people might decide to form a committee informally and request a minibus route concession. Second, a group of people might decide to incorporate themselves formally and request a bus route concession.

The procedure for obtaining recognition of a minibus route would take approximately 26 months. To obtain the bus route concession would take close to 27 months. Graphs 9 and 10 (pages 149 and 150) contain details of this exercise.

We have summed up the main results of the ILD's research into the costs of access to industry, housing, trade, and transport. As we have seen, these costs are caused by government regulations of varying nature and importance. They were doubtless imposed in a desire to correct the defects of the market and better plan or rationalize private activity but have exactly the opposite effect. They give rise to a number of costs which discriminate against people according to income, ensuring that those who are financially better off enjoy the benefits of legal protection more readily, and that those who are poor are forced to engage in essentially honest activities such as building, trade, industry, or transport without the protection of the law. What we have here is bad law.

The costs of remaining formal

Having established the relationship that exists between people and the law when they enter various economic activities, the ILD investigated this relationship for the duration of the activities themselves. During this period, too, citizens are forced to comply with a number of regulations—in order to remain legal. We have coined the phrase "costs of remaining formal" to refer to this phenomenon.

In its broad sense, this phrase covers a very widespread and complex situation. It refers both to costs directly imposed by the law—taxes, compliance with bureaucratic procedures, obligations to administer per-

Graph 8. Average Time Taken to Set Up an Informal Market

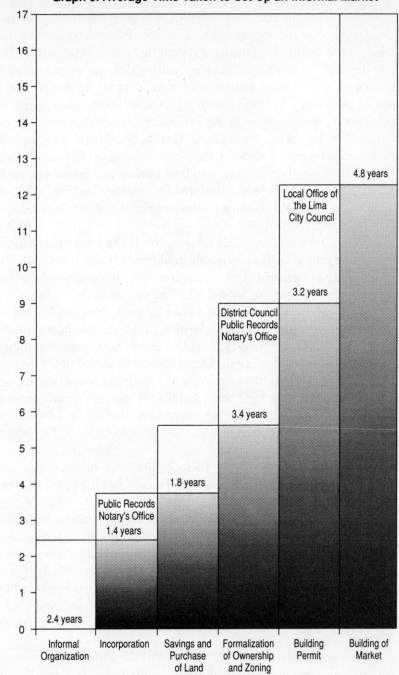

Procedures

sonnel in a certain way, and payment of higher rates for public utilities, among others—and to costs indirectly imposed by legal institutions as a whole—the instability of the legal system, insecurity of property rights, and the inefficiency of the judiciary in settling disputes or collecting debts, among others. Since it was impossible to cover all these aspects at once, the ILD decided to study indirect costs at some future stage and to concentrate for the time being on direct costs, examining the returns declared by businesses themselves. This analysis was limited to industry.

Accordingly, we chose a sample consisting of fifty small industrial firms, employing between one and four workers and engaging in activities where there is a high level of informality: baking, knitting, dressmaking, shoemaking (except rubber or plastic footwear), and furniture making and woodworking.

When they analyzed this sample, the ILD's researchers found, that remaining formal costs a small industrial firm 347.7 percent of its after-tax profits and 11.3 percent of its production costs. In other words, were it not for the costs of remaining formal, the firm's profits and therefore its savings and potential investment capital would be more than quadrupled.

The sample provided an indication of the relative importance of the costs chosen for analysis. The ILD's researchers classified these costs tentatively into tax costs, nontax legal costs, and public utility costs. It was found that 21.7 percent of the costs of remaining formal are tax-related, 72.7 percent are other legal costs, and the remaining 5.6 percent are public utility costs. In other words, for every $100 that a small industrial firm must pay in order to remain legal, $22 goes to taxes, $73 to other legal costs, and $5 to utilities.

The "other legal costs" include the cost of the administrative procedures required to remain formal. To calculate the time taken by these procedures, the ILD conducted a survey of 37 legally established companies operating in areas where there is a particularly high level of informality—for instance, foodstuffs, wooden furniture, textiles and garment manufacturing, chemicals and plastics, printing, basic metal working, mechanics, and toys. It found that companies devoted approximately 40 percent of all their administrative employees' total working hours to complying with bureaucratic procedures. On average, each of these employees devoted two-and-a-half days a week to this task—a tremendous waste of resources.

The costs of remaining formal prevent the surpluses generated by an activity from being distributed freely, and thus affect the companies' potential profits. They can use only $23.30 of every $100 of the surpluses

Graph 9. Hypothetical Procedure for Access by a Minibus Committee

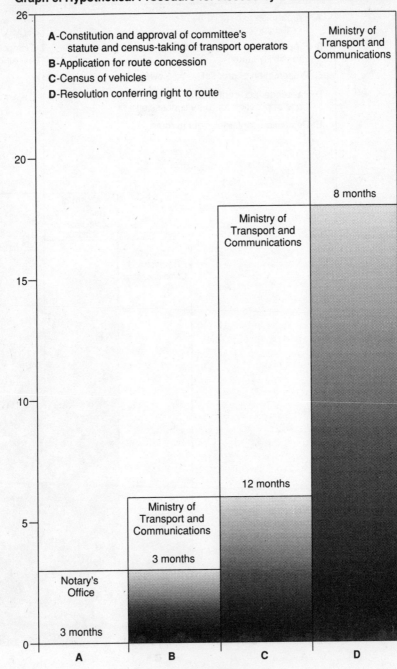

A-Constitution and approval of committee's
    statute and census-taking of transport operators
B-Application for route concession
C-Census of vehicles
D-Resolution conferring right to route

Ministry of Transport and Communications

8 months

Ministry of Transport and Communications

12 months

Ministry of Transport and Communications

3 months

Notary's Office

3 months

Average Duration of Procedure in Months

Procedure

A   B   C   D

150

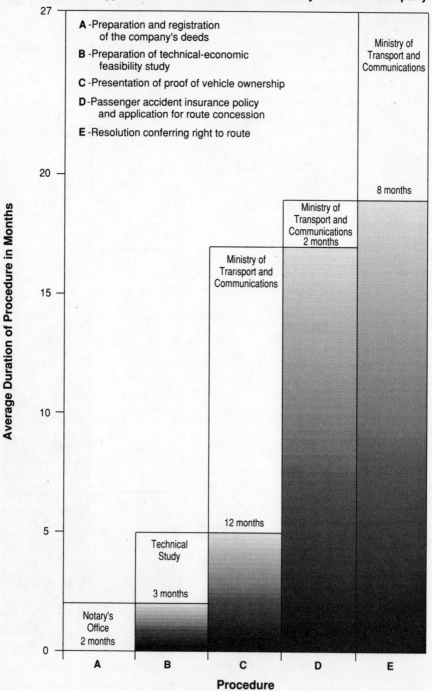

Graph 10. Hypothetical Procedures for Access by a Minibus Company

Average Duration of Procedure in Months

A - Preparation and registration of the company's deeds

B - Preparation of technical-economic feasibility study

C - Presentation of proof of vehicle ownership

D - Passenger accident insurance policy and application for route concession

E - Resolution conferring right to route

Notary's Office 2 months

Technical Study 3 months

Ministry of Transport and Communications 12 months

Ministry of Transport and Communications 2 months

Ministry of Transport and Communications 8 months

Procedure

generated and potentially convertible to profits, and they spend the remaining $76.70 on remaining legal. Contrary to what one might assume, only $17.60 of this amount goes to pay taxes; $59.10 is spent on other legal costs.

First, we can conclude that, since taxation is not the main problem, tax policy is not the prime determinant of whether companies operate formally or informally. Other legal costs are at the heart of the matter. Business people have to satisfy a number of regulations, ranging from processing an endless succession of documents in government offices to administering their staff inflexibly. This appears to have a decisive impact on a business's formality or informality. The ILD's analysis suggests that the intensive use of labor steadily increases the costs of remaining formal, prompting people to use capital rather than labor, intensively. People without capital—who are also unlikely to be able to assume the greater costs of remaining formal—desert to informality. Since it is labor, rather than capital, that is abundant in Peru, the result is an inefficient use of resources which is damaging to the whole of society. There is, in fact, a widespread trend in Peruvian legislation to favor this use of capital, and even the overcapitalization of formal businesses, through mechanisms which make formal employment more costly than the formal use of capital.

We can also conclude that the costs of remaining formal seem to have an excessive impact on the way in which businesses are run, affecting their operations and output independently of the production process itself. By altering the allocation of resources, they make production more costly, limit the mobility of factors of production, and increase the cost of transactions. This alters the profitability of a firm, regardless of its basic economic efficiency. The company's prosperity depends less on how well it does its work than on the costs imposed on it by the law. The owner who handles these costs better or manipulates the firm's relationship with the state better is more successful than the one who is concerned only with the job.

What we have here is bad law.

The Costs of Informality

As we gradually confirmed the existence of the costs of formality, we came to grasp not only why informals operate outside the law but also the real significance of the extralegal system. If informals wanted to establish a new set of laws, it was because they had lost something by operating outside and even in defiance of the law. We had to examine what they were in fact losing.

We gradually discovered that informality is not the best of all possible worlds, that it involves tremendous costs, that people try to offset these costs in all kinds of novel but inadequate ways, that lawbreaking is not, on balance, desirable, and that the apparent chaos, waste of resources, invasions, and everyday courage are the informals' desperate and enterprising attempts to build an alternative system to the one that has denied them its protection. This discovery enabled us to devise a complementary concept: the costs of informality.

We shall distinguish here between the cost of illegality, based on the evidence about the main differences between formal and informal businesses or activities, and the cost of not having a good law, the result of a more thorough process of conceptualization in which an attempt is made to identify which efficient legal mechanisms and instruments people had to forgo when they opted for informality.

We have been limited, however, to observations conducted empirically in informal places of work and residences. As a result, we can offer only a general list of limitations which illustrate, and only partially, the tremendous losses inflicted on the country by a legal structure which discriminates among its citizens. Moreover, for the purposes of this analysis, we have assumed that businesses or economic entities are either completely formal or completely informal. In real life, of course, this is not so: many formal businesses are partly informal or carry out informal activities, and vice versa. Some of the cases we investigated fell into these categories, for formality and informality are relative concepts; for the sake of simplicity, however, we will assume that informals have no legal status whatsoever and that formals are completely legal.

The costs of illegality

Our first attempt was to determine the differences between informal and formal activities or businesses and to establish the most common cost of informality.

It is clear that informal businesses devote tremendous effort to avoiding punishment by the authorities. They do so by means of a number of practices which we will consider in due course. Second, informal businesses make transfers to formal activity without any actual reciprocation from the latter, since they are excluded from its scope and benefits.

Third, informal businesses suffer the consequences of their evasion of certain taxes and labor laws.

In the pages that follow we will present the evidence we gathered on the cost of avoiding penalties, the cost of net transfers, and the costs of evading certain taxes and labor laws. We shall try to explain how the costs that differentiate formals from informals, and thus represent the costs of operating outside the law, arise in practice.

The costs of avoiding penalties

The first significant difference between an owner of an informal business and a formal one is the tremendous investment which the informal must make to avoid detection. Informals constantly run the risk of being penalized for not having obtained permits, paid taxes, or applied for the authorizations required by law. In its interviews, the ILD found that this is the main source of concern among informals. The informal business owner, who by definition has failed to comply with some or all requirements, saves the legal costs of compliance but must bear the cost of avoiding the corresponding penalties.

Informals use various strategies to avoid detection and penalties. Among the main ones, we identified dispersing their employees among a number of smaller and less visible workplaces, not advertising their goods or services, not entering certain markets which are in effect barred to them, and corrupting the authorities. When we visited clandestine factories, we found that the need to avoid detection forces informals to operate on a very small scale. They deliberately limit their operations or, if they need to grow, do so by dispersing their workers so that there are never more than ten in one establishment. While such arrangements obviously help them to avoid detection, they also prevent them from achieving efficient scales of production. This seems to be a fairly widespread consequence of informality.

Informal businesses are undercapitalized, not only because they have no access to credit but also because using certain capital goods makes them easier to detect. Furthermore, it is worth using some of these goods only if there are enough workers to handle them, and this increases the risk of detection.

Another difference between informal and formal business people, also deriving from the need to avoid detection, is that the former cannot easily advertise their goods or services and must make do with concealed, restricted methods of attracting customers, based almost exclusively on their reputation. This helps them to remain unnoticed by the authorities, but it also prevents them from building their business. According to the U.S. Small Business Administration, two-thirds of all customers are brought in by the signs displayed outside shops or factories. Advertising can also help to offset the disadvantages of a poor location, compensating for the lack of visibility with effective communication. Informals cannot exploit this advantage, either.

In order to avoid detection, informal businesses generally operate outside such legally established markets as stock markets and trade fairs. Moreover, they do not have access to the trade instruments used there, such as shares, letters of credit, or warrants. Thus, anyone interested in dealing with informals must devote more time to gathering information on potential trading partners, thereby increasing the cost of both the information gathering and the transactions. Were they to enjoy these institutional facilities, informal businessmen would be able to negotiate faster and more efficiently, and purchasers would merely have to go to specialized markets to conduct their transactions.

Another major cost of avoiding penalties is that informal businesses must devote a considerable proportion of their resources to corrupting the authorities. While the informal business owners interviewed said they paid out between 10 and 15 percent of their gross income in bribes and commissions, the owners of formal small businesses said they paid no more than 1 percent.

Since 61 percent of the hours worked in Peru are informal, there is obviously a long frontier between the informal sector and the state authorities. Some informal businesses are completely clandestine, but it is inconceivable that 61 percent of all the work done could be carried out illegally without the authorities in some way turning a blind eye. This systematic corruption undermines the principle of authority in the country as a whole. It could be argued, in strictly economic terms and with the necessary dose of cynicism, that bribes replace the taxes which the informals do not pay, for they achieve similar results. However, bribes also involve an undesirable element of misconduct which is absent from taxes.

It could also be said that bribes perform a function far closer to that of insurance, in that they attempt to eliminate the informals' uncertainty about the losses they might sustain if they were penalized by the authorities. In paying a bribe, they are simply buying security from prosecution—a kind of insurance against official penalties. However, there is every indication that these bribes are proportionally larger than insurance premiums because the actual risk of prosecution cannot be quantified. From a strictly economic standpoint, therefore, they are inefficient.

The costs of net transfers

A second difference between formals and informals is that, unlike what happens in a well-integrated economy, informals make a number of unreciprocated transfers to formals which represent net losses to informality. The existence of these transfers is fundamental to an understanding of why the apparent benefits of evading the law do not yield a greater return than legal business does. In analyzing the situation, we have made a distinction between the cost of taxation and the use of cash assets, and the cost of saving intangible assets.

It is generally maintained that informal economic activity not only competes unfairly with legally established activity, since it saves the cost of formality, but also benefits, without paying, from the public utilities offered by the state, forcing the state to transfer to formal business the entire burden of funding the public budget.

This reasoning is incorrect. The evidence gathered by the ILD shows that there are at least three major channels through which informal activities are constantly transferring resources to the government and other formal institutions: indirect taxation, inflation, and differences in interest rates.

Innumerable transactions take place daily between formals and informals. Although informals do not pay taxes on their sales, they pay taxes each time they purchase something from formals. Since formals invoice their sales, informal purchasers are paying indirect taxes. This does not always happen, for some sales take place without invoices, but there are situations where tax evasion is very difficult. The gasoline tax, for example, is largely borne by informal transport operators.

There are a large number of transactions in which informals are forced to make transfers to the government in the form of sales tax and import duty. The ILD estimates that, in 1985, informal economic activity transferred the equivalent of $813 million to the government in this form, representing 5.7 percent of the gross domestic product (GDP) for that year and 41.4 percent of all taxes levied on inputs.

Bearing the cost of inflation is another way of paying taxes. Many economists have defined inflation as a tax on money which the government levies on the private sector to finance its surplus spending or budget deficit. When prices rise and the currency loses purchasing power, private individuals cede to the state part of the value of their cash assets. This process particularly hurts those who hold more of their money in the form of cash, namely the informals, whose transactions are conducted in cash and who use the banking system less frequently—not only for fear of detection but also to protect themselves from the debasement of money—unlike those who keep their savings in hard currency or in interest-bearing accounts. The purchasing power which informals lose by keeping cash in hand is a transfer of resources to formal activity, part of which is funnelled off by the government. The ILD estimates that, in 1985, such transfers totalled $554 million—3.8 percent of the GDP for that year.

If we add the two transfers together, we find that informals transferred resources totalling $1,367 million, or the equivalent of 9.5 percent of the GDP, to the state. This amount would have more than covered the central government's entire investments for that year, which came to $465 million.

Last, transfers are made from informals to formals because of diferences in the interest rates paid for credit. According to the ILD, interest rates on the informal credit market in June 1985 were as much as 22 percent a month in Lima, as against the maximum rate of 4.9 percent that a formally established business could obtain from a bank. This disparity in the cost of money is caused by the informals' lack of access to formal credit, which forces them to accept the informal mediation of individuals who can obtain cheap, formal credit which they transfer to informal businesses at excessively high rates. This huge difference in interest rates can be attributed partly to the perceived risk of conducting a financial transaction with an informal business, and also to the fact that the market for informal capital transactions is competitive and the interest rates established tend to reflect more accurately the opportunity cost of using the financial resource.

The difference in interest rates transferred by informals to the rest of formal activity came, in 1985, to $501 million—3.5 percent of the GDP for that year. We can grasp the size of this transfer more fully if we consider that it was 1.4 times larger than the amount paid by formals in taxes on income and fixed assets.

If we add the transfer represented by the difference in interest rates to the two already mentioned, informals transferred to formals a total of $1,868 million, or around 13 percent of the GDP in 1985. This alone calls into question the superficial contention that informals contribute nothing to formal society.

One side effect of the use of cash is the cost of saving tangible assets. Fearing depreciation of their cash assets as a result of inflation which, in the period from 1983 to 1985, was way over 100 percent a year, many informals prefer to accumulate inventories rather than save money. As a result, many purchases of capital equipment, movable assets, and storable merchandise are made before the proper time. Since equipment is indivisible and the costs of capital are high, these advance purchases mean that some informals invest on a far from efficient scale.

We can see this at a glance. The overall impression created by informal settlements, street vendors' markets, and industrial workshops is that they are only half-finished. Buildings are unfinished, construction materials are piled up on the sidewalks, and equipment is incomplete. One might think that this is due to an innate Peruvian laziness, but it is not so. What it means is that informality forces informals to save in materials rather than in money and that the financial system is not working.

The costs of evading taxes and the labor laws

The third difference between formals and informals is that the latter generally do not pay direct taxes or comply with labor laws. This no doubt has economic benefits which may partially offset the cost of informality and even outweigh the benefits of formality. For instance, if the law establishes a minimum wage which is above the level dictated by the market, we can assume that informal businesses will pay lower salaries and wages. This is why informal businesses are the chief employees of unskilled labor.

The drawback for informal businesses is that this prevents them from using anything but methods with low technology and productivity. The advantage is that when the market is depressed they can hire and fire without any problems other than moral considerations or that of losing good workers. Among formals, on the other hand, labor is regarded as a fixed cost; they are prevented from responding to fluctuations in demand as flexibly as informals.

The general sales tax (IGV), however, affects both formal and informal activities. Although it appears to be a tax on gross income, it is actually a tax only on added value, which is why it is levied at each stage of production. At the second stage, for instance, one pays a tax on gross income but receives credit for the payments made at the first stage. This is a major handicap for informal suppliers of intermediate goods. The customer pays the gross tax but cannot obtain credit for the intermediate good purchased from the informal supplier. This places the informal supplier at a comparative disadvantage.

The IGV, therefore, prompts informals to conduct their activities at the two extremes of the productive process: first, activities where added value accounts for a large part of the total retail sale price, since this offers the advantage of evading the tax precisely when it reaches such a point. Second are activities which occur in the early stages of the transformation process, when the entire value-added tax can be evaded (cultivation of agricultural produce, brick manufacturing, provision of domestic services, and so forth). Informal business owners are excluded from relatively technical areas of intermediate production partly because the tax system does not allow them to benefit from the tax credit. Perhaps the greatest cost is that, in this context, the tax system militates against higher levels of productivity.

The costs of the absence of good law

Having established that there are costs to being illegal, we asked ourselves whether eliminating those costs would be enough to transform informality into the best of all possible worlds. The following exercise convinced us that this is not true and that informals suffer not only from their illegality but also from the absence of a legal system that guarantees and promotes their economic efficiency—in other words, of good law.

When clandestine factory owners do everything they can to avoid detection, when informal settlers waste time and effort on defending their property and complying with the procedures necessary to legalize it, or when street vendors cannot offer acceptable guarantees to finance a market or buy on credit, it means that they do not have the property rights or secure contracts needed to organize their economic activity efficiently. That society as a whole suffers from the adverse effects of informal activity, also demonstrates the absence of a workable extracontractual legal system.

It is essentially these three elements—property rights, contracts, and an extracontractual legal system—that a good law should provide. The absence of such a law creates an extremely burdensome set of costs which informals must bear in exchange for not paying the costs of formality.

The costs of not having property rights

Traditionally, in Peru, property rights have been understood as those which confer on their holders the power to use, enjoy, dispose of, and claim a tangible or intangible asset within the framework of the law. A more superficial interpretation has limited even this concept to movable or immovable assets. We wish to give it a broader meaning here, however, based principally on its economic importance.

Classical legal theory holds that individuals can, essentially, enjoy real and personal rights, the former in relation to things, through ownership, possession or usufruct, among other ways, and the latter in relation to other people, through contracts. This division has overcompartmentalized the real situation, for it gives the impression that there is no connection between the two groups of rights. We see the main connection as being that individuals may own or possess not only things, but also contracts. Accordingly, there is in each personal right an implicit real right which connects it precisely to the subject of that right.

This means that property rights may relate not only to houses, cars, machinery, or merchandise but also to rental agreements, foreign currency certificates and their free convertibility, and all sorts of credits, with the result that property rights can be lost not only through confiscation or expropriation but also through more sophisticated and apparently innocuous regulations such as tenancy laws, freezing of savings, or measures against speculation.

Thus, by property rights we mean all those rights, both personal and real, which confer on their holders inalienable and exclusive entitlement to them—in other words, the power to enjoy them freely, to dispose of them freely, or to use them to the exclusion of all others. Having said this, it becomes obvious that the most significant cost of the absence of a good law is the absence of secure, reliable property rights. We shall therefore explain the three main conclusions we have been able to reach and which will enable us to identify more readily the costs that the informals must assume because they do not have these rights.

Our first conclusion is that informals do not use or preserve the resources available to them as efficiently as they might if they were sure of their rights. If they cannot enforce their rights to land, housing, and equipment, their incentives for investing in them are considerably reduced. People build less if they think there is a risk that the state or another person might take away or occupy what they have built, just as no one invests in costly innovations if anyone might later appropriate their invention without compensation. The effect of all this is to reduce aggregate investment.

Secure property rights, on the other hand, encourage holders to invest in their property because of their certainty that the property will not be usurped. From a strictly economic standpoint, therefore, the true purpose of property rights is not to benefit the individuals or entities holding those rights, but to give them the incentive to increase the value of their assets by investing, innovating, or combining them advantageously with other resources, something which would have beneficial results for society.

This was confirmed by the ILD's field work in Lima's informal settlements. As we saw in the chapter on informal housing, when the Mariscal Castilla and Daniel Alcides Carrión settlements, which have similar socio-economic characteristics, were compared, it was found that the value of housing in the former was 41 times greater than in the latter because of the legal security it enjoyed. A larger sample, 37 settlements, later revealed that the ratio of the value of settlements with title and those without is 9 to 1. Everything indicates, then, that the existence or absence of property rights has a direct bearing on the level of investment.

The second conclusion is that informals cannot transfer their property easily. They cannot use it for more valuable purposes or as collateral. This limits their property's mobility as a factor of production and reduces its productivity.

The third conclusion is that informals incur substantial costs in defending their possessions and satisfying the need for public property by establishing and operating thousands of different organizations. These informal organizations involve a tremendous investment of time and other resources; moreover, they do not have the authority to force delinquent members to contribute to their operating costs.

Many of the decisions made by such organizations require a majority. But when each owner has only one vote, serious difficulties may arise because the differing intensity of each voter's preferences is not taken into account. Let us take the case of an informal settlement where there are plans to build a street costing $3,000. Of the fifty families living in the settlement, ten set a value of $200 on the building of a street and the other forty set a value of only $50. This means that the community as a whole has set a value of $4,000 on the road, making the road profitable because the valuation exceeds the cost of building it. But suppose the proposal is that each family will bear a fixed share of the cost, $60. It will be rejected because forty of the fifty families will consider themselves net losers since they value the project's potential benefits to them at somewhat less than that amount. Thus, while relatively efficient at administering individual property, people living in informal settlements lack the administrative and levying mechanisms to develop and pay for collective projects. The state would solve the problem simply by forcing everyone to pay in the form of taxes.

Of course, there are other ways to solve such problems, but they are generally more costly and less reliable. For instance, the decision may be to build roads and sidewalks only in front of houses whose owners have made their payments. But this can put a noncontributing member in a bad light. In such a situation, the informals' inability to reach legally binding agreements increases their difficulties.

In some adverse situations, a spirit of cooperation emerges which enables community leaders to demand of their members an altruism which permits surprisingly high levels of cooperation. But the fact remains that the absence of coercive mechanisms substantially reduces the potential scope of an informal partnership. In other words, although there are people who are highly altruistic, there are also conflicts of interest which cannot be resolved by informal coordination.

If we take the above three conclusions into account—that informals do not use or preserve their resources efficiently; that they cannot easily transfer their properties, use them for their more profitable purposes or offer them as collateral; and that their collective organizations are unable to compensate for their extralegality—it will be easier to grasp the cost of the absence of property rights.

We shall now turn to the cost of access to informal activity. The first is the cost of access to land for building, whether by invasion or informal sales, as well as of the long process of consolidation of rights which, as we saw in the chapter on housing, begins with the expectative property rights and ends with legally recognized property. As you will recall, informals gain access to land without simultaneously acquiring a stable legal right to either that land or anything they build on it. The threat of eviction hangs over them for a long time, until they win full recognition of their rights. Even though the likelihood that this land will be recovered by the state or by private individuals is, in most cases, fairly remote, it remains a continual threat which reduces the settlers' incentive to invest.

As a result, informals tend to invest in such items as household electrical appliances and vehicles, which are movable, rather than in such fixed items as piping, drainage, or roofing. It is not unusual to find motor cars, televisions, and other appliances in informal settlements with shoddy buildings. It is hardly surprising, therefore, that no investments are made in sanitation, with serious consequences for everyone's welfare.

The absence of public registers of the property rights of informals makes it even more difficult to establish the validity of a claim. There are a number of reasons for this. First, it is more difficult to locate legitimate debts which are backed or guaranteed by the property in question, since there is no central register of such transactions. For the same reason, it is more difficult to defend oneself against a third party's claim to the property. Third, there are valid disputes over ownership and no register in which to research their history.

Informal registers exist in many settlements, but in others they are far from complete. As a result, informal transfers of property create difficulties. For example, a person's expectative property right may be respected by neighbors and third parties because of certain personal characteristics such as being well known in the community. An unequivocal right to the property is not recognized, however. In other words, the claim to the property is based on informal ties which are very difficult to transfer to a potential buyer. In such a case, a potential buyer will have to devote time and money to ascertaining to what extent such factors bear on the validity of the expectative property right and to learning whether the buyer can defend that property with the same skill and at the same low cost as the seller. As we saw in the chapter on housing, one widespread method is to attend meetings of neighborhood organizations and be introduced by the seller as the new owner of the land, agreeing to the terms of the invasion contract and any supplementary agreements.

By extension, the same reasons inhibit the use of property as collateral, one of the various benefits traditionally conferred on property owners. This is because a lender must make the same costly investments as a purchaser in order to make sure that the property is under the borrower's control and that, in the event of a default, the property can be obtained with the same rights as those enjoyed by the present owner. This increases the interest rate charged by lenders for loans guaranteed by an expectative property right or its equivalent; worse still, it may simply prevent such transactions from taking place.

The difficulty of transferring an asset always reduces the incentive to invest further in it, since informals must possess property for a long time before their right to it can be legally recognized. Formals, on the other hand, can add to the value of an asset without envisaging long-term possession, since their right is recognized from the outset. There are formal contractors who invest in land in order to develop it, build on it, and sell it as soon as possible. The contractor can even specialize in large-scale development and infrastructure, thus taking advantage of the economies of scale offered by mass production. This is an advantage which informals do not enjoy.

The few informal contractors that do exist undertake such operations only at considerable risk. A customer who has pledged to buy a building can have a change of mind and withdraw at any stage of the project, and there is no legal means of obtaining compensation. The purchaser can make down payments and in the end not receive the house that was contracted for.

Finally, informals are forced to reverse the procedure followed by formals: instead of acquiring land legally, developing it, building on it, and finally moving in, they begin by moving in, then building, then developing, and it is only at the end of a lengthy process that they acquire legal ownership of the land. Such a process is obviously totally uneconomical.

The costs of the inability to use the contract system

Economically speaking, contracts are means of organizing and transferring property rights, for they enable parties to pool human and material resources in order to produce goods or services which can then be used to maximum advantage. As such, they are another of the mechanisms that a good law must provide.

Contracts can be classified schematically into two groups: those binding two or more parties among themselves through the pledging of assets, and those which, while also binding on the parties through the pledging of assets, create a separate legal entity for consolidating and executing the relationship. The former are ordinary contracts, such as sales contracts or contracts of deposit, and the latter are partnership agreements creating such business organizations as limited companies, limited liability trading companies, or cooperatives. An efficient state can facilitate the ways in which property rights are transferred and organized between private individuals, either by requiring all agreements reached between the parties to be enforceable before the state authorities, or by providing them with legally authorized forms of standard business organization.

It is precisely these facilitative legal instruments that informals lack and the absence of which is so costly to them. Let us first consider the costs associated with the inability to make full use of ordinary contracts, and then those resulting from the absence of formal business organizations.

The empirical work done by ILD's researchers demonstrated clearly that it would be difficult for a court to enforce the contracts used by informals, either for lack of evidence—these contracts are generally oral—or because the parties are inhibited by the relative illegality of their activities. The result is that informals try to minimize the damage they may suffer from one party's failure to comply with a contract. They must forgo setting up businesses larger than they currently operate or they may resort to an alternative to legal coercion to enforce contracts.

Contracts which are legally enforceable lend credibility to people's pledges and sometimes specify the penalty a defaulting party must pay. The mere fact that contracts can be enforced encourages the parties to make reasonable commitments that they can fulfill and discourages unrealistic pledges intended to persuade the other party to make a commitment. A legal system which gives all citizens ready access to efficient law courts is a proven and appropriate means of facilitating transactions between people.

Another advantage of legally enforceable contracts is that they enable the parties to enter into beneficial long-term commitments. For instance, if a business owner has the contractual assurance that a customer will buy a given quantity of goods over a period of time, the owner will be able to invest in the machinery and equipment needed to produce the goods and, at the same time, pay off the debts incurred in financing such machinery.

The owner of an informal business who invests in machinery, on the other hand, assumes a far greater risk either because of the fear of detection or because the contract is difficult to enforce. Depending on how the owner evaluates the risk of noncompliance by the customer, the decision may be not to invest in the equipment, to the detriment of both the business and the rest of society. The customer cannot be sure that the owner of an informal business will honor the prices originally negotiated, either. The owner, if the customer has no alternative source of supply, may raise the original price on the very day on which the goods are to be delivered. Fearing such a situation, the customer assumes the risks of the agreement only if the profit is sufficiently great. These limitations so increase the cost of transactions that some of them simply never take place.

It was also observed that the cost of not having legally enforceable contracts increases when a business is being conducted on a large scale. For instance, the owner who wants to obtain the capital needed to purchase more machinery must first offer certain guarantees to lenders. Since it is highly unlikely that an informal will have the necessary documents, lenders cannot be sure that they know all there is to know about the borrower's debts and commitments. They charge higher interest rates than they charge formal businesses because this is the quickest way to cover the risk involved in the absence of formal guarantees. Informality, then, virtually prohibits the use of economies of scale in almost any situation.

However, as we saw when we described the extralegal system in the three previous chapters, informals have managed to generate a set of norms to regulate their activities. While these ingenious substitutes arouse the enthusiasm of some social scientists, they do not function as well as an efficient legal system. Our interviews enabled us to identify the alternative methods used by informals to increase compliance with contracts. One is to invest time, effort, and money in cultivating long-term friendships. An informal business owner who is committed to purchasing from a supplier on a continuous basis hopes to encourage the supplier to make each delivery on time. This works for both parties, for the purchaser has the same incentive as the supplier to honor the commitment. To penalize noncompliance, either party may resort to publicizing the other's default to third parties, thus damaging a reputation. There is nothing very new about this: even among formally established businesses, adverse publicity is an important coercive method which works best when it is used in a relatively small and well-defined circle where everyone knows each other.

This informal method of coercion has definite limitations, however. First, it takes a lot of time and effort to establish a reputation or a sustained relationship, and the latter is restricted to parties wanting to enter into a contract. People who have only recently become established in a market are not trusted by suppliers or purchasers because they have not established a reputation. We found that suppliers often do not provide newcomers with the same quality of products or do not supply them on time, because they give preference to established customers. Only when newcomers have conducted an appreciable number of transactions can a potential long-term relationship become an efficient incentive. In early transactions, the informals incur higher costs because their lack of reputation prompts other parties to breach contracts and charge high interest rates and high prices.

Even if a newcomer is gaining a reputation, we have seen that, for reasons that are difficult to predict, another party may choose not to comply with the contract. As everyone is aware of this risk, owners of informal businesses tend to diversify their sources of supply and sales markets more than formals. Instead of buying a thousand fasteners from one supplier, an informal garment maker will buy two hundred from five different suppliers. The suppliers are thus producing at inefficient levels, making unit costs higher and proportionally reducing their opportunities to employ workers.

Even after a good commercial relationship has been established, one of the parties may lose confidence in the other. Before a relationship ends, it is very possible that one of the parties may act in bad faith. If the fastener supplier believes that the garment maker will not reorder, the supplier may decide not to deliver the final consignment even though a down payment was made. The garment maker, on the other hand, may not pay for the final consignment because it no longer seems necessary to maintain the relationship. If both parties are aware that they can breach the contract with impunity, the situation can easily deteriorate. Such fears may be enough to prevent the commercial relationship from ever getting off the ground, or to prevent both parties from making as much profit as they could have made had they been able to sign a formal contract.

Another alternative used by informals to increase compliance with contracts is to invest a lot of time in investigating or monitoring the other party. In our example, the garment maker may try out every one of the fasteners ordered. This procedure may be reasonable in the context of an informal business, but it is a costly way to achieve an objective which, in the formal sector, would merely require a guarantee of quality. In the absence of such a guarantee, the owner of an informal business has to be constantly on the alert, whether or not the goods are defective. This is a waste of resources.

Another way of reducing the possibility of a breach of contract is to deal only with relatives or people from the same region. Owners who have suffered a breach of contract will turn to their families, neighbors, or other friends in the justified expectation that the group will pressure the guilty party to offer compensation for the damage done. Similarly, a person newly arrived in the city soon realizes that it is difficult to find anyone other than a relative or someone from the same region who will enter into a contract. It appears, from the interviews we conducted, that the most successful migrants are those who had established, influential relatives when they came to Lima.

We also noticed a widespread tendency to "incorporate" friends into the family in order to make relationships more secure. An older person with whom a close but respectful relationship is established is often called "uncle," and a close friend of the same generation is called "cousin." It takes a fair amount of time and resources to establish and cultivate a wide network of friends, "uncles," and "cousins," and this hinders the development of wide, efficient markets. As a result, production, labor, and capital markets tend to cater to small groups of people who have been recommended rather than remain wide open and so achieve both economies of scale and increasingly efficient specialization. This reduces the purchaser's ability to compare costs and quality among a large number of suppliers and also reduces the producers' incentives to operate more efficiently and expand their markets.

Another alternative way to increase compliance with informal contracts is to organize collective bodies, such as neighborhood organizations, street vendors' associations, or minibus committees to execute agreements or contracts between their members. The group replaces legal institutions and the state's power to ensure that agreements are executed as agreed. However, the coercive capacity of such organizations is always less than a good judicial system. It is also costly and difficult to establish mechanisms parallel to the judiciary which enable the community to review and determine the validity of a complaint. Moreover, these private tribunals cannot force witnesses or parties from outside their community to give testimony, and they are therefore less competent to establish the fact, settle a dispute, or solve problems between members of different groups. These organizations also have to cover the cost of devising their own rules and publicizing them among members of the community.

The drawbacks of informal systems do not mean that reputation is not an important incentive for complying with contracts, however, even among formals. Formal operators are more prepared to do business with or lend credit to people with whom they have more than just economic ties, and formal buyers also investigate and monitor the quality of materials bought from their suppliers. The difference between formals and informals is one of degree: reputation is more important and contractual uncertainty is greater when access to efficient tribunals is limited.

The last alternative used by informals to ensure that contracts are honored is the threat, and occasional use, of violence. If we assume that our garment maker has only recently gone into business and can do very little to ruin the reputation of a well-established fastener manufacturer who has breached a contract, there may be no alternative but to send some thugs to beat up the supplier. In an informal market, where there is a lot of movement, there is a fairly large demand for coercion against those who breach contracts. Violence is used for several purposes. Instead of paying a group of thugs to ensure compliance with a contract, something which is already undesirable, business owners often pay thugs to ensure that violence is not used against them. Since there is nothing to prevent this violence from also being used against formally established business owners, the situation also imposes costs on society as a whole.

Their informality also prevents owners of informal businesses from reaping the benefits of legal partnerships. They thus lose an important means of pooling their resources and increasing their economic worth. It is these two functions which make legally established business organizations, whether limited companies or cooperatives, so important economically.

Economic value is created by transforming inputs into outputs. Shoemakers, for instance, take their labor (work hours), money (financial capital), tools and leather (physical capital) and transform them into shoes. One person, working alone, can produce relatively little, which is why it is important to divide the work among several people; two or more people can often do a job far more efficiently if they work together than if they work separately. As a result, the key to creating value is to pool labor, capital, and ideas on an efficient and lasting basis. Let us take an example to illustrate the importance of this process.

An employee who sells his or her labor to a business owner for a long period of time will naturally come to specialize in this particular line of work. As time passes, however, the worker runs the risk that this specialized labor will be less useful to other employers, and will therefore demand a measure of job security from the employer. The owner, who has invested in training the worker, may therefore agree to conclude a long-term employment contract with the worker in order to protect that investment.

The situation becomes more complicated when it involves financial capital, since a very short-term loan, perhaps one that has to be repaid within a week, does not allow a business owner to develop an idea, put it into practice, and then reap the benefits. Furthermore, financing a business may require dozens or hundreds of lenders or investors, all of whom will be aware of the possibility that the borrower may later be unable to repay them, and none of whom will be able to supervise the owner directly. This is why we have business organizations. Such organizations make it possible for long-term commitments and transactions between employees, customers, lenders, suppliers, and investors to be defined in a partnership agreement, so that they can be combined, executed, and supervised through such responsible intermediaries as the managers and directors of the business.

Business organizations are, thus, a combination of standard contracts which legal institutions make available to people so that they can conduct their transactions more efficiently. We might say that they are like mass-produced garments, but made as the interested parties would have wanted them if they had the time and imagination to have them made to measure. By establishing rights and obligations among a number of parties within an operating framework which permits inputs to be pooled on a productive and long-term basis, the law is a requisite for any major investment.

The difficulty of obtaining access to legal means of organizing inputs and distributing risks, sharing responsibilities, and conducting long-term economic activities is a tremendous limitation of informal activity, for it forces production to remain very small, reduces the range of goods provided, and permits the use of few technological advances. Informal owners cannot pool several people's property, administer it collectively, and ensure that the business survives the death or withdrawal of a member or of the manager. It is hardly surprising that the ILD was unable to find any large informal businesses operating with substantial capital and modern technology.

Among the many advantages possessed by business organizations are limited liability, shareholding, and share capital. We shall consider briefly what it means to informals to be excluded from these benefits.

In partnership agreements, formal business owners can limit the risks of their own commercial participation in a business whose liability is limited to a specific amount of capital. Owners of informal businesses, however, cannot limit the risks of their operations by establishing a legal entity separate from themselves and, as a result, cannot limit their liability to the amount of their share in the ownership of the business. Their personal finances have no protection if the venture is unsuccessful.

Because they do enjoy these benefits, formal entrepreneurs can assign resources more easily, establish definite spheres of activity, and divide their business ventures among different business organizations so that the possible failure of one business will not affect the others. Moreover, limited liability makes it easier to deal with a commercial, financial, or industrial partner because it makes it possible to define the scope of the business and the limits of the guarantees without having to investigate all of the owner's possible relations; the other parties simply have to examine the books and accounts of the business with which they are dealing.

Financiers are generally reluctant to deal with informals and do so only at very high interest rates and on limited occasions, for they have no way of limiting the scope of their relationship to a legally defined financial sphere, which would obviate the need for them to inspect all the possible assets and liabilities of the informal who is requesting financing.

The owners of informal businesses cannot use the share system, either. Since they have no shares, they cannot transfer ownership of the business simply by selling deeds representing its capital. They also cannot use this system to share the risks of the business among different partners. Nor can owners of informal businesses enjoy the rights inherent in shareholding. There are no shares to pledge as collateral for a personal obligation, no shares that can be encumbered with an usufruct so that a third party can reap the benefits while the owners retain their ownership; no shares with which minority partners can protect themselves; and no way to challenge, in court, management decisions which are thought to violate individual interests.

Nor can the owners of informal businesses increase their capital by bringing in new partners, because they do not have an abstract mechanism like stocks for sharing ownership. Since shareholding does not exist among informals, they cannot buy part of a business—only machines and individual elements of it.

Similarly, the owner of an informal business cannot convert debts into shares, thus losing the possibility of overcoming temporary difficulties by relinquishing part of the business rather than the entire business, a possibility which the law offers to formally established businesses.

Last, since they are not legally established, informal businesses have great difficulty in obtaining insurance policies to reduce their risks. While an informal, like any citizen, can obtain insurance for himself or herself, additional requirements are usually imposed on businesses: official accounting, stock-keeping, and proper registration, for example. Insurance companies also impose what they call "ethical" requirements, under which policyholders must comply with the laws in force. When a minibus crashes and the operator's vehicle is destroyed, when an informal's factory burns down or a house collapses, the loss is irreparable. If they had insurance coverage and could share their risks among a large group, today's owners of informal businesses could extend their activities.

In sum, if such facilities were accessible to the owners of informal businesses, they would be able to increase their business and organizational capacities and obtain greater financial resources to run and expand their operations. Private investors would then have more ways of investing their capital and increasing and diversifying its returns. These facilities cannot be perfected in a country like ours, because of the restrictions on capital markets, the defective administration of justice, and many other institutional shortcomings. Not even major companies fully enjoy these legal facilities in Peru.

The costs of the inefficiency of extracontractual law

The third cost arising from the absence of facilitative law has to do with the inefficiency of extracontractual law. This type of law relates to damages not covered by contracts and thus protects everybody's interests.

Informal activities affect the community as a whole, without there being an administrative apparatus to correct them. In other words, they are costly to the public at large.

Let us consider transportation. As we saw in the chapter on informal transport, the care with which minibus operators drive their vehicles affects the well-being or safety of many other people. Theoretically, the minibus operator could negotiate with the other drivers and pedestrians travelling around the city each day and reach an agreement to take care and prevent accidents which took all their interests into account. In practice, however, this is unworkable: for a two-mile route alone, the driver might have to negotiate with more than a hundred other drivers and, depending on the location, perhaps thousands of pedestrians, in addition to first ensuring that it is actually they and not others that will be encountered on this route. Some authority would first have to establish the rules of the game (all vehicles should proceed on the right, pedestrians should walk on the sidewalk and cross only at pedestrian crossings, and so forth).

Traditionally, it is the state's function to reduce the risk of damage or injury resulting from any individual's activity. There may also be private solutions, insurance for instance. The two solutions may be combined: the law may require individuals to take out insurance policies to provide compensation in case of accident. Compulsory insurance of minibuses can cover the risks to passengers, pedestrians, and the drivers of other vehicles. They, by dealing with an insured business, are negotiating with a legally liable party whose negligence can be satisfactorily compensated by insurance. Furthermore, the insurance company would automatically put pressure on the drivers by increasing their premiums if they had many accidents or were manifestly irresponsible, and might in extreme cases cancel a policy.

We can also gauge the importance of extracontractual law from the differences between the development of informal housing and informal transport. As we saw, in both cases, the informals' behavior reflects their energy, initiative, and organizing skills, elements essential to success in business.

Both activities begin with invasions prompted by the perception of opportunities and the desire to satisfy an expanding market. However, Lima's residents generally view informal transport as doing them more harm than informal housing, for informal settlers can control their settlements far better than minibus drivers can control the public consequences of their actions. The residents of informal urban developments are both the builders and the occupants of their homes, and thus the ones most likely to suffer from the consequences of untoward actions. Anything harmful is immediately perceived and can be corrected. As sociologists would say, informal settlement dwellers are able to "internalize" the consequences of their actions.

By contrast, minibus operators are only one of many groups affected by the urban transport system which they themselves established. The users of this system as well as those who use the public thoroughfare daily, as pedestrians or passengers of other vehicles, also have an interest in seeing it operate properly. Since they do not belong to minibus operators' organizations and are far too heterogeneous a group to organize in their own interests, however, their only means of protection would be through the law. When this is not available, what we get is a minibus service which is good and efficient in terms of fares but tremendously insensitive to the rights of other users of the public thoroughfare. Because the minibus operators have no way of internalizing their problems, as settlement dwellers do, a system of extracontractual law is needed to represent the interests of others. But it does not exist.

When there is no extracontractual law to cover informal activities, or such law is inadequate or improperly used, informal economic activity can be very costly to the larger community. This reduces the value of its social contribution and increases its uncertainty. As we saw in the chapter on transport, the high rate of deaths and injuries and the serious deficiencies in safety—and there are analogous problems in other informal economic areas—prove beyond a shadow of a doubt that the law is inefficient. Moreover, in such a situation, lawbreaking becomes so widespread that even formals begin to follow suit and safetly levels plummet dramatically, endangering society as a whole.

The National Economic Consequences of the Costs of Formality and Informality

Having gained an idea of the costs of both formal and informal activities, we discovered that this division of activities has other adverse effects on the economy in general, the main ones being declining productivity, reduced investments, an inefficient tax system, increased utility rates, limited technological progress, and a number of difficulties in formulating macroeconomic policy.

Declining productivity

As we saw when considering formal businesses, excessive government interference results in a great waste of resources. Businesses must devote considerable time to complying with government regulations, and the many restrictions affect the flexibility of decision making and cause resources to be used inefficiently. Productivity declines.

It is difficult to be productive when government restrictions hamper the pooling of resources, when taxes and tariffs distort the price of materials and products, and when price controls distort production incentives. The same is true when red tape, including accounting requirements and other procedural rules, increases costs and when labor laws render the mobility of labor virtually impossible, making it extremely costly to engage new staff.

Informals may sometimes be able to use their resources more efficiently than formals. We know that when informal businesses avoid regulatory impediments, they are more productive than formals. We also know, however, that the costs of informality, including more expensive capital and the absence of facilitating legal instruments, generally result in lowered productivity. The fact that these businesses are more labor intensive than capital intensive reduces their productivity still further, as ILD's researchers found: they calculated the informals' productivity as a third of the formals.

Furthermore, when labor and social regulations increase the cost of labor, formal companies will respond by using less labor and more capital. In other words, their ratio of labor to capital will be lower. This means that formal businesses do not take advantage of the country's most important productive resource—its labor—and that the country offers its citizens fewer opportunities for employment.

In informal activity, on the other hand, the ratio of labor to capital is too high. Informals have too much labor and formals have too much capital. This produces an arbitrary and inefficient specialization of the country's resources, for productivity becomes optimum only when decisions are based on the best combination of employment and capital.

Reduced investment

Informal activity is known to have two consequences which reduce aggregate investment. First, informal businesses use more labor-intensive technology, which significantly reduces capital investment in general, for business is moving to informality. Second, in view of the difficulties which informals face in enforcing their contracts, and the high rate of return which financiers require of informal investors, there will be little long-term investment in production. The cost of formality also results in lower levels of investment.

We conclude, from the difficulties which both formals and informals face in achieving optimum economies of scale, that there is a lower level of investment in Peru's economy than there would be if the legal system functioned efficiently.

The inefficiency of the tax system

When taxes are collected, the main burden rests on the relatively small group of people who are still operating formally, the state squanders vast resources on detecting evasion, and unnecessary distortions occur throughout the economy.

Businesses which are relatively large and therefore forced to operate formally pay more taxes than they would if informality did not exist, since the total tax burden is borne by a smaller tax base. This discourages many companies from expanding. In Peru, the development of industries which need to be large in order to operate and therefore cannot operate informally, is constrained. Second, tax evasion is so widespread that the state has to invest in a large number of costly strategies in order to detect evaders, who in turn expend resources on trying to avoid detection.

Let us pause for a moment to consider the unnecessary distortions in the tax system and in the economy in general. It is a well-known economic principle that any noncorrective tax is inefficient in some way. A tax on wages, for instance, may encourage people to work fewer hours. A tax on property makes property less desirable and encourages some businesses to use less land and invest in fewer buildings of their own. Taxes distort economic choices, which is why one goal of the tax system should be to minimize these distortions, taking particular account of the costs of collecting and administering taxes.

One way to do this is to keep tax rates low. For example, a 90 percent tax on profits or earnings will prompt many people who might have been prepared to invest in some productive activity to do nothing instead. A tax of only 10 percent, on the other hand, might significantly reduce the distortion.

In Peru, where the government is so committed to satisfying needs by intervening directly and where there are few formals whom the system can tax in order to cover these costs, tax rates are increasing. Formal activity, in consequence, becomes less and less attractive and informality continues to grow. However, since the government persists in its efforts to obtain more revenue, it increases the taxes levied on formal activity and creates a vicious circle: increased informality, reduced formality, maintenance of the level of public spending, need to increase taxes on formal activity, greater incentives to operate informally, and so on.

Increased utility rates

The same is true of public utility rates. It is estimated that almost half of Lima's water and electricity supply is unaccounted for. While there may be some leaks, most of these losses must be attributable to the informals, who tap the water and electricity supplies illegally. Most informals do not pay directly for these utilities, with the result that informality increases the rates for those who obey the law.

Again, much of formal activity is made up of businesses which remain formal only because they are too big or too well-known to desert to informality. Burdened by tremendous governmental requirements, they demand more and more privileges in return. Their poor performance and their need for privileges are consequences of the vicious circle we described above. We can see this even in formal export firms, which are taxed fairly heavily. Their disadvantage can be offset only if the Peruvian government reimburses, in the form of subsidies or subsidized interest, that part of their taxes which is attributable to a higher level of informality. (The situation is further complicated by the fact that such privileges violate international GATT agreements banning the subsidy of exports and provoke reprisals from importing countries in the form of antidumping laws or countervailing duties.) The net result is to raise the level of taxation of that part of the formal sector which is not engaged in the export business and which will therefore shrink.

The distortion grows, then, as the circle continues. As tax rates increase, the inefficiency of the tax system becomes more marked. Taxes on employment discourage the recruitment of workers, added-value taxes discourage investment in formal production companies in general, and so on and so forth. According to the ILD's calculations, if this vicious circle continues and other conditions remain constant, informal production will account for 61.3 percent of the GDP recorded in the national accounts by the year 2000.

Limited technological progress

The existence of informal activities undermines technological progress for a number of reasons, the main ones being the small size of the businesses, their lower level of interaction in production, and their inability to protect technological innovation.

We have seen that fear of detection, the absence of property rights, and the difficulty of enforcing contracts are all responsible for the small size of informal businesses. Although economists disagree about the size required for a business to make innovations, there can be no doubt that a relatively innovative business will be larger than informality would permit. We also know that one of the most usual ways of benefitting from an innovation is to increase sales. It makes no sense for a business which must avoid detection to increase its scale, however, for this would expose it.

Since innovative activity has positive consequences for the entire community, the losses resulting from its relative lack are borne not just by the businesses involved but by the entire country, which would otherwise be able to reap the benefits of technological progress.

Difficulties in formulating macroeconomic policy

The macroeconomic decisions that a government makes—for instance, those relating to the size of the deficit or the rate of growth of the money supply—are largely determined by measurement of the performance of the economy. The existence of informal activities makes it extremely difficult to obtain precise information about national economic performance and introduces an excessive element of speculation into political decision making.

If informal activity were a constant proportion of total economic activity, the margin of error might not be so great. However, informal activities, at least in some areas, have grown more rapidly than formal ones; as a result, their growth rate has been underestimated. The ILD found that Peru was 28.7 percent richer than the national accounts indicated in 1985. It is also likely that underemployment, unemployment, and inflation are overestimated, since some workplaces are not registered and the relatively low prices of informal transactions are not taken into account.

Although those in charge of macroeconomic policy are surely aware of the phenomenon, the fact is that the size and growth of informality make it more difficult to achieve an acceptable degree of accuracy in determining the level of economic activity and that they introduce a greater element of uncertainty into the task of designing macroeconomic policy.

The Law as a Determinant of Development

So far, we have seen that Peruvians are forced to assume excessively high costs in order to operate legally or, if they are unable to do so, that they have been left out of the system. This means that they cannot take advantage of the country's good laws, namely the facilitating instruments provided by the law to make economic and social activities more efficient: property rights, contracts, and extracontractual law.

Facilitating instruments provided by the law

The importance of property rights has been emphasized by various economic historians who believe that the boom in technological innovation in the West, and the massive investment that made it possible, began only at the end of the eighteenth century, when property rights were perfected and made independent of politics. Douglass North, for instance, provides copious evidence that the wave of major inventions in Europe began only when a system of patents was established to protect intellectual property rights. The importance of these patents resides in the fact that, with the exception of a handful of accidental discoveries, most innovation entails expensive research and education, costs which are worth assuming only if they can later be recouped. Before the Industrial Revolution, these costs outweighed the benefits later obtained. It was only when an ingenious legal instrument, exclusive patent rights, appeared that a legal basis emerged for defining intellectual property. This not only facilitated research for innovative purposes but also created a powerful incentive for increased investment in education, research, and the search for innovative solutions to technological problems.[5]

Contrary to the belief widespread in Latin America, the economic importance of property rights is not that they provide assets which benefit their holders exclusively, but that they give their owners sufficient incentive to add value to their resources by investing, innovating, or pooling them productively for the prosperity and progress of the entire community.

The well-known example of the lake with vast reserves of fish illustrates this idea. If no one owns the lake, only its value as a source of food will be used, not its value as a hatchery. There will be no reason for fishers to limit their catch unless they can be sure that any fish they do not catch will not be caught by others and that, in the long run, once the fish have reproduced, they themselves will be able to benefit from their earlier sacrifice. The most likely outcome is that the reserves of fish will soon disappear. On the other hand, if someone had property rights to the lake, the owner would calculate its value both as a source of food and as a hatchery, because of the knowledge that the fish not caught today would reproduce and that many more could be caught tomorrow. It is the owner's profit motive which leads to the conservation and, thus, the maximization of the value of the fish reserves. The potential commercial benefits are the main incentive for making the necessary investment and trying to predict the economic trends that will determine the relative value of the resource. Naturally, the rest of society is also interested in seeing that this process of prediction and investment is carried out properly so that there will be no shortage of fish tomorrow.

This example is applicable, mutatis mutandis, to any resource to which property rights have not been granted, for instance, state wasteland on the outskirts of cities which can be used for both social purposes (housing) and economic purposes (workshops, factories, commercial businesses). Land, street, and route invasions have, in some ways, been the spontaneous means used by informals to create extralegal property rights in the absence of a good law. If the extralegal system did not generate these rights, there would be no incentive for the informals to develop and give economic and social value to these resources.

In tracing the history of contracts, Douglass North and Robert Paul Thomas point out in their masterful book that the Industrial Revolution in Europe was made possible by the fact that states substantially improved

[5] Douglass North, *Estructura y Cambio en la Historia Económica* (Madrid: Alianza Editorial, 1985).

compliance with contracts and significantly reduced the private costs of executing them.[6] The contract system was not created by the state, however. What happened was simply that, over the years, the authorities gradually came to recognize that the private sector's customary trade practices, many of them informal, were efficient and well established, and gave them force of law so that any breach of the terms of a contract could be prosecuted and penalized. As we shall see in the conclusion of this book, this procedure is extremely efficient since, instead of trying to shape reality to its wishes, the state converted into legal norms practices which had proved their feasibility. That feasibility had been partly established by the gradual emergence, in Europe's main cities, of public notaries who specialized in witnessing and registering contracts and mediating trade disputes, ensuring that agreements between producers and merchants were executed more efficiently. They also helped facilitate negotiations by establishing fixed rules and models which were used to adapt contracts to a variety of transactions.

The outcome of all this is that today, among formals and above all in the developed Western countries, where there is no need to avoid detection by the authorities, the confidence created by enforceable contracts makes people more prepared to take risks and these contracts have become requisite for long-term investments. Since innovation is the riskiest investment, if a government cannot give its citizens secure property rights and efficient means of organizing and transferring them—namely contracts—it is denying them one of the main incentives for modernizing and developing their operations. This is precisely what happens to the informals.

The developed countries' capital markets could also not have functioned as efficiently as they did if the state had not been prepared to require by law that instruments of credit be honored. Over the years, law courts began to recognize bills of exchange, promissory notes, and letters of credit. When the legislators agreed that such instruments could be made out to the bearer and not necessarily to a specific person, the innovation streamlined financial operations, for it enabled a lender or creditor to transfer assets to a third party and thus give economic agents a further mechanism for making payments and granting credits. This made it possible to engage in transactions taking place on two separate dates: that of the delivery of the merchandise or loan and, later, that of

---

[6] Douglass C. North and Robert Paul Thomas, *The Rise of the Western World* (London: Cambridge University Press, 1973).

payment or reimbursement. And as the legal security of transactions increased, so too did the volume of trade, the possibilities of financing production and innovation, and the access of new people to productive activities.

In other words, the modernization of the market economies which required that production and labor become more specialized and transactions more sophisticated, came about because the law made it possible to reduce the costs of a transaction. The aforesaid costs include all those which, independently of the transaction itself, are needed to conclude that transaction, namely, the costs of negotiating or executing contracts, providing and transferring property, transferring capital, recruiting labor, and distributing or insuring against risks—but above all, the costs of entering, remaining in, or remaining outside the legal system. The evidence presented throughout this chapter is that, in Peru, the costs of transaction, for formals and informals alike, are excessively and absurdly high, resulting in a tremendous waste of resources which can be halted only if the legal system begins to lower these costs efficiently.

It is clear that the absence of a properly understood and applied set of extracontractual laws, combined with the lack of property rights and contracts, is partly to blame for the fact that the damage done by the informal activities of Peruvians is not shouldered by those responsible for it but by third parties. This anomaly, which reduces the social value of those activities, can be corrected if extracontractual liability, the third pillar of any good legal system, is enforced.

Basically, what property rights, contracts, and extracontractual liability do is reduce uncertainty for people who want to invest their labor or capital in the development of existing resources. It would be hard to think of anything which discourages investment as much as uncertainty. No resident of an informal settlement will invest much in a home if there is no secure ownership of it, no street vendor is going to improve the environment if eviction is feared, and no minibus operator will respect public order on a route to which rights are not recognized. The people we interviewed feel there is a constant risk that the law will be forcefully used against them and that their activities will be abruptly interrupted. It should be pointed out that the costs of informality also affect formals and particularly increase the uncertainty of the costs of remaining formal, for there is no property right, contract, or extracontractual liability which can be regarded as constant when the state can use the legal system arbitrarily.

We might gain a better understanding of the uncertainty created by the absence of facilitating legal instruments by relating it to the function of insurance. Let us suppose that, each year, there is one possibility in a thousand that a motorcar valued at $10,000 will be stolen. The hypothetical annual cost of a theft would be $10, or one-thousandth of the $10,000. If the owner of this car does not care about the risk, it will not matter whether the car is insured, at a cost of $10 a year, or that there is one chance in a thousand of losing it, a cost of $10,000. The fact is, however, that few people are indifferent to this risk. Most people, if they have the means, will pay far more than $10 to offset the possible loss. The widespread purchase of insurance, throughout the world, shows that people do not like uncertainty and are prepared to pay a high price to avoid it. The uncertainty which the law does not undertake to dispel discourages effort and encourages people to find other ways of reducing their risks.

Formals reduce their risks in different ways—by distributing shares and liability among business partners, diversifying their commercial portfolio, establishing precise limits to their liability, and buying insurance policies. They may also reduce their risks by connivance and by the constant use of intermediaries to gain official protection against unforeseen events. Generally speaking, none of these methods of reducing uncertainty is accessible to informals, with the exception of small-scale diversification and a certain capacity for political negotiation won by some of their unions. They try to reduce it by other means which, as we have seen, include paying bribes, minimizing investment, overinvesting in movable assets, diversifying or decentralizing production, or trading with and employing mainly relatives, friends, or people they know from the same region. In particular, the payment of bribes, which among the informals we interviewed came to between 10 and 15 percent of their gross earnings, is indicative of the fear created by uncertainty.

If they were given property rights and could be sure that their contracts were enforceable, and if extracontractual liability were adjudicated efficiently, this uncertainty would be reduced and the value of informal economic activity would increase systematically. Greater certainty would increase the value of both the labor and the capital of the nation. In any country, uncertainty or legal instability reduces the volume of long-term investment and investment in plant and equipment. People save less and invest the little they do save in such socially unproductive goods as jewelry, gold, or luxury property. The flight of capital from countries like Peru is only one more result of the desire to avoid uncertainty.

Of course, not all uncertainty can be eliminated, but there are certain types of uncertainty which are completely unnecessary, for instance, those suffered by informals because they lack facilitating legal instruments. An appropriate change in the requirements of the law to make such instruments universally available would immediately reduce the amount of uncertainty.

Incentives, specialization, and interdependence

We have spoken of good laws and bad laws, a good law being one that guarantees and facilitates the efficiency of the economic and social activities it regulates and a bad law, one that disrupts or totally prevents it. Using the term as we have throughout this chapter, we can say that Peruvian laws are predominantly bad because those who drafted them did not take into account their costs and the way in which they stifled economic activity. The most tangible proof of the unsuitability of these laws is that the vast majority of the economically active population has chosen to operate informally and a minority have chosen to take their professional expertise and their capital elsewhere. In other words, they have chosen to operate outside these bad laws, which entail such high costs and such complex regulations.

It is not enough that a good law be neutral and not encourage people to operate informally. It must also do at least two other things: it must create incentives for people to seize the economic and social opportunities offered by the country; secondly, it must facilitate the specialization and interdependence of individuals and resources.

Let us first show why incentives are important. As we saw earlier, the urban economy increases the opportunity to earn more but, in order to do so, it is essential to increase the value of the opportunities perceived. However, the value of these opportunities is determined by the legal system. For example, a maze of red tape must be negotiated in order to use waste land legally. The economic value of the land is directly affected by the cost of complying with the red tape. If a house is built on the land, its value will be determined by the extent to which one can be sure that third parties will not take it over, either violently, through invasion or vandalism, or through more subtle encroachment such as the restrictions which the state may impose on the use or transfer of property. In other words, the land may be the basis for a house, but its value and its development will decrease as the difficulties of obtaining it by adjudication, making it secure, confirming title to it, and selling or renting it increase.

Thus, the actual value of an economic opportunity is not the value it would have if it could be realized without cost, but rather its estimated value, taking into account the cost of the red tape, the degree to which it can be protected against third-party appropriation, and the ease with which it can be sold. The less costly the transaction and the more secure the right to enjoy the fruits of investment, the greater the real value of an economic activity. A law that is efficient in dealing with these elements will encourage people to identify and seize existing opportunities and will systematically increase the value of economic activity.

Second, a good law must also encourage the specialization and interdependence of individuals and resources. In any society, certain individuals are better equipped than others to perform specific productive tasks. Similarly, certain material resources are more productive if they are used for some purposes than for others. It is an economic maxim that if, instead of trying to meet their needs directly, members of a society specialize in the tasks they are best able to perform and exchange among themselves the fruits of their labor, everyone will achieve a higher level of well-being. Specialization of material resources also increases well-being because their social benefit is maximized if they are used for purposes which increase their value for all parties and not just for those who possess them.

In order for the members and resources of a society to specialize, however, those investing the resources must be sure of a return on the investment. This will happen only if all the members are sure that the transaction will benefit them, that what they receive in exchange for their labor or products will bring them greater benefits than they could have obtained alone. This is why economists say that exchanging resources increases their value and, consequently, the well-being of all.

However, this specialization of individuals and resources cannot take place if individuals are isolated and do not trust one another. Isolation and mistrust rule out specialization because, by definition, specialized persons need others to supply their requirements. As a result, it becomes essential for producers to trust the system of exchange, which means that the system of exchange must be organized in such a way that it provides security to everybody. There can be no denying that the law, and the institutions safeguarding it, are the principal source of this trust.

The law, then, allows citizens to specialize because it enforces property rights, promotes reliable contracts which enable these rights to be organized and transferred, and attributes liability when it is not established by a contract. These three elements are essential if a society is to make the best use of its citizens' initiatives and labor and of its material resources. The main idea underlying this viewpoint is that, if the state provides good laws, it makes specialization and exchanges far easier, enabling human and material resources to be used in the best possible way. An appropriate system of property rights, contracts, and extracontractual liability can spontaneously generate the efficient use of resources without a bureaucracy to decide or authorize how the resources must be used. Citizens dependent on this system will have sufficient incentives to produce, through a multiplicity of efforts and private transactions, an economic system which is exceptionally sensitive to the opportunities for development.

This is a crucial proposition, for traditional academic thinkers still believe that the causes of development are purely economic achievements—technological progress, accumulation of savings, investment in human capital, reduction of transport costs, economies of scale—when in fact these are not the initial causes. None of these alleged causes explains why, in some countries, people are more innovative, save more, are more productive, and are prepared to run greater economic risks. Are we inhabitants of underdeveloped countries genetically or culturally incapable of saving, innovating, taking risks, or running industries? Or are these "causes" of development not the causes at all, but in fact development itself? Is the real cause an official set of legal and administrative institutions which encourages technical progress, specialization, exchanges, and investment? The evidence gathered in this book points in the latter direction.

It is because of bad laws, then, that both formals and informals are only incipient, interdependent specialists whose potentialities will remain limited as long as the state fails to give them the incentives needed for progress, namely good laws.

Is the law the only determinant?

So far we have analyzed the legal aspects of the problem of informality. We should now ask ourselves whether there are other aspects of the problem.

Peruvians in general, and informals in particular, have specific preferences, skills, and patterns of behavior which can be regarded as social, cultural, or ethnic factors that dictate the existence of informality. They also have preferences for specific goods and services, which can be regarded as economic factors. All of these elements certainly combine with the legal situation to influence, and even determine, the characteristics of informality. For instance, it may be more complicated and therefore more costly for a person from a rural society to comply with certain legal requirements than for a person who is accustomed to life in an urban society. On the other hand, people who find the social, ethnic, or cultural characteristics of informals repugnant, will make a greater effort to enter and remain in formal activity than those who are attracted by or indifferent to these characteristics.

The problem is one of determining how much these factors contribute to the phenomenon, whether they are essential or secondary. Let us take the invasion of state waste land as an example. What explanation can we find for this phenomenon, if we view it from a cultural or social standpoint? Is it an age-old practice which reflects Peruvians' partiality for getting together and invading other people's property? Of course not.

From a legal standpoint, on the other hand, the explanation is perfectly clear. When it takes seven years and several thousand dollars to obtain land for housing, most people, regardless of their skills, education, and attitudes, will invade land and acquire it informally. If the red tape were reduced, there might still be people who would prefer to invade land and risk all the adverse consequences, but they would be a minority.

Let us view the problem from another standpoint. If the cultural differences between formals and informals are really so great, how are we to explain the fact that so many informals are ready to try to find a way of formalizing their activities and, moreover, that so many people operate both formally and informally at the same time? The ingenious, productive, and innovative way in which Peru's informals work, their determination to win legal recognition, the existence of an extralegal system of norms, and what they produce and consume seem to indicate that, from an economic and social standpoint, informals have very similar aspirations to formals. Although no one denies the relative importance of social, cultural, or ethnic factors, we simply have not found any evidence to bear out the theory that they explain why a large sector of the population operates outside the law.

The legal system so far seems to be the best explanation for the existence of informality. From this standpoint, the choice between working formally and informally is not the inevitable result of people's individual traits but, rather, of their rational evaluation of the relative costs and benefits of entering existing legal systems.

The law and national development

All the evidence suggests that the legal system may be the main explanation for the difference in development that exists between the industrialized countries and those, like our own, which are not industrialized.

It sometimes seems as if experts in developed countries automatically assume that their legal institutions exist in every country. This is not the case, however. The debate about development will therefore have to be reformulated to take the importance of legal systems into account. We cannot continue to close our eyes to the fact that not all of a society's decisions are determined by its cultural characteristics or economic systems.

How many investments could people in the United States and Western Europe have made without clearly defined and secure property rights, a system of extracontractual civil liability, and a system of justice which protected their property? How many innovations would they have made without patents or royalties? How many assets, long-term projects, and incentives for investment would they have managed to create without enforceable contracts? How many risks would they have run without limited liability systems and insurance policies? How much capital would they have accumulated without enforceable guarantees? How many resources would they have been able to pool without legally recognized business organizations? How often would they have gone bankrupt and had to start all over again if they had not been able to convert their debts into shares? How many businesses and private institutions would have survived for generations without hereditary succession? Would they have been able to industrialize without economies of scale? We sincerely believe that development is possible only if efficient legal institutions are available to all citizens. This belief is strengthened when we consider that, despite the informals' efforts and sacrifice, informality is characterized essentially by the absence of such institutions.

However, we do not seek to underestimate the importance of the country's cultural identity. The way in which Peruvians use their economic opportunities and demonstrate their preferences for certain goods and services rather than others reflects the country's culture and ideology. Certainly, the Japanese, for all the far-reaching recent technological and economic changes in their country, also continue to be culturally identifiable. As we have seen, Peru's traditional customs, its regard for reputation, family ties, communal activities, and concepts of hierarchy and status are put to imaginative use by the informals. There is no reason, after an appropriate reorganization of the country's legal institutions, that the rest of the country's social mechanisms should not continue to be influenced by Peru's cultural heritage.

This heritage will, in turn, always determine the nature of our development and the range of creative possibilities offered by it. How many of these possibilities can actually be realized and how many Peruvians will be able to benefit from them will, however, depend primarily on the country's legal institutions.

It is simpler and cheaper to bring the formals and informals together by changing the law than by trying to change the characteristics of the people. To show the informals how the existing laws operate, or to try to convince them that they will increase their social standing by accepting the mercantilist system inherited from Spain, would be to alter their culture drastically. It makes more sense to adapt the law to reality than to try to change everyone's attitudes, for the law is the most useful and deliberate instrument of change available to people.

CHAPTER SIX

The Redistributive Tradition

We have seen how the law affects the efficiency of the economic and social activities it regulates. We must now ask ourselves why bad laws predominate in Peru and what effect this has on the country. Why does the law disrupt efficiency? Why does it limit or prevent production instead of promoting it and making it cheaper? Why does it force a large proportion of the population to work informally and impose extremely high costs and absurdly complicated requirements on the formal sector? Why does it not foster confidence in the system of social exchange? Why does it fail to encourage citizens to seize economic opportunities that would facilitate the specialization and inter-dependence of individuals and resources? In other words, why does our legal system make us poor?

There appears to be a tradition among our country's lawmakers of using the law to redistribute wealth rather than to help create it. From this standpoint, the law is essentially a mechanism for sharing a fixed stock of wealth among the different interest groups that demand it. A state which does not realize that wealth and resources can grow and be promoted by an appropriate system of institutions, and that even the humblest members of the population can generate wealth, finds direct redistribution the only acceptable approach.

In legislating from a purely redistributive standpoint, however, our lawmakers fail to see that, in addition to its immediate distributive effect, any law will affect the functioning of the productive system as a whole. Such an approach does not consider how the law can alter the individuals' economic decisions and opportunities.

The ILD's research into lawmaking revealed that the authorities rarely consider the positive or negative consequences of their decisions. Their emphasis is on reconciling different special interests, favoring those which are considered appropriate and redirecting resources to them through legal channels. Each time the government grants a privilege or tax exemption, reduces prices, gives a certain type of worker permanent protection from dismissal, or grants an exclusive concession to a certain kind of business, it automatically creates costs and benefits which deprive others of incentives and opportunities. For instance, if the state controls the price of bread and decides to fix its price at a level which allows a smaller profit margin than is available through other activities, it may bring about an immediate redistribution of money from producers to consumers, but it will also have created a disincentive for baking bread, causing many to desert the industry for a more profitable one.

In addition to its overall economic impact, however, the redistributive tradition has created in Peru a society where almost all the country's vital forces have organized in political and economic groups, one of whose main aims is to influence government in order to obtain a redistribution which favors them or their members. This competition for privileges through the lawmaking process has resulted in a widespread politicization of our society and is directly responsible for the existence of the bad laws which give rise to the costs of formality and informality.

This trend has reached such an extreme that organizing to obtain the unearned income[1] which the state may hand out or transfer through the legal system, or at least to protect oneself from this process by forming what we call "redistributive combines," is not restricted to spheres traditionally associated with political activity—political parties, the mass media, or informal organizations—but extends to business corporations and even families. Changes in the composition and leadership of boards of directors can often be attributed to a change of government. Nor is it unusual to find families in which father and son, brothers and sisters, even husband and wife join or form ties with different political parties or the armed forces in order to get ahead. Another symptom of this need to form redistributive combines is the plethora of political newspapers and magazines in Lima. Many publications have been created specifically to safeguard their shareholders' interests.

These combines are always fighting to ensure that any new laws will not harm their interests and will, if possible, directly benefit them. As a

---

[1] By "unearned income" we mean a favor or income obtained from the state not as payment for a productive contribution but as a result of some perhaps temporary privilege. See Richard Webb, "Democracia y Economía de Mercado," in *Ponencias y Debates de un Simposio* (Lima: Instituto Libertad y Democracia, 1983).

result, the state legislates almost exclusively to distribute unearned income
and has transformed us into a democracy of pressure groups. Businesses
channel their natural competitive zeal into establishing close ties with the
political and bureaucratic authorities instead of into a contest to serve
consumers better. Established business owners fight to maintain the
privileged situation they have managed to achieve over the years, while
new owners, who also want a slice of the pie, fight to win partial advantages
through political participation. A legal system whose sole purpose is
redistribution thus benefits neither rich nor poor, but only those best
organized to establish close ties with the people in power. It ensures that
the businesses that remain in the market are those which are most efficient
politically, not economically.

This politicization of Peruvian society means that all problems are
handled primarily according to the procedures established by the government, rather than according to other standards such as economic efficiency, morality, or justice. Everything is left in the state's hands, and
society inevitably becomes bureaucratized and centralized. Politicization,
centralization, and bureaucratization can all be traced to the same source:
redistributive laws.

The legal system changes as the relative position of those who manage
to influence the government changes. This is why we often hear that our
legal system lacks uniformity and stability, our laws are negotiable, there is
legal anarchy, and what matters is not what you do or want but what
politician or bureaucrat you know. Nor should it be surprising that bribery
and corruption are characteristic results of a legal system in which
competing for unearned income has become the predominant form of
lawmaking. Both our traditional history and the history of the informal
activities we described in earlier pages are replete with examples of this
state of affairs.

However, each time an election takes place, voters assume that, if
the electoral process is an honest one, the candidate who comes to power
will not succumb to pressure and the technocrats responsible for carrying
out the laws the victor proposes will be a group of untainted, disinterested
individuals ready to achieve, through some mysterious process, the best
and impartial results. All of this is an illusion. There is no established
method or theory which enables a politician to decide in a vacuum
whether middle-income housing or highways between the capital city and
the provinces is needed more, how much emphasis to place on
hydro-electric plants instead of refineries, or whether to give greater
subsidies to those who work and invest in the region of Puno or those who

export added value. All such decisions are in fact simply political value judgments.

And, as we shall see, none of these political judgments can be justified on the basis of pluralism or open debate. In Peru, 99 percent of the central government's rules, which are the means by which wealth is redistributed, emanate from the executive branch, which adopts them without public consultation or control. It is the executive's ability to legislate redistribution without any debate in Parliament or elsewhere that enables redistributive combines to interfere in lawmaking. This also explains why, in countries like ours, property rights are not protected against the political powers-that-be.

Thus, redistributive laws ultimately politicize all sectors of the population, which try to organize in order to live at other's expense. Consumers press for prices below competitive levels, wage earners press for wages above them, established business people try to prevent or delay any innovation that might damage their position, and employees exert pressure to keep their jobs and avoid replacement by more efficient workers. The system has forced all of us to become experts in obtaining protection or advantages from the state.

Laws designed to redistribute wealth to consumers do not do what they are supposed to do: quite the opposite. Attempts to reduce the price of essential goods ultimately cause prices to go up. Research carried out by the Instituto Libertad y Democracia (ILD) showed that, between December 1980 and June 1985, prices of controlled foodstuffs increased 31.4 percent more than prices of uncontrolled foodstuffs. This is because any state-imposed price-control system necessarily involves politics and red tape and thus the possibility that, once they have been isolated from market forces, prices will in fact be controlled by redistributive combines. All this causes a tremendous waste of resources. Not only must redistributive combines and the state maintain an entire system for negotiating, creating, and administering redistribution, but society as a whole has to suffer the consequences of negotiation, increased bureaucratization, and a rigid institutional system.

Redistributive combines devote much of their efforts to directing their intermediaries and go-betweens, holding receptions, and using legal studies to win privileges, instead of improving their transactions. Some of the country's best talent and our business people's best hours are spent on waging redistributive wars instead of achieving real progress. Even elite provincial business people have to establish close ties with the redistributive powers in the capital. A significant proportion of the country's formal provincial firms have their managerial offices and executives in the capital rather than on site, simply because their executives can gain more by visiting politicians and bureaucrats than by concentrating on increasing their businesses' productivity. The redistributive legal system has thus helped to centralize economic activity in Lima.

Compared with business people in other developing countries, Peru's executives have to invest more effort in obtaining political information than technical information, something which calls for acquaintances in political and bureaucratic circles, in order to obtain the information needed to take the right decisions. The only winners are those who get the information. Competition for technical information, on the other hand, benefits not only the person who obtains it but also enables anybody to improve the quality or lower the cost of a product.[2] The concept of an oligarchical society conjures up precisely the kind of society which encourages the creation of redistributive combines that take turns or share in controlling the functioning of the state but, in so doing, mismanage the country's resources because, instead of concentrating on production, they devote themselves to competing for the unearned income handed out by the state.

Second, Peruvian society is forced to suffer the consequences of a legal system which is based on redistributive transactions, brought about by combines, which gradually institutionalize the acquired rights of specific groups. As a result, the law's beneficiaries are no longer individuals but successful combines. As we shall see in the next chapter, this characterized the mercantilist states of earlier periods, where groups—guilds, aristocratic families, or large commercial associations—and not individuals had rights. It is this that distinguishes ours from today's market economies.

Third, the elected politicians no longer make decisions about many issues. As regulations and controls proliferate and grow increasingly complex, the responsibility for them and the actual power to make decisions about redistributive mechanisms gradually descend through the civil service maze until they reach lower bureaucratic levels. Since these bureaucrats who deal directly with the combines are some of the country's lowest-paid employees, it is almost inevitable that they will sell themselves to the highest bidder.

Fourth, since the legal system can be used to defend or appropriate whatever one takes a fancy to, and since everything that is redistributive is

[2] See T. G. Congdon, Trade Policy Research Centre, London, 1985.

also negotiable, the state also comes to legislate in detail on virtually every activity in the country.

Fifth, the institutional system is particularly rigid and immutable. The laws enacted as a result of a redistributive agreement between the state and a combine establish a legal system which gradually becomes untouchable because the combine will demand that it be maintained and its demand is supported by the bureaucracy.

In contrast, laws which are not enacted for redistributive purposes can easily be improved or replaced by the state until the objectives for which they were created are achieved. In a redistributive state, whose regulations and policies are governed by transactions overseen by combines, it is extremely difficult to undo what has been agreed on, even if what has been agreed on has failed to achieve positive results: it has become an acquired right. Combines force the legal system to steadily accumulate laws which prevent access to formal activity, increase the cost of remaining formal, and make it virtually impossible to simplify regulations and reduce bureaucracy.

Last, the constant pressure to distribute and redistribute society's resources through law-making has made Peru's legal system increasingly obstructive and complex and thus the main spur to informal activity.

According to Mancur Olson,[3] a costly legal system suits redistributive combines because it enables them to obtain advantages which are obscured by a web of legal norms and which neither the press nor the political opposition is able to perceive clearly. When a privilege is identified and a law is enacted to eliminate it, the plethora of regulations becomes even more complicated. Human ingenuity is boundless and people will always be able to get around the new law by using the infinity of regulations that already exist. Civil servants, politicians, and competitors, for their part, will find a way of eliminating the law again, and this will create an endless cycle of competing regulations.

Olson cited the progressive income tax, which always includes mechanisms that reduce the impact of the tax rates, mechanisms that are accessible only to people who have the resources to penetrate the maze of tax legislation, as one type of law well suited to redistributive combines.

Something similar occurs with tariff protection. A high tariff makes a product more expensive for those who use it and forces those who do not enjoy protection to pay for those who do. However, it may also prompt the

[3] See Mancur Olson, *The Rise and Decline of Nations: Economic Growth, Stagflation and Social Rigidities* (New Haven: Yale University Press, 1982).

former to seek protection to offset the cost of the latter's protection. In the long run, this results in arbitrary and inefficient tariffs, in the open politicization of economic incentives, and in foreign-trade regulations which are so complex that they rule out participation by citizens who are technically but not administratively equipped, such as informals.

In countries where the legal system is essentially redistributive, international economic activity is a breeding ground for redistributive combines, because the foreign trade of countries like Peru is dominated by legal instruments which favor those skilled in politicking and red tape. I am referring to such far-from-simple legal instruments as differential controls or exchange rates, a variety of indirect taxes and surcharges on imports, direct taxes on imported goods, licenses, quotas, lists of authorized and unauthorized goods, advance payments on imports, explicit and implicit subsidies, tax reimbursements, bilateral and countervailing agreements, and direct investment regulations. Special mention should be made of exchange controls. Such controls encourage the public to buy strong currencies on the black market. In these circumstances, importers tend to overvalue their merchandise in order to remit more currency abroad. The government, for its part, retaliates with increased controls in order to close the hatch through which resources are escaping.[4] The end result is that the new regulations generate more procedures, more bureaucracy, more corruption and, ultimately, more informal activity.

The same thing happens when, in the zeal to redistribute resources to users of formal credit, bank interest rates are fixed below the inflation rate (negative interest), creating an excess demand for such credit and making relatively little money available for loans. In these circumstances, instead of allowing capital to flow automatically to the most productive business—the only ones able to pay real interest rates and offer the best guarantees of success—the state imposes other criteria for distributing credit. The state tends to favor the winners of redistributive wars, who will ultimately benefit from the scarce but relatively cheap savings resulting from negative interest rates. When the redistributive criterion is applied to the price of money, credit becomes politicized and subject to discrimination and red tape.

It is simply untrue that, in Peru, we are all equal before the law, because no two people pay the same tax, no two imports are taxed in the same way, no two exports are subsidized in the same way, and no two individuals have the same right to credit.

[4] T. G. Congdon, p. 11.

In Peru, political influences on redistribution have been encouraged by the fact that the executive branch is the nation's primary source of laws. Since 1947, the state has produced nearly twenty-seven thousand laws and administrative decisions annually. The executive branch has become the main channel for competition for unearned income. Once the administration is elected or established, there is no effective way of monitoring its lawmaking activities or the privileges it redistributes. We can see the importance of this from table 1, which lists all the norms and decisions enacted between 1947 and 1985 by the legislative and executive branches. The executive branch enacts, without consultation, over 98 percent of all the decisions adopted by the two branches. Parliament, whose pluralism and openness to press and public scrutiny may lessen the possibility of arbitrary legislation, issues a little over one of every hundred laws promulgated in Peru. As a result, most decisions are made without democratic consultation and, what is worse, the vast majority of them are specific resolutions which are almost never published.

In an exploratory survey conducted by the ILD to gather information on the way laws are currently made in Peru, we found that the initiation, preparation, and promulgation of laws were not at all subject to established procedures. According to one person we interviewed, "They depend on each minister." That is, they differ in each sector and, when there is a change of minister, new procedures are introduced. A lawyer interviewed in the same survey said that "Nowadays, no laws are enacted to serve a general purpose." She and other interviewees referred to excessive interference in the content of laws by private interests. What we have is a system of lawmaking which is highly susceptible to the influence of economic or political power, wielded through two complementary bodies: on the one hand, the senior officials in each ministerial office, who have exclusive control over the initiation, drafting, and adoption of legislative proposals; on the other, advisors, vice-ministers and the minister, who often consult outside advisors—mainly lawyers close to them who represent private interests.

In the same survey, members of the executive branch interviewed by the ILD acknowledged that they regularly consult redistributive combines when they plan to legislate in an area affecting them. Such consultation takes place because the state lacks the sufficient professional staff. One official mentioned the following examples: "If the minister for industry plans to draft a law on the automobile industry, he doesn't have a single specialist on the subject in the ministry. As a result, whether he likes it or not, he is ultimately forced to accept the proposal put

TABLE 1.   Norms and Decisions of the Central Government

Year	Legislation	Norms and decisions of the executive branch	%
1947	132	8,759	(98.52)
1948	58	19,583	(99.70)
1949	309	37,639	(99.19)
1950	308	21,531	(98.59)
1951	113	35,471	(99.68)
1952	241	42,515	(99.44)
1953	147	32,323	(99.55)
1954	118	29,353	(99.60)
1955	343	40,753	(99.17)
1956	164	30,864	(99.47)
1957	184	31,190	(99.41)
1958	185	22,792	(99.19)
1959	230	30,314	(99.25)
1960	188	36,932	(99.49)
1961	341	46,810	(99.28)
1962	541	38,242	(98.61)
1963	415	27,072	(98.49)
1964	579	38,375	(98.51)
1965	507	23,598	(97.90)
1966	504	26,030	(98.10)
1967	407	17,515	(97.63)
1968	590	19,286	(97.03)
1969	728	20,950	(96.64)
1970	625	25,976	(97.65)
1971	540	27,679	(98.09)
1972	621	34,127	(98.21)
1973	609	35,623	(98.32)
1974	566	39,623	(98.59)
1975	315	32,552	(99.04)
1976	391	28,978	(98.67)
1977	294	20,704	(98.60)
1978	351	20,096	(98.29)
1979	435	14,170	(97.02)
1980	397	15,789	(97.55)
1981	381	13,700	(97.29)
1982	191	13,186	(98.57)
1983	210	13,653	(98.49)
1984	302	15,230	(98.06)
1985	420	17,078	(97.60)
Annual average	358	26,822	(98.68)

SOURCE: Instituto Libertad y Democracia

forward by the companies, which obviously reflects their own best interests."

A lawyer who worked for the Revolutionary Government of the Armed Forces (1968–1980) and today is in private practice, said that the state bureaucracy which remains is poorly qualified and is undergoing an economic and moral crisis which makes it particularly susceptible to bribery. According to him, the bribe required to obtain a law benefitting an individual must not be "discussed" at the lower levels of the administration, but with members of the minister's office. Bribery elicits the necessary favorable report in an individual's file and helps to maintain the dialogue.

A lawyer in the office of the minister for the economy in the democratic government which ruled the country from 1980 to 1985 said that lawmaking has reached such levels that "there is no time to think." This is so: to its surprise, the ILD found that resolutions and decrees arriving for signature by the minister or the president are not accompanied by a file containing technical reports and other opinions, but simply the text of the law in question. And, as we can see from table 1, the total number of such laws has never been less than thirteen thousand a year since 1948.

Our legal system, then, does not seek to establish the regulations needed to safeguard and delimit rights and obligations protecting everyone's property and encouraging everyone's transactions, for it does not reflect a desire to create wealth-producing institutions but, rather, an obsession with the direct administration of daily occurrences. Consequently, it is the result of constant competition for unearned income and of our rulers' personal priorities and opinions, and it is made up of the bad laws which regulate the costs of formal and informal activity. It hardly favors the opening of legal institutions to marginal populations.

All of this causes discouragement, uncertainty, and corruption, and fosters social unrest. In the redistributive state, discouragement sets in when, from an early age, Peruvians realize that wealth is not so much the result of labor as of political wheeling and dealing. As they grow older, young Peruvians find that the people who begin to get rich are often not the ones who invest labor or capital in productive enterprises but those who have managed to gain some political influence. The most experienced among them—those who have heard the promises of left- and right-wing governments—grow discouraged because they know from personal experience that the best way to get ahead is to win a favor from the state.

Uncertainty is constant in the redistributive state, for Peruvians are aware that the executive branch, which issues some 110 regulations and decisions each working day, can change the rules of the game at any moment without prior consultation or debate. Peruvian law is unstable and unpredictable because it depends on who wins the redistributive wars. The flight of resources to informality and of Peruvian talents or capital abroad reflects the rejection of the system and a desire to work or save and invest in countries with more predictable legal systems, i.e., fewer arbitrary legal redistributions. Whether these redistributions take the form of open expropriations, such as assigning private land to a housing project, or concealed expropriations, such as freezing bank deposits or instituting discriminatory exchange rates, people cannot be sure just how much their assets and liabilities are worth. They cannot fully enjoy the fruits of their labor or anticipate when a redistributive regulation will remove them from the market.

In the redistributive state, the enviable capacity to be generous with other people's money is an invitation to corruption. In the struggle for wealth and favorable redistribution, no means are spared. And as corruption grows, so does anarchy. In a country where the law can be bought, where both left- and right-wing political parties agree that it is the state's prerogative to regulate and legislate in detail, and where the false ethic of redistributive justice has evaded and consigned to oblivion the ethic of productive justice, there are no secure property rights and no legal incentives for creating wealth. The inevitable hallmarks of the resulting system are instability and anarchy.

CHAPTER SEVEN

The Parallel with Mercantilism

As we have seen how the redistributive tradition defines our society, it has become clear just how far we are from being a market economy. So we must ask ourselves, What kind of system do we have? Is it one shaped by factors specific to Peru or Latin America? Is it a reflection of our own particular cultural identity? Is it unique?

In actual fact, the redistributive tradition is not exclusive to Peru and Latin America, it cannot be attributed solely to our cultural characteristics, nor is it historically unique. It characterizes a system of social organization in which Peru, Latin America, and possibly a large proportion of Third World countries seem to be immersed at present, as the developed countries were before them—namely, mercantilism.

The Characteristics of Mercantilism

As is well known, "mercantilism" is the name given to the economic policies pursued in Europe between the fifteenth and nineteenth centuries. According to the UNESCO *Dictionary of Social Sciences*, "mercantilism is . . . the belief that the economic welfare of the State can only be secured by government regulation of a nationalist character." According to others, who emphasize the role of the private sector in mercantilism, it is the "supply and demand for monopoly rights through the machinery of the

201

state. . . ."[1] The European societies of that time were politicized, bureaucratized, dominated by redistributive combines, and impoverished. The parallel between twentieth-century Peru and the European mercantilism of earlier centuries is a valid one.

Being a system in which the government of a highly regulated state was dependent on elite groups which were in turn sustained by state privileges, mercantilism was vigorously opposed both by Karl Marx, the father of communism, and by Adam Smith, the father of economic liberalism. Smith viewed mercantilism as a system in which merchants and industrialists demanded, and the state provided, their own regulations and sources of income.

Mercantilism was a politically administered economy in which economic agents were subject to specific, detailed regulation. The mercantilist state did not let consumers decide what should be produced; it reserved to itself the right to single out and promote whichever economic activities it considered desirable and to prohibit or discourage those which it considered inappropriate. According to Charles Wilson, "the mercantilist system was composed of all the devices, legislative, administrative, and regulatory, by which societies still predominantly agrarian sought to transform themselves into trading and industrial societies."[2] To achieve its objectives, the mercantilist state granted privileges to favored producers and consumers by means of regulations, subsidies, taxes, and licenses.

Mercantilist governments viewed their intervention on the side of private interests as justified, for in those days it was inconceivable that a nation might prosper through the spontaneous efforts of its citizens. Modern-day Europe inherited from the Middle Ages the belief that all humans were born sinners and that those in power had the duty of guiding the destinies and actions of their subjects in order to save them from themselves. From this standpoint, well-being and order were conceivable only if individuals and their organizations were regulated by the state and subordinated to its highest interests. Left unsupervised, commercial and industrial activity would inevitably result in poverty, hunger, disease, and death.

It was the duty of medieval rulers to intervene directly in their subjects' economic activities, assigning and redistributing their resources through strict regulations which determined, inter alia, the weights and measures used in trade, "fair" prices for producers and consumers,

[1] Robert B. Ekelund, Jr., and Robert Tollison: *Mercantilism as a Rent Seeking Society* (College Station, Tex.: Texas A&M University Press, 1981), chapter 1.

[2] Charles Wilson, *Mercantilism* (London: Routledge & Kegan Paul, 1963), p. 26.

minimum wages to protect employees, and maximum wages to protect employers. The anticipation of future needs was absolutely prohibited because it was regarded as "speculation."

The mercantilist era was born when European industry and international trade began to expand and some military costs began to decline. Much of the economic scarcity that had characterized the Middle Ages began to disappear and private business activity gathered momentum. Since the medieval system of government was the only one that Europeans knew, however, they applied its antiquated political methods to the new forms of increasingly important private economic activity. The commercial and industrial revolutions of Western Europe thus took place in a context of widespread state intervention in the economy and detailed regulation of production.

At the beginning of the mercantilist era, increased private production, large taxes, and massive regulation provided the state with considerable revenue. Although the mercantilist government believed that the new prosperity would make the nation great, the decisive factor was the power of the state. Since it was not those who governed, however, but the entrepreneurs whose activities they authorized who produced the wealth, the entrepreneurs soon gained much of the state's power. A large proportion of mercantilist writing consisted of arguments in favor of created or private interests, and it was the influence of merchants that ultimately gave the name "mercantilism" to the policies pursued by governments in those days. European mercantilism was characterized by the close ties that existed between an ever-present state and a privileged and exclusive entrepreneurial clique. Let us examine some characteristics of this phenomenon which is so strikingly paralleled in contemporary Peru.

Access to enterprise

Just as in Peru today, in mercantilist Europe the pursuit of formal enterprise was reserved for a chosen few. The entrepreneur always required express authorization from the king or government. In England, this was known as the "charter" of privilege.

> Whatever the financial form, however, it was the collection of rights and privileges which reflected the deal between the state and the merchants. The latter got the official backing of the government in opening negotiations with the rulers of a new era of trade; a monopoly of an area; control of entry and thus, it was hoped, the ability to maintain profits; the right to keep out retailers. . . ; and the creation of a corporate entity to lobby for

the interests of the group. The state, for its part, got something which war and inflation made it want in ever-growing amounts: a source which it could tap for money and especially for loans of cash.[3]

As a result, access to enterprise was limited to individuals or groups who had political connections and could repay the king or his government for the privilege of operating a legal business. Businesses were like milk cows who supplied the government with the funds it needed to achieve its power objectives. Often, the state not only levied the taxes agreed in the charters but also demanded that it be made a shareholder in enterprises called mixed companies, and be given loans and donations. In so doing, the mercantilist state taxed consumers indirectly.

Sometimes, the state also set up its own businesses to meet its needs or that of the group in power—as, for example, the "royal manufactures" established in eighteenth-century Spain, following the French Colbertist model. These royal factories, forerunners of modern state-owned corporations, fell into two groups: those producing goods for national defense, such as artillery pieces, and those producing luxury goods, such as tapestries, glassware, and porcelain. Most were inefficient, operated at a loss, and disappeared in the late-eighteenth and early-nineteenth centuries.

As the years passed, other legal ways of establishing businesses and favoring their owners developed. In the seventeenth century, for instance, the English state granted some citizens the privilege of forming "legal entities" which could survive the death of their members or enabled them to litigate impersonally or separate the owners' private interests from the interests of the businesses themselves, so that they could acquire resources more efficiently than any individual. Private association was so great a privilege that, in England, citizens who formed associations without obtaining express authorization from the king or his government were prosecuted. When the English began to group together to acquire and administer resources, even without privileges, the English state viewed this as an attack on its authority and the established order. In 1720, it promulgated the Bubble Act: although its stated aim was to "discipline private initiative," its real aim was to help the larger businesses by limiting the ability of small companies to compete for capital.

In Spain, the Cortes and the police were used to prevent "unfair competition" by law or by force. Holders of privilege sometimes took the law into their own hands to punish anyone who tried to break their monopoly. According to Larruga, in 1684 the residents of Pastrana opened

[3] D. C. Coleman, *The Economy of England, 1450–1750* (Oxford University Press, 1977), pp. 58–59.

a ribbon factory modeled on foreign factories. All went well until, in 1690, the residents of the nearby town of Fuente de la Encina decided to follow suit, arousing the indignation of the people of Pastrana, who enjoyed an exclusive privilege within a radius of twelve leagues. After a protracted dispute, the residents of Pastrana took up arms, attacked the town of Fuente de la Encina, seized the factory's lathes and implements, and took the workers by force back to their own town, treating them like prisoners of war.[4]

Most historians agree that while production was geared to the interests of the influential merchant classes, it also met the state's needs: the state's connections with a number of well-established, hand-picked, readily identifiable merchants enabled it to obtain and control, fairly easily, the income it needed to keep its coffers full and to pursue the policies it deemed necessary. So, although the case for state regulations, subsidies, and intervention on behalf of specific merchants or industries was argued very convincingly—for instance, a given activity was essential to national defense or such protection was required to help an industry grow—the fact is that they also responded to the state's need for identifiable sources of income which it could tax without major difficulties. An industry run by large numbers of small entrepreneurs or agricultural producers was difficult to control and still more difficult to tax. The state did not have the know-how and the mechanisms of a market economy to deal with a widespread entrepreneurial class. Mercantilism reconciled the aims of the privileged classes with the fiscal needs of their governments.

Excessive legal regulation

As in Peru today, legal regulation was excessive in the mercantilist state. According to Gregory King, seventeenth-century English demographer and statistician, the need to contend with the law was so great that in 1688 approximately 3 percent of England's population were lawyers.[5] As the regulations benefitting certain activities became more detailed, with the addition of more technical specifications to protect certain industries, the body of regulations in mercantilist countries grew inordinately. Governments have always used detailed, precise regulations for redistributive and discriminatory purposes, but this tendency got completely out of hand with the advent of mercantilism and its manifestations: the growth of cities, the

---

[4] See Francisco Cabrillo, *Notas para el ILD* (Madrid: Meca, 1985).

[5] Gregory King, *Natural and Political Observation* (G. E. Barnett ed., 1936).

expansion of international trade, the discovery of new countries, and the sophistication of newer techniques of production. To protect their monopolies and also to ensure a stable supply of labor, the English restricted the introduction of new methods of production. In 1623, for instance, the Privy Council of the English Crown commanded that a needle machine be dismantled and that all the needles produced therewith be destroyed.

Laws were also passed to ensure the consumption of the goods produced by monopolies. In 1571, a regulation required all citizens to wear an English woolen cap on Sundays. In 1662, a regulation required that corpses be buried in English woolen textiles, an order that was confirmed in even greater detail in 1666, 1678, and 1680.[6]

In France, the drafting of regulations was codified by Colbert, minister of finance to Louis XIV, between 1666 and 1730, when all the regulations on production were to be found in four volumes totalling 2,200 pages, plus three supplementary volumes covering virtually all economic activities. For instance, there were 51 articles on textile production while the three main sets of regulations on textile dyeing consisted of 317, 62, and 98 articles respectively. In 1737, the instructions regulating the Lyons silk industry came to more than 208 articles.

Mercantilist regulations differed from earlier ones in that they were not dictated by the king but resulted from consultations with privileged economic groups or merchants. It is hard to imagine that the king of France would have known how many types of thread or needle had to be used to manufacture textiles in Lyons, Paris, or Semur: the people who gave him this information were the manufacturers. The regulations were essentially mechanisms for preventing competitors from entering the market. An instance of overregulation with especially adverse effects occurred during the seventeenth and eighteenth centuries. The English, who had already begun to liberalize their regulations, developed the production of cotton prints which were far cheaper than the traditional calicoes. Between 1686 and 1759, in an effort to protect their textile industry, the French passed a number of laws prohibiting the use and production of such fabrics. By the end of the period, these laws were contained in two statutes, some eighty ordinances, and an even greater number of administrative norms.

According to historian Joseph Reid, another reason for overregulation was the mercantilist state's determination to keep the rural population from

---

[6] Eli Heckscher, *Mercantilism* (London: E. F. Soderlund ed., George Allen & Unwin, 1934), Vol. 1, p. 265.

migrating to the cities, in order to ensure that sufficient food was produced to feed the entire population. Reid and other historians believe that a more important reason to control prices and to keep the rural population in the countryside was to keep the poor peasants moderately content and geographically dispersed in order to consolidate the government's power.[7]

Another reason for overregulation was the desire to redistribute the national wealth. To do this, kings established price ceilings in times of scarcity and price thresholds in times of plenty, so as to keep scarce goods accessible and plentiful products profitable. For instance, it was traditional to establish a maximum price for bread when wheat harvests were poor and the price tended to go up. Although it seemed reasonable to keep the price of a basic necessity low, it was clear, even in those days, that in the long run price ceilings did not help disadvantaged groups but in fact steadily raised the real price of bread by encouraging producers to produce less, thereby making bread accessible only at very high prices on the black market or else forcing people to wait on breadlines to get it at the official price.

Public and private bureaucracies

Just as in present-day Peru, mercantilist bureaucracies increased the costs of transactions instead of reducing them. The government of Louis XIV (1661–1715) introduced "industrial inspectors" whose sole function was to monitor compliance with industrial regulations. In the sixteenth century, Europe's cities, particularly the centers of public government, grew significantly. Reid and other historians attribute this to the fact that it was there that privileges were granted and negotiated and, of course, where the bureaucracy lived.

The bureaucracy grew because the raison d'être of the mercantilist state was to redistribute wealth according to its fiscal and political interests and thus to encourage, discourage, or prohibit different economic activities and agents. The task of deciding who should prevail and who should not was an arduous one—even for kings. It required the skillful analysis and documentation of lawyers and accountants, who had to prove that their proposals were the ones most suited to the state and its aims. If it is difficult for a banker to choose to whom to lend money, imagine the problem of a mercantilist government that had to decide what to promote and what to ban throughout a country.

[7] Joseph Reid, *Respuestas al primer cuesticrario del ILD* (Lima: Meca, 1985).

The initial allocation of resources and the corresponding regulations, taxes, and subsidies were only the beginning of the mercantilist bureaucracy's work, for those who did not benefit from redistribution began to look for ways of making the government pay attention to them also. This required an entire private apparatus for currying governmental favor, which in turn generated more regulations to correct earlier decisions, and more bureaucrats to administer regulatory mechanisms and ensure compliance with the decisions made.

Thus, the administrative apparatus of mercantilist states ceased to have autonomous objectives and instead administered the relations and ongoing negotiations between the guilds, redistributive combines, and the state.

Redistributive combines and guilds

Just as in Peru, the most powerful private businessmen in mercantilist Europe organized themselves into redistributive combines which gradually established a pseudo-bureaucracy of private go-betweens, made up of lawyers, accountants, and other individuals engaged in what we now call "public relations," whose main job was to file petitions with governments. One type of redistributive combine was made up of the guilds—associations of producers which might today be regarded as "cartels." Their aim was not to promote the technological development of their industries but to use "monopoly power and often political power to serve their interests."[8] They sought to control entry to the legal exercise of their profession or activity, limit competition as far as possible, fix prices, regulate the market, control and standardize conditions of employment, and, wherever possible, control with their go-betweens the policies pursued by the government.

Peru: A Mercantilist Country?

As we have shown, there are important similarities between the system in mercantilist Europe and the system of redistributive law in Peru. Both are characterized, to a greater or lesser extent, by authoritarian lawmaking; an economic system in which the state intervenes directly; obstructive, detailed, and *dirigiste* regulation of the economy; poor or nonexistent access to enterprise for those who do not have close ties with government;

[8] Mancur Olson, *The Rise and Decline of Nations: Economic Growth, Stagflation and Social Rigidities* (New Haven: Yale University Press, 1982), p. 125.

unwieldy bureaucracies; and a population which organizes into redistributive combines and powerful professional associations.

We might conclude that Peru's is a predominantly mercantilist system which has little to do with a modern market economy. However, spokesmen for the traditional right wing are always confusing the two systems in their attempt to rationalize the commercial and business activities of those they represent and also to win the sympathies of devotees of the private sector in the West. The Westerners often do not realize that their Latin American counterparts function in economies governed by politics rather than markets. The traditional left also confuses the two systems, but they conclude that, although private ownership of the means of production predominates, the development the country needs has not been achieved, proving that capitalism has failed and that a collectivist model is needed. What they both succeed in doing is to discredit the idea of development through a formal private sector simply because, in alluding to it, they are in fact referring to an outdated mercantilist system. No thought is given to the idea that what private individuals or the state produce depends on the legal institutions of a country and that the incentives in a market economy and in a mercantilist system have radically different consequences.

Each of these systems encourages different entrepreneurial abilities. In a market economy, the ability to produce is encouraged because what prevails is competition; in a mercantilist economy, the ability to win privileges and use the law to one's own advantage is encouraged, because the determining factor is state regulation. In a market economy, consumers are served efficiently and economically; in a mercantilist economy, it is the public and private bureaucracies that are well served, generally at the cost of the rest of society. In a competitive economy, the entrepreneur must satisfy a customer who is interested only in the quality, price, and accessibility of a product and not in the attributes of its producer. In winning the favor of the state in a mercantilist environment, on the other hand, the entrepreneur's astuteness and sociability are the crucial attributes that win beneficial state laws and policies. The ability to organize an argument with conviction, coherence, as well as with publicity or discretion, are important, but the goal may also be achieved by social attentions or bribes.

In the mercantilist economy, entrepreneurs and workers spend an increasing amount of time politicking, complaining, flattering, and negotiating. Each must wait on line to see the bureaucrats. More lawyers and more go-betweens are recruited and the complicity of more journalists is sought, while the government must recruit more bureaucrats and conduct more studies in order to deal with them and justify its decisions. This is why, in a mercantilist economy, many people who could have been merchants work in the ranks of public and private bureaucracies—an economic disgrace because, unlike genuine workers, bureaucrats and lobbyists do not increase production or investment by their efforts.

Perhaps the greatest difference between the two systems lies in the ease of access to the market. In market economies, anyone can enter the market, produce, distribute, or obtain government authorization without the intervention of third parties. In mercantilist economies, access to the market is restricted. Special licenses or permits are required for virtually everything, creating a constant need for assistance from a privileged private group or from the authorities who guard the administrative gates. Having to waste 289 days on red tape before being able to operate an industry, or having to wait almost seven years before being able to build a house, are the obstacles which the mercantilist system erects against entry to the market.

As we shall see later, mercantilist institutions had to be eliminated or overcome before the modern market economies of the West could function. The European mercantilist economy was costly because it had to support a large number of unproductive bureaucrats and lawyers who served only to wrap, unwrap, and rewrap its country's subjects in laws which controlled, distributed, redistributed, and assigned the privileges which strengthened the state and favored certain entrepreneurs. The mercantilist economies of Western Europe were far less wealthy than the market economies which succeeded them because the energies of their bureaucrats, lawyers, and business people were, economically speaking, wasted. Although some favored industries grew more as a result of mercantilist privileges than in the subsequent market economy, their growth had an adverse effect on development because their output was achieved by uneconomical means and their success encouraged others to try to win the same advantages by seizing power or obtaining favors instead of by creating wealth.

The Decline of Mercantilism and the Emergence of Informals

Mercantilism gradually disappeared from Europe because of its inefficiency, for the profits made by redistribution and the use of resources for that purpose instead of for improving production reduced the value of countries' total earnings. Not only did mercantilist countries become impoverished, they also fostered conflict among their citizens and so undermined their social structures that, through evolution or revolution, European mercantilism gradually disappeared.

We believe that "Peruvian mercantilism" is experiencing a decline similar to that undergone by European mercantilism between the end of the eighteenth century and the beginning of the twentieth century, for they share many traits. From this standpoint, it is particularly important to examine the earlier decline and what courses the different European countries then took, whether voluntarily or by force of circumstances. This will enable us to reflect on Peru's future.

From what we know, we can conclude that the decline of European mercantilism began with the mass migration of peasants to the cities. The migration occurred mainly because of rural poverty and because people began to realize that it was in the cities that contact could be made with the powers that redistributed the national wealth and where the most protected industrialization was occurring.

Then, as now, institutional rigidity and excessive administrative obstacles and confusion prevented the formal private sector or the public sector in the cities from creating jobs as fast as they were needed to absorb the arriving peasants. Informals began to proliferate in Europe. Legions of peddlers invaded the streets, smuggled and illegally produced goods invaded the markets, and illegal suburbs flourished on the cities' outskirts. Persecution of the informals by the authorities caused such marginalization and dissatisfaction among them that there were outbreaks of violence. Then, as now, as the informal economy grew, the burden of taxation began to fall on an increasingly narrow sector of the population, the formal sector, and it had no choice but to reduce its costs and taxes by buying a large proportion of its inputs from informals,[9] creating increasingly large public deficits. As a result, both informals and formals began to disobey the law, triggering the political instability that constant lawbreaking engenders and undermining the authority and legitimacy of the mercantilist state.

As the European countries' normal industries began to stagnate and illegal activities became increasingly widespread, the mercantilist system itself declined. Europeans emigrated to colonies, former colonies, or countries which had undertaken more successful reforms. Many of those

---

[9] This practice was so widespread that, in Great Britain, the term "putting out system" was coined to denote it.

who could not or would not emigrate entered informal industry or joined violent subversive movements. Formal business people became increasingly vulnerable and the power of guilds and redistributive combines gradually waned. The political authorities responded to the crisis by appealing for a return to morality, prosecuting lawbreakers, and enacting more laws against lawbreaking, thereby further hampering society with their regulations. Opportunities for corruption of public officials increased, while confused governments, unaware of the cause of their problems, tried to mitigate the effects of the crisis by offering handouts, distributing foodstuffs, organizing public soup kitchens, and giving peasants incentives to remain in or return to the countryside. Their efforts proved inadequate: unrest, fatalistic propaganda, the contrast between rich and poor in urban areas, criminality, violence, and the state's consequent loss of social relevance eventually spelled the end of most European mercantilist systems, replacing them with market economies or communist collectivism.

The factors which caused or characterized the decline of European mercantilism bear some similarity to the situation in contemporary Peru and therefore warrant further consideration.

Migration to the cities

De Vries, Coleman, Clapham, Heckscher, and, in general, most writers on the subject link the end of mercantilism in Europe to the mass migrations to its cities, to the growth of the population as a result of a decline in plagues, and to a reduction in rural incomes as compared with urban incomes.[10]

In the seventeenth and eighteenth centuries, strict controls on industry enabled the French state to levy high taxes to finance public works. Workers in the cities began to receive fairly high wages for carrying out the various works ordered by the different kings. It did not take many people to put up palaces and public buildings, but those employed to do so were well paid. Since these urban wages were relatively high and direct and indirect taxation in the countryside was very steep, the more ambitious peasants migrated to the cities, especially to Paris. Then, during the latter

[10] Jan De Vries, *Economy of Europe in an Age of Crisis, 1600–1750* (Cambridge: Cambridge University Press, 1976); D. C. Coleman, *Revisions in Mercantilism* (Methuen and Co., Ltd., 1969); J. H. Clapham, *The Economic Development of France and Germany, 1815–1914* (Cambridge: Cambridge University Press, 1963); Heckscher, *Mercantilism.*

part of the nineteenth century, rural poverty and industrial subsidies led to industrial growth in, and mass migration to, the cities.

In England, the first wave of migration began relatively early, in the seventeenth century, and was so massive that the Settlement Act of 1662 sought to halt it by giving justices of the peace in the cities the power to order migrants to return to their parishes in the countryside. In 1697, in the face of continuing migration, a law was passed allowing migrants to move within the country only if they obtained a certificate of settlement from the authorities in their new place of residence. Attempts were also made to discourage migration by helping poor and retired people only if they returned to their parishes of origin. None of these measures proved very successful.

The emergence of informal activity

When they arrived in the cities, migrants from the countryside found that there were not enough jobs for them. Restrictive regulations, not the least being difficulties in obtaining permission to expand or diversify activities, limited the capacity of formal businesses to grow and, thus, their ability to provide jobs for the new laborers. Most migrants initially found themselves without jobs, and some entered domestic service or worked only on a casual basis.[11] There are great similarities between the residents of the poor neighborhoods surrounding Peru's iron and steel and industrial plants and the paupers who settled precariously on the outskirts of Europe's mercantilist cities, awaiting admission to a guild or employment in a legal business in order to obtain the stable income which dealing with the state was supposed to guarantee.

Migrants who did not find legal employment, and their descendants, gradually began to open workshops in their homes. Many of these jobs were not full-time and, as Coleman indicates, "much industrial work consisted of the direct processing, with little capital equipment beyond simple hand tools."[12] In the beginning, city dwellers despised the work done by these people outside the guilds and the system. In Spain, the colloquial expressions *"eres un puñetero"* or *"vete a hacer puñetas,"* alluding pejoratively to the supposedly ignoble occupation of making *puños*, or cuffs, for shirts in small informal workshops, are still used.

Since it was the only feasible alternative, however, informal activity

[11] Reid, *Respuestas.*

[12] Coleman, *The Economy of England.*

spread quickly. Heckscher quotes a comment by Oliver Goldsmith in 1762: "There is scarcely an Englishman who does not almost every day of his life offend with impunity some express law . . . and none but the venal and the mercenary attempt to enforce them."[13] Two French decrees (of 1687 and 1693), also cited by Heckscher, recognized that one reason why production specifications were not complied with was that these workers were illiterate. As a result, they could not meet even the simplest legal requirement of the textile industry, that cloth manufacturers append their name on the fore-pieces of the cloth. But while many of these workers may not have known how to read or write, they were efficient. Adam Smith comments that "If you would have your work tolerably executed, it must be done in the suburbs [informal settlements] where the workmen, having no exclusive privilege, have nothing but their character [reputation] to depend on, and you must then smuggle [without being seen by the authorities] it into the town as well as you can."[14]

There were constant clashes between the authorities and these small entrepreneurs. The preambles to laws and ordinances of the period frequently refer to noncompliance with laws and regulations. According to Heckscher, the import of printed calicoes from India was prohibited in 1700 in order to protect England's woolen manufacturers. Despite a ban on their use, enterprising English manufacturers went on producing such calicoes, always managing to find exceptions or loopholes in the law. One way around the ban on printing cotton-based fabrics was to use fustians—English calicoes made with a linen warp. Thus, the new manufacturers gradually gained or created industries, forcing the established industries to change or go out of business. Informals were also prosecuted and punished in Spain. In 1549, Emperor Charles I promulgated a number of ordinances. One of the penalties imposed in the twenty-five laws was to cut the selvedges off a fabric sample with scissors so that informals could not sell their fabrics without telling the buyer why the inspectors had mutilated them.

Clashes between the state and informals did not stop at lawbreaking, however. State repression was fierce and, at least in France, extremely brutal. Restrictions on the access of new producers and new goods to the textile sector in the mid-eighteenth century were plentiful and harsh. Laws prohibited the French public from manufacturing, importing, or selling

[13] Heckscher, *Mercantilism*, vol. 1, p. 323.

[14] *Ibid.*, p. 241. The bracketed words are ours.

cotton prints, and penalties ranged from slavery and imprisonment to death. The informals remained undeterred, however. Heckscher estimates that more than sixteen thousand smugglers and clandestine manufacturers were executed by French authorities under laws prohibiting the illegal manufacture and the import of printed calicoes, not to mention the far larger number of people who were sent to the galleys or punished in other ways. Heckscher also mentions that, on one occasion in Valence, seventy-seven informals were sentenced to be hanged, fifty-eight were to be broken on the wheel, six hundred and thirty-one were sent to the galleys, one was set free, and none were pardoned.

According to Ekelund and Tollison, the reason the authorities prosecuted informals so harshly was not only to protect established industries but also because multicolored prints made taxes more difficult to collect.[15] It was easy to identify manufacturers of single-colored textiles and thus verify whether they were paying all their taxes while, thanks to the new printing system, calicoes could be made with a variety of colors, making it much more difficult to identify their origin. Fiscal zeal was one of the main features of mercantilism.

The state relied heavily on the guilds to help it enforce the law by identifying lawbreakers. However, since instead of adjusting the law to include the informals, the authorities made the laws more stringent, they forced many people who wanted to enter or remain in informal industry to migrate to the suburbs, the informal settlements of the time. When the English Statute of Artificers and Apprentices of 1563 fixed wage rates for workers, which were to be adjusted annually by reference to the prices of certain basic necessities, many informal business operators moved to outlying towns or established new suburbs (informal settlements) where state supervision was less strict and regulations more lax or simply inapplicable. By setting up business outside the cities, the informals were able to escape the control of the guilds, whose jurisdiction extended only to city boundaries.

After a time, informal competition had increased to such a point that formal business owners had no alternative but to subcontract part of their production to suburban workshops. This further narrowed the tax base, causing tax levels to rise. This in turn exacerbated unemployment and unrest and, above all, prompted greater migration to the suburbs and increased subcontracting to informals. As producers fled the cities and the number of informals grew, the guilds began to weaken. Some informals

[15] Ekelund and Tollison, *Mercantilism as a Rent Seeking Society.*

did so well that, through political pressures and bribes, they gradually won the right to enter formal business.

The guilds fought back. Under the Tudors, numerous laws prohibited the establishment of informal workshops and services in the suburbs. However, the informals' numbers and their skill at avoiding detection thwarted all these efforts. Some of the most notable failures recorded by historians were those of the hat and coverlet makers' guilds in Norwich, England, who, after a protracted and highly publicized campaign, were unable to enforce their exclusive legal right to manufacture the goods in question.[16]

What happened was that the state, as in Peru today, gradually retreated before the advance of informality. In England, where the transition from a mercantilist economy to a market economy was fairly peaceful, new laws gradually authorized rural and suburban industry. After a time, the authorities were forced to recognize that many suburbs and towns had been established specifically to avoid control by the state and the guilds. In Sweden, King Gustavus Adolphus founded a number of cities and towns in order to forestall the informals and thus incorporate them into the legal system.

As long as the mercantilist system endured, however, most of the efforts made by European states to control the proliferation of informal activities failed. In England, the state was forced to yield before the evidence that new industries were developing primarily in places where there were no guilds or legal restrictions. It was widely acknowledged that the cotton textile industry boomed because it was subject to somewhat more liberal regulations than the woolen textile industry. A distinction was even drawn between the entrepreneurial abilities of the inhabitants of suburbs and those of cities governed by mercantilism. In 1588, a report to Lord Cecil, minister to Queen Elizabeth I, described the citizens of Halifax, one of the new informal settlements, as follows:

> They excel the rest in policy and industry, for the use of their trade and grounds and, after the rude and arrogant manner of their wild country, they surpass the rest in wisdom and wealth. They despise their old fashions if they can hear of a new, more commodious, rather affecting novelties than allied to old ceremonies. . . . [They have] a natural ardency of new inventions annexed to an unyielding industry.[17]

[16] Heckscher, *Mercantilism*, vol. 1, pp. 239–44.

[17] *Ibid.*, *Mercantilism*, p. 244.

The informals of those days were not only establishing new towns near the cities but also building within the cities. In Germany, it was necessary to pass a test and obtain legal approval in order to build. None the less, Clapham tells us that "whole districts could be found in which plenty of houses were being built, though there was no one in the district legally qualified to build them."[18] Migration also brought informal trade to the cities. In England, according to Coleman, in the decades following the Restoration, some traditionalists began to complain about the growing numbers of peddlers and street vendors, the disturbances that took place in front of shops, and the appearance of new shopkeepers in many small cities. Formal traders tried in vain to rid themselves of the newcomers. In Paris, the legal battle between the tailors and the secondhand clothes dealers lasted for more than three hundred years and had not even ended by the time of the French Revolution.

Thus, the informals began to undermine the very foundations of the mercantilist order because they were competitive and aggressive and viewed the authorities as their enemies. In those countries where the state outlawed and prosecuted them instead of absorbing them, progress was delayed and unrest increased, spilling over into a violence whose best-known manifestations were the French and Russian revolutions.

The collapse of the guilds and redistributive combines

The increase in informal activities inevitably weakened the mercantilist guilds whose main function was to control access to formal enterprise. Coleman attributes the guilds' decline to the "increasing labor supply, changing patterns of demand and expanding trade; the growth of new industries and the considerable extension of rural industry organized on the putting-out system."[19] Moreover, in countries which made a peaceful transition from mercantilism to a market economy, the state stopped supporting the guilds with exclusive privileges when it realized that allowing the employment of informal immigrants in the cities was preferable to unemployment, even when the employer was not recognized by a guild. In England, the political instability that accompanied the decline of mercantilism meant that fewer and fewer people applied for admission to the guilds, thereby setting the stage for the state to drastically alter the way in which business was conducted.

[18] Clapham, *Economic Development of France and Germany*, pp. 323–25.

[19] Coleman, *The Economy of England*, p. 74.

Corruption

Like the guilds, the bureaucracy also declined. Although mercantilism initially ushered in a long period of economic growth in Europe, its excessive controls meant that it was always accompanied by corruption. By the end of the eighteenth century, its entire apparatus had been weakened and in some places was completely corrupt. Heckscher mentions an ordinance which, in 1692, stated that in many places inspectors went to places of production merely to collect the dues on which they had agreed with the guilds and did not examine the goods at all. Almost all production supervisors, whether they belonged to the guilds or were appointed by the state, were continually accused of corruption and of neglecting their duties, a situation that was attributed to lack of civic respect for the law.

According to Reid, even the English Parliament, which by the end of the seventeenth century also had the power to authorize the establishment of businesses, was known to receive bribes in return. As we mentioned earlier, Oliver Goldsmith, in the mid-eighteenth century, said that none but the venal and mercenary attempted to enforce the law. The justices of the peace appointed in the suburbs and vested with administrative functions had little incentive to enforce laws and regulations which had been drafted in the cities and were unacceptable to suburban residents. Thus, in 1601, a speaker in the House of Commons defined a justice of the peace as "a living Creature that for half a Dozen of Chickens will Dispense with a whole Dozen of Penal Statutes." In those days, as in Peru today, public officials sought to blame their legislative failures not on bad laws but on inadequate enforcement. A pamphlet of 1577 stated: "So that I conclude better laws in these points cannot be made, only there wants execution." Referring to the breakdown of the mercantilist system, Joseph Reid says that mercantilism was infected by the widespread corruption that permeated all its institutions and divided the population into those who could outwit the system and those who could not. He sees it as inevitable that a system of legal institutions which encouraged some people to break the law and made others suffer from it would lose prestige among both.[20]

Unrest and violence

In the end, the mercantilist system caused considerable unrest in Europe, above all because its legal institutions no longer responded to a more

---

[20] Joseph Reid responds to the second questionnaire submitted by the ILD. Typewritten memoranda. ILD Library, 1985; Heckscher, *Mercantilism*, vol. 1, pp. 247, 251.

complex and changing urban reality. The rigidity of mercantilist institutions in fact excluded migrants from the economic potential of which, on reaching the cities, they now had their own version. There were other reasons for unrest, however. Migration, the difficult task of adapting to urban life, overcrowding, and the diseases which the migrants brought with them also aggravated the unrest. Coleman observes that, as early as the sixteenth century, there were complaints in the English Parliament about the "multitude of beggars" and the great increase in "rogues, vagabonds and thieves" in the cities.[21]

The unrest also had its roots in overregulation: the more regulations there were, the more were infringed and the more were enacted to prosecute those who infringed the earlier ones. Lawsuits proliferated, smuggling and counterfeiting were widespread, and governments engaged in violent repression. "The fact was that the age was one of violence when the pursuit of economic ends constantly demanded the backing of force." There was endless street violence and fighting. It was a period in which it was easy to provoke ideological or partisan violence because people were without hope and only a handful were able to get ahead, usually by means that were not apparent.[22]

Since government controlled everything, people placed all their expectations in it. This gave rise to a pattern typical of mercantilist life: when wages went up faster than food prices, merchants called for wage ceilings; when food prices went up faster than wages, workers demanded a minimum wage and a price ceiling on foodstuffs. Prices, incomes, and wages were fixed by political pressure and action, a situation which discouraged industrial and agricultural production and hiring so that neither minimum nor maximum prices were able to solve the problems of scarcity, food shortages, and unemployment.

Amidst such crises and unrest, those with the greatest energies and self-confidence chose to emigrate or to join revolutionary movements. In the centuries in which mercantilism prevailed, many Italians, Spaniards, French, and other Europeans emigrated to other lands in search of a better future. In France, the persecution of the Huguenots and of informals in the textile sector prompted many entrepreneurs and skilled workmen to emigrate, mainly to England and Holland, where they and their hosts managed to prosper.

As early as 1680, there were references to the fatalism brought on by

[21] Coleman, *The Economy of England*, pp. 18–19.

[22] Wilson, *Mercantilism*, p. 27.

the impossibility of achieving substantial economic progress: "the generality of poor manufacturers believe they shall never be worth ten pounds . . . ; and if it so be they can provide for themselves sufficient to maintain their manner of living by working only three days in the week, they will never work four days."[23]

State charity

Disconcerted by the growing numbers of migrants in the cities and the prevailing unrest, the authorities tried to keep the peace by distributing food among the poor, above all milk, grains, and soup, and persuading them to return to the countryside. When the English government adopted a number of laws on the subject in 1662, 1685, and 1693, it imposed as a condition for receiving such relief the requirement that citizens settle in their place of birth or in their last place of fixed residence. The aim was to prevent families and laborers from migrating to the cities in search of employment. But when the system proved unworkable and migrants continued to flood to the cities, a new Poor Law was adopted in 1834: it stipulated that urban paupers could and must be removed to their rural birthplace, where they would receive relief.

This system did not work either, however, partly because unemployment increased and the bureaucracy that administered poor relief became corrupt and ceased to function. Migrants also always managed to find ways of returning to the cities. However, the system of aiding those who remained in rural areas discouraged families and the infirm from migrating, so that it tended to be young unmarried people that went instead. There was thus a steady influx into the cities of able-bodied people who might become successful entrepreneurs or violent revolutionaries.

Collapse

Mercantilism collapsed in most West European countries between the end of the nineteenth and the beginning of the twentieth century, when the contradictions of a system that was incapable of governing a more complex and urbanized society reached their peak. Mercantilist economies ultimately stagnated because their elite entrepreneurs specialized in exploiting regulations which favored them over new methods of production, and because those who could have produced more were discouraged or

[23] Coleman, *The Economy of England*, p. 105.

prevented from doing so by the law. As formal businesses were gradually stifled by taxes and regulations and informals openly defied the law and voiced dissatisfaction at being pushed to the margins, the stage was set for collapse. Productive structures ossified at pretty much the same rate as the cities were encircled by the migrants' precarious settlements, the streets were invaded by peddlers, beggars, and thieves, the markets were overrun with the informals' smuggled or illegally manufactured goods, and civilian life was disrupted by violence.

While mercantilist society and the circumstances of its decline were similar in all the countries studied, the outcome was not always the same. Generally speaking, those European mercantilist countries which made the transition from bad to good laws gradually calmed down and were able to prosper far more easily than those which resisted change. Countries which were more amenable to compromise adopted rules that enabled their citizens' creative energies to be tapped. By encouraging interdependence and specialization, easing access to property and enterprise, reducing the obstacles created by overregulation, and allowing an ongoing and more direct say in government and lawmaking, they made the transition to a market economy with a minimum of violence and a maximum of well-being.

Good laws enunciated and granted political, economic, and social freedoms. These, in turn, increased competition and the possibility of comparing alternatives and controlling abuses. The discretionary powers of bureaucracies were reduced and the legal and economic systems were depoliticized, thereby diminishing the power of redistributive combines, corruption, and discouragement. The time previously wasted on cultivating contracts and dealing with red tape could now be devoted to production. Once the legal system was adapted to the realities of a diverse and pluralistic society, widespread popular entrepreneurship, and an economy that was rapidly evolving technologically, both it and the state regained social relevance. This enabled the state to reduce the level of informal activity, control violence, and gradually dispel uncertainty.

Countries which resisted change and insisted on preserving their mercantilist institutions were unable to adjust their legal systems to reality and continued to oppose their people's needs and aspirations. Almost all of these countries underwent violent revolutions, some of which ultimately brought about the necessary institutional changes, while others led to totalitarianism and still others allowed some mercantilist elements to remain, but only at the cost of prolonged institutionalized repression of the citizenry.

It might be useful to distinguish among the different situations generated by the failure of mercantilism in order to learn from the past. We shall divide these situations into two kinds: peaceful and violent. England is an example of the first. To illustrate the second, we shall briefly describe the experiences of three countries: France, which ultimately established a system of democracy and widespread entrepreneurship; Spain, which alternated between institutional repression and attempts at liberalization and maintained a semimercantilist system for a considerable number of years; and Russia, where repression and confrontation ultimately led to a totalitarian system. The trait common to all was the wide gap between the countries' legal institutions and their economic and social life. However, nothing of what follows purports to determine to what extent this gap between the law and reality, or the emergence of informal activity, explains the collapse of mercantilism.

England: a peaceful solution

England's transition to a market economy was not without suffering or violence, for it is obviously no easy task to do away with traditions and privileges without encountering resistance. However, its evolution was far more peaceful than that of the three other countries we shall discuss.

Although England's transformation was spontaneous, it developed with almost systematic regularity between 1640 and 1914. Instead of undergoing a political revolution which gave rise to sudden change, a number of measures gradually transferred decision-making power from the state to private citizens. The country very gradually rid itself of the authoritarian powers of abusive redistribution, absurd regulations, privileges, and excessive controls; it also gradually legalized informal productive activities and gradually extended to the population universal access to the benefits of the legal system.

This evolution was the outcome of a number of fortuitous events and circumstances specific to England. One of these was the fierce rivalry between the crown and Parliament which, from the seventeenth century onward, competed for control of the economy. What one restricted, the other allowed. Even the competition between the different kinds of law courts meant that a party could win back in one court what had been lost in another. The sheer fact that unduly restrictive regulations had to be invoked before different courts made it more difficult to invoke them and more difficult to enjoy the privileges they conferred.

The restrictions on access to enterprise began to be relaxed only when

Parliament, in an attempt to compete with the king for the same sources of income, decided that it too would grant the privilege of establishing an enterprise, in return for credits and bribes. In the early nineteenth century, a steady evolution toward more practical ways of granting rights of access to enterprise began. In 1825, Parliament repealed the Bubble Act. In 1833, it authorized anyone, and not just freemen, to set up shop and trade in the City of London. Authorization to set up a business without a special permit and then through automatic registration was given in 1832 and 1844, respectively. In 1862, England finally ushered in the era of widespread entrepreneurship in Europe, when Parliament authorized any registered business to become a limited liability stock company. From then on, there was a significant increase in wages in England and a steady drop in prices for goods and services, so much so that working-class living standards rose 100 percent in the second half of the nineteenth century.[24]

Thus, because of Parliament's steady attacks on the privileges granted by the executive branch, competition between the courts, and open defiance of economic legislation by a growing number of informals, the monopolies gradually lost the regulatory protection that sustained them. By the end of the nineteenth century, almost the entire population had free access to property and to business activity. And, as mercantilist laws gradually lost ground, the customary popular laws that everyone accepted gained strength. These were the laws giving citizens the freedom to do things that were not detrimental to others and those guaranteeing access to private property and the right to protect it from third parties. The first of these freedoms meant that people could set up their own business and use their talents for their own benefit. The second meant that those who generated wealth could enjoy the fruits of their labor and investments without the fear of direct or indirect expropriation through arbitrary regulation.

Customary law and contracts both gained ground. As mercantilist regulations lost their validity and competition between the courts hindered their application, the value of contracts increased and, in the absence of other resources, the courts decided to enforce them. Thus, the English gradually obtained the means to cooperate voluntarily—which meant their right to private property, contracts, and business organizations. England's geography also militated against mercantilism. The fact that it was an island made it difficult to combat smuggling by sea, so that its industry was

[24] C. R. Fay, *Great Britain from Adam Smith to the Present Day: An Economic and Social Survey* (New York: Longmans, Green, 1928), p. 397.

forced to be competitive. Moreover, its geographic rivalries with the Irish and Scots made it possible for the latter to simply refuse to enforce English laws that placed them at a disadvantage. Nor could the mercantilist system be imposed for any length of time in rural areas whose inhabitants had little incentive to comply with regulations which benefitted only guilds and monopolies in the cities. Last, since local authorities vied with one another to attract new industries to their districts, conditions were not conducive to exclusive regulatory systems.

Opposition to the state's redistributive power also grew when opposing factions saw that unrest evaporated as the economy was depoliticized, regulations were simplified, individuals were given a freer hand, and the populations' energies and expectations were directed toward private effort rather than to the state.

France: a first violent solution

The excessive violence of France's transition to a market economy is in sharp contrast to England's relatively peaceful evolution. Although the French Revolution opened the doors to change, the liberalization of France's economy did not come with the Revolution itself: it took many more decades and a number of changes before France was able to achieve a measure of equality of economic and social opportunities. Although he did not completely defeat the mercantilist system, Napoleon managed to democratize access to enterprise, to some extent, by making all French citizens equal before the law. During the remainder of the nineteenth century, France gradually made the transition from mercantilism to a market system.

Reid suggests that the violence of the French Revolution was directly proportional to the mercantilist repression that preceded it. From this standpoint, no European country, with the possible exception of Russia, better illustrates the extremes reached by mercantilism in the sixteenth, seventeenth, and eighteenth centuries. The system of monarchic controls and the regulations governing France were so obstructive, the repression of informal activity was so cruel, and the absence of representative institutions was so patent that violence might in fact have been difficult to avoid. Other writers take the view that regulation was no more restrictive in France than in England but that, unlike England and other European countries, France had an efficient police and administrative apparatus which made people pay dearly for any violation of mercantilist laws.

By the late eighteenth century, it was clear that French mercantilism had impoverished the country, stifling its industriousness with a web of excessive laws, and that resentment was growing against the small but all too visible group of wealthy nobles and bourgeois. When persecution of the informals reached its peak, economic stagnation became acute and the police responded to lawbreaking with naked repression. Mercantilism was one of the main reasons for the French Revolution in 1789: "The revolutionary principle took practical shape, with exceptional force and speed, in the French Revolution. . . . the Revolution consisted in . . . a repudiation of the traditional legal order. The existing State institutions were stripped of their authority and denied any *a priori* validity." After their triumph, one of the first things the revolutionaries did was to abolish all privileges and attack the mercantilist legal system. Taxes and "the inspection and regulation of manufacturers . . . naturally came under the hammer."[25]

The French Revolution had an almost immediate effect on the rest of Europe, whose governments tried to forestall similar outbreaks. According to Heckscher, the rest of western Europe "borrowed" from the French Revolution in order to avoid its excesses and undertook reforms which gradually brought them market economies and democratic political institutions.

Spain: a second violent solution

Like other European countries, nineteenth-century Spain undertook the reforms needed to become a market economy. Unlike most, however, its progress was slower because its successes were all too often canceled out by its failures. Between the adoption of the liberal Constitution in 1812 and 1898, there were repeated clashes between those who wanted to modernize the economy and absolutist forces who wanted to preserve the mercantilist tradition. The modernizers can be said to have won since it was during this period that the basis was laid for the modern part of Spain's economy.

Shortly after Isabel II was proclaimed queen, the guilds and the *Mesta* were abolished in 1834 and 1835, respectively. Private banks were then permitted, the establishment of stock companies was encouraged by extending the principle of limited liability, and order was restored to the chaotic tax system. Little by little, up to the end of the nineteenth century,

[25] Heckscher, *Mercantilism*, vol. 1, pp. 456, 459.

major attempts were made to give everyone access to Spain's economy. Between the loss of the colonies of the Philippines, Cuba, and Puerto Rico, at the end of the last century and 1959, however, economic liberalization remained at a standstill. Amidst violence, repression, and dictatorships, policies were reinstituted which were heavily influenced by mercantilism.

Mercantilism's political recovery began to gather momentum particularly after the end of the First World War and reached its peak under the dictatorial government of Miguel Primo de Rivera (1923–1929), when the constitutional monarchy was abolished. During this period, protectionist tariffs were reinforced, governmental industrial development was encouraged, the market was controlled in a monopolistic fashion, and major state corporations were established. At the same time, important redistributive combines reemerged, allying themselves with the political authorities and benefitting widely from governmental privileges. Faced with the resurgence of mercantilism and its corollary—recession and socialist protest—Spain's influential classes viewed the alternative of an extreme left-wing government as a serious threat. Instead of liberalizing their society, however, they chose to repress it with the help of the right wing's most radical forces, triggering the Spanish Civil War that lasted from 1936 to 1939.

The war over, privileged economic and traditionalist groups allied themselves with public officials, the military and the Falange to establish a state system which, using extensive regulation and controls, tried to run Spanish society oppressively. Between 1940 and 1959, a corporative neomercantilism which combined principles of traditional mercantilism with others of fascist corporativism, much in vogue at the time, prevailed. All were united in their opposition to a market economy and a liberal society, and in their belief in the need for mercantilist policies. Accordingly, their approach was one of economic self-sufficiency and forced industrialization, using interventionist policies that included control of prices, production, and external trade.

Such intervention led once again to a system of compulsory licenses and authorizations for engaging in virtually any economic activity. Since a considerable discretion was involved in the granting of such permits, this created a favorable environment for bribery and strong ties among the government bureaucracy, civil servants, and privileged private corporations. Such controls, plus ration cards and massive bureaucratic intervention, caused an economic strangulation which prompted a vigorous resurgence of informal markets, so much so that Dionisio Ridruejo wrote at the time that the system was turning most Spanish citizens into criminals by forcing them to live outside the law.[26]

Harsh reprisals were enacted after the end of the Civil War. The Act of 16 October 1941 imposed the death penalty for certain offenses committed by informals, even though more than five thousand people had already been sentenced to labor gangs and thousands more had been punished with fines. Repression was especially harsh in the enforcement of the earlier 24 November 1938 Penal law and Procedures for Currency Offenses and supplementary legislation. Violations of the provisions on exchange controls were so frequent that they had to be judged by special magistrates, in trials which offered the accused few guarantees. The same procedure was used to enforce the Contraband and Fraud Act of 20 December 1952, which was widely violated. In housing, evasion of rent and of controls on the transfer of property was constant and, when detected, severely punished.

In 1959, however, Spain again began to move toward a market economy. It ended its isolation from the rest of the Western world and embarked on a program to reduce government regulation, liberalize prices, reduce the controls that were obstructing production growth, and ease various labor laws and restrictions on foreign trade. There were a number of reasons for this change. First, the existing system was strangling economic growth: Spaniards' per capita income was a third that of other Europeans, a fact that was clear to the Spanish workers who migrated to market economy countries, and to groups of young technocrats and economists who convinced the government that massive growth was occurring in other Western countries and that Spain was being left further and further behind.

This position was reinforced by the successes of the European Common Market and the stabilization and liberalization plan then being introduced by economist Jacques Rueff in France, as well as by the growing influence on Spanish politics of such international agencies as the International Monetary Fund (IMF) and the Organization for European Economic Cooperation (OEEC), and, although the process of liberalization came to a standstill again in 1964, Spain now seems embarked on an irreversible transition to a market economy. The Spaniards' standard of living has improved substantially and Spain seems destined to increasingly resemble Western Europe rather than the Latin American mercantilist regimes it created.

[26] Cabrillo, *Notas para el ILD.*

Russia: a third violent solution

In Russia, the end of mercantilism was brought about by a violent revolution which resulted in tremendous bloodshed, a totalitarian system, and a collectivist economy. The result is evidence that, the more the forces of change are repressed and the greater the level of unrest, the more likely it is that professional revolutionaries will seize power and impose totalitarian systems. Russia is a good example because, unlike other European countries which undertook the necessary reforms after the Napoleonic Wars, authoritarianism persisted there, as did economic and social unrest. Until 1905 at least, the absence of representative government, a harsh judicial system, and a repressive and cruel police force facilitated neither economic development nor the search for alternatives. Access to the market was difficult and special permits from the Tsar were needed in order to do business or obtain employment.

During the last third of the nineteenth century, rural poverty and industrial subsidies enabled cities to industrialize to some extent, but massive peasant migration to the cities ensued. Just as in the rest of Europe, Russia's authorities and owners of formal businesses were unable to expand their mercantilist industries fast enough to absorb all the potential formal businessmen and workers. This created all the elements characteristic of the decline of mercantilism until, in 1905, there were violent clashes with the authorities; only then were some reforms carried out to give people greater access to enterprise and political decision making. These reforms did not work, however, and the expansion of industrial employment in Russia proved inadequate since, for the most part, it remained stifled by regulations and bureaucracy.

When the productive system failed and was unable to supply the goods the country needed during the First World War, the stage was set for revolutionary forces, with popular support, to remove the Tsar from power—as they did in February 1917—and for the Bolsheviks to take control in October of the same year. Shortly before this, when the Mensheviks had mentioned the need to encourage private enterprise, the Bolsheviks had retorted that "capitalism" had already been tried in Russia and had failed. Of course, the Bolsheviks, doubtless without realizing it, were referring to a mercantilist economy, for Russia had never had a market economy.

*   *   *

If there is any single conclusion to be drawn from the European experiences we have described above, it is that it was after mass migration that the contradictions of mercantilist systems became sharper, their economies stagnated, their laws lost social relevance and their authorities were no longer able to govern.

Those countries which gradually altered their institutions were able to adjust their laws to reality, make a more or less peaceful transition to a market economy, and prosper. Those which resisted were plunged into widespread violence, civil war, political adventures, revolutions, and constant unrest. The unworkability of mercantilism and the disorder it created were a breeding ground for repressive caudillos and dictators, whether these were people like Robespierre, Fouché, and Napoleon in France or Primo de Rivera in Spain. The terrible thing about violence and institutional chaos as a means of transition is, of course, that the possibility of controlling its outcome democratically and peacefully is lost. Thus it can happen, almost by chance—thanks to a pitched battle or perhaps a bureaucratic intrigue—that a Franco or a Stalin will emerge triumphant from the fray. In almost all cases, the immediate result has been repression, and the long-term outcome has depended not on a popular and democratic consensus but rather on the convictions or convenience of a leader and on the conspiracies of those who, in times of disorder or repression, are the most skillful at establishing close ties with the powers that be.

The lesson to be learned from Europe is that a declining mercantilist government which resists the necessary institutional changes is opening the door wide to violence and disorder. It may delay the final outcome at the cost of repression and considerable suffering, but sooner or later the contradictions will probably be solved either by a communist dictatorship or by coexistence within a democratic system and a market economy.

CHAPTER EIGHT

Conclusion

Revolutions, genuine revolutions, not those which simply change the political forms and members of the government but those which transform institutions and alter property relations, advance unseen for a long time before bursting into the sunlight impelled by some fortuitous circumstance.

—ALBERT MATHIEZ
THE FRENCH REVOLUTION

The Social Relevance of Legal Institutions

Peruvian mercantilism is in decline. It is almost impossible that it will regain social relevance and that the situation will not continue to deteriorate. Even at the time of this writing, although Peru's legal institutions were temporarily revitalized by the expectations customarily aroused by the election of a new president, the mercantilist system continues to decline: on October 8, 1985, two months after a new government took office, the minister of the interior informed Parliament that there had been 282 land invasions in Peru so far that year, 153 of which had occurred during his term of office. During the same year, the government had approved only 3 legal adjudications of land.

That our legal institutions are in crisis is due partly to their gradual loss of social relevance in the face of the incursions of informality into all areas of everyday life. In housing, for instance, the authorities have had to come up with different legal solutions for the adjudication of property seized by invasion and have been forced to give informal settlements some kind of legal recognition, albeit discriminatory. More recently, they have even resorted to actual invasion to build their own housing projects. In urban transport, the state has also had to accept the result of invasions of routes of transportation by pirates and minibuses. Similarly, virtually all Peru's municipal governments must today negotiate with street vendors and accept the fact that, for every market built by the state, street vendors build twelve.

Taken together, all these setbacks show that legal institutions have ceased to provide the means to govern society and to live in it. Mercantilism has ceased to represent Peruvian society. Moreover, lack of access to the protection and opportunities which legal institutions ought to provide seems to give most Peruvians the feeling that the system is unfair and that institutions discriminate among the population rather than unite it.

Before the massive migration of recent decades, the state took advantage of the remoteness of the Andean population, scattered and isolated in agricultural communities or estates, to enforce the order which it had established. There was no need to heed the conduct of these groups in order to determine whether the state was socially relevant. This was the legacy of the Spanish Conquest and the viceroyship, during which the country's geography became an integral part of a system of coercive social control. The privileged were ensured of a plentiful supply of agricultural labor and rural populations could be kept away from urban settlements. Moreover, the population's dispersal made it difficult for them to organize uprisings or to form a revolutionary mass in the cities.

In the last four decades, however, with migration and the quintupling of the country's urban population, the situation has altered dramatically. The agrarian reform carried out by General Velasco Alvarado in the 1970s completed the dismantling of the socio-economic system which had dominated and isolated the rural population and made it possible to use force selectively against them. Nowadays, most Peruvians are in the cities and have no interest in going back, because the economic and social reasons which prompted them to move to the cities are too powerful. They can no longer be manipulated in isolation.

These migrants want to engage in the same activities as formals but, since the legal system prevents them from doing so, they have had to invent ways of surviving outside the law. As their numbers and the obstacles they face increase, their institutions and extralegal norms proliferate, creating a massive breach through which an increasingly large proportion of even the traditionally formal population has been escaping from the oppressive world of legality. There can be no denying that informal institutions and the protected space they have created now enable anyone to confront the mercantilist state instead of succumbing to it.

The incursion of informal activity in the past forty years has been so gradual that its effect has been felt only slowly. The mercantilist system did not lose its social relevance overnight, but in a gradual and almost imperceptible manner. Thus, when in July 1980 the military handed the reins of government back to civilians, they did so because they no longer had sufficient social relevance to remain in power. Nor should it be forgotten that on July 28, 1985, when former President Fernando Belaunde Terry relinquished office to his successor, President Alan García Pérez, he did so in virtually identical circumstances: his party's candidate had won barely 6.24 percent of the vote.

It is hardly surprising that Peruvian governments, succeeding one another without ever sharing social objectives, are marked by a lack of continuity. This is because, following the familiar mercantilist tradition, politicians begin by creating redistributive expectations most of which, because of the limitations of the system, will ultimately not be satisfied. Since presidents thus become highly unpopular by the time they leave office, their successors are forced to advance innovative programs and are unable to preserve what some call a "national project." The absence of governmental continuity weakens the system and makes an extremist solution increasingly attractive, thereby undermining the state's social relevance. It also reduces the grace periods which the population allows new governments, so that while a new president may arouse new expectations, this does not necessarily mean there is renewed faith in the system of government.

Violence

It is now clear that the central problem is not whether formal institutions should or should not incorporate the informals for humanitarian reasons, but whether they will manage to do so in time to avoid the violent destruction of representative democracy. It is essential, therefore, that political and social scientists investigate whether the lack of opportunity and the absence of legal facilities and protection for the majority of Peruvians is contributing importantly to the violence in the country. If this is found to be so, we might say that two uprisings are currently taking place which question the social relevance of the mercantilist state: a massive but peaceful one initiated by the informals and another isolated but bloody one initiated by subversive groups, particularly the Communist Party of Peru, called "The Shining Path."

The poorest and most discontented members of the population are not prepared to accept a society in which opportunities, property, and power are distributed arbitrarily. People realize that the country's legal institutions do not allow them to fulfill rational expectations or afford them minimum facilities and protection. The frustration engendered can easily result in violence, either in complicity or relative indifference to it. After all, if the main reason for the existence of legal institutions is to protect individual rights and property from third parties, permit orderly access to productive activity, and facilitate harmonious interaction with other individuals, it is understandable that, when people are discriminated against, many will rebel.

It is obvious to even the most formal and peaceful of citizens that the existing legal system—the red tape, the widespread mistreatment on waiting lines, the bribes, the rudeness—are a Kafkaesque trap which prevent their and the country's resources from being used efficiently. This is unacceptable to the poorest, because the most discriminatory laws and institutions are those governing economic activities—the main channel for upward mobility. The resulting frustration, at best, gives rise to informal activity; at worst, to criminality and subversion. Aggression is a human response to frustration which, in turn, is caused less by suffering and poverty than by the difference between what people have and what they think they are entitled to.

Something similar occurred at the end of Europe's mercantilist regimes: the limitation of opportunities to those with the requisite political contacts engendered fatalism and despair. Those who refused to be defeated, those with energy and self-confidence, chose one of two solutions: emigration or revolution. Where emigration occurred on a massive scale, for instance in southern Italy, it took with it those who would have been catalysts for change. Where the choice of emigration did not exist or was rejected, the state and the police had to wage a protracted struggle against violent rhetoric and terrorism, battles which made their economies unproductive and destroyed incentives for investment.

If opportunities for mass migration, such as those available in Mexico, do not exist and the necessary institutional reforms do not occur, the most likely outcome of a failed mercantilist system will be violence in one or another of its manifestations: revolution or repression. After all, we know that it is mainly young people from rural areas who are drawn to the cities, because they do not have to take a family with them. Since those who migrate are the most enterprising, they may also prove to be the most aggressive and belligerent. Both their age and the difficulty of establishing personal relationships and a home far from their place of origin make them the easiest prey to the rhetoric of violence. Casual employment with no future gradually wears down their tolerance and buries their hopes.

Mercantilism has almost always ended in violence and there is no reason to think it will be any different in Peru, especially if the authorities persist in remaining inflexible. It can be argued that, while some countries such as Russia abandoned mercantilism violently, other countries, like Spain, seem to be moving toward a market economy after several decades of authoritarian rule. But these nations were never free of violence, and it was largely their neighbor's influence which helped them to complete the transition peacefully.

In Peru, these safety valves do not exist. The possibilities of subversion are greater now than they were then. Technology has made weapons more efficient and easier to carry. Our vast urban areas, with their infinite nooks and crannies and discontented residents, enable the violent underground to mobilize and hide very easily. Sad to say, there is no valid reason to suppose that mercantilism will not continue to provoke violence in Peru.

The Survival of Mercantilism

A revolution against mercantilism, which has been gathering momentum for decades but has only recently begun to affect it seriously, is on the move, and this revolution is informality.

Whether because of the legacy of colonialism or because of the absence of a genuine decentralizing feudal experience, the fact is that mercantilism has lasted here at least a century longer than in Europe.[1] However, some of the phenomena we associate with its overthrow are now emerging: informal activity, frequent invasions of property, widespread lawbreaking, the first elements of a market economy, the anarchy resulting from negotiating for laws and bureaucratic favors, and many of the factors which preceded and shaped the European Industrial Revolution. There is no large-scale informal industry, but no such industry existed when the Industrial Revolution first began in the developed countries or, indeed, until the obstacles to popular participation in enterprise began to be removed and a beneficial legal system appeared which made modern production possible.

Although the basic elements of economic and social revolution already exist in Peru, the country's legal institutions are clearly still mercantilist: popular access to private enterprise is difficult or impossible for the popular classes, the legal system is excessive and obstructive, there are massive public and private bureaucracies, redistributive combines have

[1] See Claudio Véliz, *La Tradición Centralista de América Latina* (Barcelona: Ariel, 1984).

a powerful influence on lawmaking, and the state intervenes in all areas of activity.

Without falling into the trap of simplistic historicism, we must not forget that our present is also the result of a long mercantilist tradition that came to us from Spain. The politicians' idea that our government must consist of a centralized, monopolistic authority does not seem to have changed much since then. On this point, Donald M. Dozer observes that:

> Acceptance of the supreme and overriding power of the state, then, is the inheritance of Latin America. The Roman law and its derivative, the Napoleonic Code, which form the basis for the legal system of Latin America, exalt the authority of the state. Despite the successful resistance of the Latin Americans to Spain, Portugal, and France in their wars of independence, the tradition of government absolutism and centralized authority of the state as the decisive factor in human life, which Philip II, Pombal, and Napoleon exemplified, casts its long shadows over modern Latin America—not only as an idea but also as a basis for action.[2]

The powers which tradition and the legal system vest in our rulers, even if they are democratically elected, give them absolute authority over economic and social activities and make it illusory to think that there might be some property right or transaction which cannot be arbitrarily harmed by the state. The state has virtually all the legal instruments it needs to interfere in the institutions which are supposed to lend stability to business activities: it runs an administrative apparatus which expropriates or freezes private resources, has unrestricted rights over any property which has not been assigned to private individuals, and has central control of import and export tariffs and licenses, currency exchange, and prices, and most savings and credit. It also controls exporters by means of countervailing agreements and the allocation of subsidies, controls buying and selling by state monopolies, and controls virtually all the imaginable—and apparently harmless—means of discriminating and redistributing the country's resources according to arbitrary political criteria. All these powers are generally hidden behind the magic words "planning," "promotion," "regulation," and "participation." For all practical purposes, most of the people do not have rights that can be effectively defended against the state.

As a result, although the protagonists of our economic life—the state, private enterprise, and consumers—are the same as in a market economy, the state's tremendous power and its ties with certain private individuals make the relationship among them essentially mercantilist. The state's

[2] Donald M. Dozer, *Are We Good Neighbors?* (Gainesville: University of Florida Press, 1959), p. 276.

legal authority over property and economic activity is so boundless that, in the fullest sense, Peru has never been a country of owners but at most one of usufructuaries. This makes it worthwhile for owners of businesses to devote a large proportion of their resources to infiltrating the bureaucracy and thus protect their interests, rather than to devote themselves to improving output. In keeping with the good old mercantilist tradition, institutions offer them greater incentives to serve politicians than the consumer.

Political Voluntarism

With all this power, it is hardly surprising that our rulers should believe that their will is the dominant factor in causing things to happen. We shall call this belief, so typical of mercantilist regimes, "political voluntarism." Its ideological basis is to be found in that school of legal thought which considers social institutions to be the outcome of deliberate government action.

This, of course, is an illusion. No human being or ruler can comprehend the entire process of social evolution, still less in a changing society like ours. The authorities who undertook massive public housing programs in the capital city never imagined that, its capacity for indebtedness and its entrepreneurial apparatus notwithstanding, the state would be able to invest only the equivalent of one dollar for every sixty dollars invested in the houses in informal settlements. Lima's mayors never imagined that, in the last twenty years, they would be able to build only one market for every twelve markets built by informals. Those in charge of Lima's urban transport system never dreamed, as they tried to plan it more than twenty years ago, that informals would today be providing 95 percent of the service. What these figures show is that progress does not come about purely through state action. This is one of our main conclusions and one which may create some surprise, since it challenges the widespread notion that our rulers are able to know and do everything. Political voluntarism makes it hard to understand how things can happen when people other than those in power want them to happen.

Those who expect things to change simply because rulers with greater determination and executive skills are elected are guilty of a tremendous conceptual error—the assumption that, in an urban society swamped by migration, a ruler can know everything that is going on in the country and that a new social order can be built on this presumed knowledge. In such a society, with millions of people whose specialization makes them interdependent, with complex systems of communication between producers and buyers, creditors and debtors, employers and employees, with a constantly evolving technology, with competition and a daily flow of information from other countries, it is physically impossible to be familiar with and directly run even a small fraction of national activities.

The government's ability to intervene everywhere is thus limited. Although great opportunities may exist for doing good, this does not mean that it is possible to do so directly from a position in government. Rulers are finite and limited beings who face vast and innumerable problems. As soon as they devote attention to one problem they are automatically turning their backs on many others. They are forced to choose between operating on a large and a small scale, between the general and the specific, between the all-embracing and the diverse. If they choose to deal with specific problems, they will be unable to rule the country and will be doomed to failure. No amount of enthusiasm will increase their powers, and they will be able to achieve only what a majority of Peruvians, out of conviction or self-interest, are prepared to do voluntarily. It is not rulers who produce wealth: they sit behind desks, give speeches, draft resolutions and supreme decrees, process documents, inspect, monitor and levy, but they never produce. It is the population that produces.

This is why good laws are so important. When legal institutions are efficient, rulers can reap major benefits with minor actions. To do so, they must discard the bad laws of mercantilism, which seek to regulate every issue, every transaction, every property, and replace them with efficient laws which promote the desired ends. Only good laws can reduce reality to workable, manageable dimensions. Only legal institutions that have proved their effectiveness can reduce the tremendous imbalance that exists between the simplicity of a ruler's mind and the complexity of Peruvian society.

Political voluntarism might have worked in small, primitive economies, but it does not work in modern urbanized societies. In a dynamic, unpredictable economy of millions of people, human ingenuity in creating inventions and new techniques, or in avoiding governmental controls, is so great that it would be impossible for a government to take specific action at the same speed as society operates. This is why Western Europe's voluntarist governments disappeared with the collapse of mercantilism. It was impossible to have an Industrial Revolution until an economy administered almost exclusively by politicians was abandoned.

Left- and Right-Wing Mercantilists

The weight of the redistributive tradition is such that, as we see it, Peru's so-called democratic left- and its right-wing parties are primarily mercantilist and thus have more in common than they imagine.

No left- or right-wing leader, on assuming national or local office, ever took the opportunity to alter the impediments to humble people's access to formal society. Instead, both sides resorted to mercantilist instruments. Both intervened directly in the economy and promoted the expansion of state activities. Both strengthened the role of the government's bureaucracy until they made it the main obstacle, rather than the main incentive, to progress, and together they produced, without consulting the electorate, almost 99 percent of the laws governing us. Both failed to delegate to private individuals the tasks mismanaged by the bureaucracy, either because they did not have sufficient confidence in the population or because they did not know how to hand responsibility over to it.

There are, of course, differences between right-wing mercantilism and left-wing mercantilism: the former will govern to serve foreign investors or national business interests, while the latter will do so to redistribute well-being to the neediest groups. Both, however, will do so with bad laws which explicitly benefit some and harm others. Although their aims may seem to differ, the result is that in Peru one wins or loses by political decisions. Of course, there is a big difference between a fox and a wolf but, for the rabbit, it is the similarity that counts.

Because they govern with mercantilist systems, the traditional left wing and right wing are both concerned more with transferring wealth than with laying the institutional bases for creating it. Having failed to create the conditions for millions of migrants to join the formal productive process, left-wingers and right-wingers alike are disconcerted by the poverty rampant in their cities and resort to the old mercantilist ploy of handing out disguised forms of charity in quantities which ultimately prove ludicrously inadequate. Today, both the left and the right-wing view informality as the problem. Neither seems to have realized that the problem itself offers the solution—to use the energy inherent in the phenomenon to create wealth and a different order. Perhaps this is because converting a problem into a solution smacks of alchemy, or perhaps they are opposed to private initiative on a large, popular scale. Like all good mercantilists, they both feel secure only if the answers come from a higher authority within the centralized order.

A particularly good example of this tendency is the regulation on street vending, described in the chapter on informal trade, which Lima's municipal government, controlled by the Marxist left wing, enacted in 1985 through Ordinance 002. If, instead of overregulating the street vendors, the authorities had removed the obstacles to their activities and made it easier for them to form business organizations and obtain formal credit so that they could build more markets, by 1993 all of today's street vendors would be off the streets.

The irony is that, while the mayor dealt popular initiative this discriminatory blow, he openly encouraged private contractors to build markets right in the center of Lima. Thus, the policies pursued by the left wing in the municipal government were essentially mercantilist rather than socialist and did not differ significantly from what the right wing would have done in the same circumstances.

The traditional left and right wings also advocate a protective and exclusive order, and neither has proposed measures to integrate newcomers and enable them to compete. Instead of seeing how people can gain control of market forces and make them serve the country's social interests, they try to replace those forces by the system of government which preceded the Industrial Revolution in Europe.

In dealing with the problem of informality, little thought has been given to ways of reforming the legal order to adapt it to the new realities of production. No one has ever considered that most poor Peruvians are a step ahead of the revolutionaries and are already changing the country's structures, and that what the politicians should be doing is guiding the change and giving it an appropriate institutional framework so that it can be properly used and governed. As a result, the main political choices available in Peru have placed electors in a terrible dilemma: they are being asked to elect an increasingly powerful state in the form of either a right wing which often openly favors certain private groups or of a left wing which is moving resolutely toward a state capitalism which might prove even more oppressive than the mercantilist system.

It is also clear that many owners of formal businesses, overwhelmed by the costs of formality, feel safer collaborating with an interventionist government with which they can come to an agreement than advocating an impersonal market economy in which there is no omnipotent ruler who can intervene on their behalf. For them, the private sector is capitalism without competition, a combination of state support and private control—mercantilism.

Despite all this, the rhetoric of our traditional left and right wings is very similar to their foreign supporters'. Perhaps they themselves are confused, but the result is that they have been able to create the illusion abroad that what is taking place in Peru is the pluralistic political confrontation characteristic of party politics in Western democracies—that the right wing wants to strengthen private enterprise and protect public freedom, and the left wing wants to help the poor and remedy social injustice in Peru.

They are mistaken, however. The traditional right wing does not represent the principles which underlay the Industrial Revolution, nor are its actions based on a social philosophy which would be acceptable in a liberal* context. In Peru, economic liberalism has been adapted to give superficial coherence to conservative mercantilist policies, instead of spurring the attack on mercantilism as it did in Europe. When they need to appear favorable to the West, our governments appoint "pure" liberals to strategic positions, who apply their theories at the macroeconomic level without altering the legal institutions that discriminate internally, and they remove such liberals from office when they begin to arouse too much criticism from the mercantilist establishment.

Like the conservatives, Peru's liberals agree that discriminatory state intervention is essential because of our country's "cultural backwardness." Thus, while in macroeconomic matters they keep up with the latest jargon and workings of orthodox liberal economics, when it comes to internal social and economic matters, their legal mechanisms are exclusive and far from liberal. This creates a kind of internal legal apartheid characterized essentially by the full legality of the activities of part of the population and the relative legality of the rest. This is how, in addition to laws on urban development, we come to have provisions on informal settlements; or a legal system for formal transport and exceptional rules for minibuses; or commercial laws for formal establishments and ordinances for street vendors. The traditional right wing never considered the possibility of having the same laws for everybody. Believing that the mercantilist status quo was already an advanced liberal society which needed only foreign capital and perhaps a superior culture and race, they devoted most of their energies to defending the dominant class and its culture and traditions. They never searched for the reforms and institutions indispensable to the development of a modern economy open to all sectors of the population.

Something similar happens with the extreme left wing because,

---

*"Liberal" is used here in its original, European sense as standing for less concentration of power and greater opportunities for individual initiative.

although it has managed to win the sympathies of the poor, its actual economic projects lead unmistakably in the direction of state capitalism and take no account of popular effort, initiative, and potentiality. In this, they are quite reactionary. We believe that such an approach will ultimately undermine the possibilities that a left-wing government will come to power by democratic, nonviolent means.

We are thus faced with a strange paradox: most traditional left-wingers and right-wingers believe that what we have in Peru today is a liberal status quo. On this assumption, mercantilist business owners turn to Western governments and their allies in the foreign private sector for help in preserving a system which allegedly reflects that existing in the West. The left wing, for its part, asks their ideological allies abroad for help in abolishing a liberal system which they claim has failed and is therefore unworkable. Both are mistaken: Peru is not a liberal society. It is a mercantilist society.

Thus, when conservatives and those to the left of center in the United States take a position on the Peruvian conflict, the former supporting the right wing and the latter the left wing, they do not realize that neither of them is really supporting anything other than mercantilism in one of its various manifestations. Both sides lose, because they give monopolistic control of change to extremists. Those who back the traditional right wing lose more, however, because they become defenders of the status quo and thus identified with injustice and misery. Neoliberalism—called "neoconservatism" in the United States—is not even represented in the local political spectrum and has almost no influence on Peru's intelligentsia.

The Promise of Human Capital

Perhaps the most serious distortion caused by the mercantilist approach to reality is that it has obscured the tremendous human capital and potential development of the migrants. The right and left wings alike have nursed the antibusiness prejudices of the populace.

The romanticism of the left wing makes it generally praise and even venerate ordinary people, provided that they confine themselves to a strictly dependent role and possess neither ideas nor the ability to organize with others. It sees such people as passive objects in need of assistance programs similar to those required by the disabled and unemployed. It is as though left-wingers appreciate workers only when they lack the ability to get ahead on their own. This attitude is little different from the paternalism of right-wingers, who also sympathize with people of popular extraction as long as they confine their activities to loyal servitude, handicrafts, or folklore, but reject them as soon as they open their own businesses and charge for their services, negotiating their prices according to the dictates of the market. Then, the reaction is to say that their prices are "exorbitant" and that the enterprising worker is a "thief" or "rascal." Both right- and left-wingers acknowledge the right of mestizos from the high plateaus to live among us only as long as they need us to organize or employ them.

Competitive business people, whether formal or informal, are in fact a new breed. They have rejected the dependence proposed by the politicians. They may be neither likable nor polite—remember what many people say about minibus drivers and street vendors—but they provide a sounder basis for development than skeptical bureaucracies and traffickers in privileges. They have demonstrated their initiative by migrating, breaking with the past without any prospect of a secure future, they have learned how to identify and satisfy others' needs, and their confidence in their abilities is greater than their fear of competition. When they start something, they know there is always a risk of failure. Every day they face dilemmas: what and how are they going to produce? What are they going to make it with? At what prices will they buy and sell? Will they manage to find long-term customers? Behind every product offered or manufactured, behind all the apparent disorder or relative illegality, are their sophisticated calculations and difficult decisions.

This ability to take risks and calculate is important because it means that a broad entrepreneurial base is already being created. In Peru, informality has turned a large number of people into entrepreneurs, into people who know how to seize opportunities by managing available resources, including their own labor, relatively efficiently. This is the foundation of development, for wealth is simply the product of combining interchangeable resources and productive labor. Wealth is achieved essentially by one's own efforts. It is earned, little by little, in an active market where goods, services, and ideas are exchanged and people are constantly learning and adjusting to others' needs. Wealth comes from knowing how to use resources, not from owning them.

This new business class is a very valuable resource: it is the human capital essential for economic takeoff. It has meant survival for those who had nothing and has served as a safety valve for societal tensions. It has given mobility and productive flexibility to the wave of migrants, and is in fact doing what the state could never have done: bring large numbers of outsiders into the country's money economy. The benefits which this new business class offers Peru far outweigh the damage done it by terrorists and mercantilists. The overwhelming majority of the population has one goal in common, to overcome poverty and succeed.

We face two challenges: what can we do to prevent informal energies from being kept in check by a punitive legal system and how can we transfer the vitality, persistence, and hopes of the emerging business class to the rest of the country? The answer is to change our legal institutions in order to lower the cost of producing and obtaining wealth, and to give people access to the system so they can join in economic and social activity and compete on an equal footing, the ultimate goal being a modern market economy which, so far, is the only known way to achieve development based on widespread business activity.

A country's entrepreneurial reserves do not automatically function properly, they do so only if prevailing institutions allow them to. We have only to look at all those Peruvians condemned to poverty and mediocrity in their own land who, on emigrating to other countries, become successful because they are finally able to operate with the protection of proper institutions. What determines a society's economic system is the way its legal institutions operate. If business activity is restricted to a select group, the economic system will be a mercantilist one. If it is restricted to a state technocracy, it will be state capitalism, a collectivist system. But if every citizen, regardless of his or her origin, color, sex, occupation, or political orientation, can in practice be in business, then we shall have a genuinely democratic economy, a market economy.

Where we place business initiative in our society is therefore extremely important. If it is placed at the disposal of all Peruvians, we will be able to tap the vast entrepreneurial reserves that are developing throughout the country. The more people are able to participate in the economy and detect opportunities, the greater the potential development. The great strength of a market economy is that it relies on the people's ingenuity and capacity for work, instead of on the limited contribution of an arbitrarily chosen elite. What is needed is to make the transition from a system in which individuals are subordinated to the aims of the state, to one in which the state is at the service of individuals and the community.

An Agenda for Change

We have seen that the transition away from mercantilism in Peru while avoiding repression requires bringing the legal system closer to reality. This book shows that the present system of lawmaking has been unable to keep pace with events and that this has given rise to growing discrimination against Peruvians of humble origin and caused the law itself to fall into disrepute.

Finding a peaceful way out of mercantilism, then, means readjusting our primitive legal institutions to permit the peaceful interdependence and development of individuals within an increasingly complex and hetero-geneous society. Since the Spanish Conquest, no change has been so forceful and far-reaching as the one Peru is experiencing today. We are no longer made up of self-reliant communities, but are becoming increasingly interdependent. This change will continue, and we must devise legal institutions and means of government which will allow us to cooperate peacefully during the long and perhaps interminable process of transfor-mation.

To do so, we must draw on what actually works. More specifically, we must draw on the extralegal system which, as we have seen, most of the population accepts. This system, which regulates property rights and contracts and is enforced through decentralized informal organizations, arose through a process of voluntary adaptation to new circumstances. The main extralegal norms are more general and abstract than those of the mercantilist system because they are a response to the emergence of an urbanized society, which is larger and more fluid than traditional society. They are the result of a process of spontaneous adaptation to a life which requires greater interdependence and coordination.

These norms are not perfect. They lack effectiveness *erga omnes* and therefore the means of enforcement. They are not codified and lack the technical terms that might refine them. There can be no doubt, however, that they are socially relevant, for a considerable number of people comply with them voluntarily. Economic theory indicates that such voluntary compliance occurs only if the extralegal system is relatively more efficient than the formal system. No society likes to obey rules which do not suit it: that these rules are efficient is shown by the fact that they are widely observed. Moreover, this extralegal system is utterly Peruvian, the fruit of national experience. The spontaneous generation of extralegal norms by the informals has initiated a reform of the status quo, pointing the way that legal institutions must go if they are to adapt to new circumstances and regain social relevance.

The challenge, then, is to come up with a legal and institutional system which reflects this new reality, which allows the economy that has sprung up spontaneously to function in an orderly fashion, which enables competitive formal business people and merchants to produce with security instead of obstructing them, and which transfers to private individuals those responsibilities and initiatives which the state has thus far monopolized unsuccessfully. All of this would enable the legal system to regain social relevance.

Our present legal institutions give us no way of knowing what Peru's vast and diverse population mean by well-being or by appropriate solutions to their problems. In the last forty years, this population has constantly surprised its rulers with its aspirations and achievements. Partly, this is because different Peruvians have different objectives and change them in the rapid process of evolution, diversification, and individualization we are undergoing. But it makes it clear that there is no need to try, for the umpteenth time, to get the country to agree on common objectives: a "national project" to achieve precise objectives is impossible in a country as heterogeneous and populous as ours. Rather, the country's legal institutions should provide the means for private individuals to decide for themselves what objectives they want to pursue and, provided that they do no harm to others, ensure that the law enables them to achieve their ends. The Peruvians' worth lies more in their differences than in their similarities. Instead of embarking on the impossible task of agreeing on objectives, therefore, we should agree on the means to achieve any legitimate objective.

We perceive these means as being essentially two in number. The first is the means to tackle existing institutional problems in order to remove the obstacles which currently prevent formals and informals from integrating and getting ahead. The second is the means to tackle future institutional problems, which would involve changing the way in which we make laws. We shall now examine both of these.

Existing institutional problems

To start with, the formals and the informals should be integrated into a single economic and legal system which outlaws discrimination so that the entire population can make full use of its creative energies.

When people talk about integrating formals and informals, some mean "informalizing" the formals in order to free them of legal restrictions, while others mean "formalizing" the informals in order to reduce the adverse consequences of informality. Such integration would, in fact, mean both: removing unproductive restrictions from the legal system and incorporating everyone into a new formality.

History shows that in countries where the migrants were integrated and institutions were created which gave each member of the population the chance to participate and engage in production, a developed society emerged. In countries where success began to come from producing goods and services which the country needed instead of from receiving privileges from the state, there was progress, prosperity and, of course, integration. In countries where legal institutions remained unchanged following migration, on the other hand, greater prosperity was not achieved, unrest grew, and violence often erupted.

It is no easy task to change legal institutions. To do so, it is essential to identify the country's most pressing and crucial problems, see what legal institutions give everyone access to opportunities in the most efficient manner, which ones foster the entrepreneurial qualities needed to create wealth, and which others foster coordination among individuals and the efficient use of resources.

In this connection, the extralegal system shows us that what Peruvians want, first and foremost, is firm property rights, reliable transactions, and secure activities. They want facilitative legal instruments, which they do not now have. Second, they want to avoid obstructive legal norms as far as possible. Third, they want to replace the state with informal and private organizations in many areas. A minimum program for integrating the country would thus require simplifying and decentralizing the governmental bureaucracy and ultimately deregulating, or depoliticizing, national productive life. Let us now consider these points.

Simplification

By "simplification" we mean taking steps to optimize the functioning of legal institutions so that the duplicative and unnecessary parts of laws can be reduced or eliminated. Simplification does not affect the roots or the mercantilist system, just some of its consequences.

Simplification requires that we identify the kind of legislation which is doing the most harm—raising the cost of entering and remaining in formal activity, as well as the cost of informality. Such costs waste resources, limit the extent to which formals can adjust to changing economic circumstances, and prevent informals from developing their capacities to the full.

These three problems affect not only the businesses directly concerned but also consumers, who must pay higher prices because of the costs created by the web of regulations and who suffer a reduction in the quality of goods because businesses function less efficiently. It also harms the employees and suppliers of formal businesses, who obtain less for their contribution because it is not used efficiently.

Simplification means using techniques already well known as "de-bureaucratization" in developed countries. These include replacing rules which specify how to fulfill certain requirements by rules stating the ends to be achieved. This would lighten the burden on those who must obey the laws in question, because instead of having to meet certain requirements before they can do something, they will instead be monitored afterward to see whether they are complying with the law. Such procedures, which emphasize ex post facto monitoring rather than prior paperwork, reduce red tape without abandoning necessary controls but also provide more efficient means of enforcement.

Simplification is also made possible by automatically monitoring the relevance of laws which have been adopted but whose efficiency and necessity remain to be proven. This is done by enacting "sunset laws," laws which are to endure for only a specified time. This period over, a law lapses automatically unless experience with it warrants its renewal.

The quantity of paperwork produced by the government can be reduced by tying paperwork reduction programs to budget allocations—less red tape would mean more funds—or by giving the public access to the bureaucratic information so that it becomes aware of the legal or customary bases for bureaucratic praxis and thus can pressure the bureaucracy to eliminate harmful and unnecessary administrative practices.

For the most part, simplification means reducing the cost of being productive without changing the political system. When Peruvian governments talk about reducing bureaucracy, they usually mean simplification. They are prepared to change the law, but only if this leaves their political power intact.

Decentralization

By "decentralization" we mean transferring legislative and administrative responsibilities from the central government to local and regional governments and bodies in order to put the authorities in more direct contact with reality and the problems to be solved. This means giving local governments the authority to legislate, without prior control by the central government, on all those matters which can be handled at the regional level—to enact those laws that will not have an adverse effect on the rest of the country.

Decentralization is not "deconcentration," with which it is often confused. When a branch of the Agricultural Bank is opened in Piura or the Constitutional Guarantees Court is located in Arequipa, this is not decentralization: it is deconcentration. Decentralization means actually transferring lawmaking and decision making to local government. Deconcentration is simply transferring some functions from the center to the provinces, but decentralization involves relinquishing a degree of decision-making power to them.

Like simplification, decentralization does not basically alter the mercantilist system, because collusion between governments and privileged citizens can take place at the local level just as well as at the national level. Decentralization can play a very important supplementary role in an agenda for change, however, because it enables local governments to compete and enables the population to compare those who facilitate productive life and those who do not. The jurisdiction which offers a better system of laws will be rewarded by the people who settle or do business in it and others will try to emulate it, thereby improving the quality of lawmaking throughout the country.

Furthermore, if informality results from a lack of communication between government and the governed, things should improve if more decisions are made at the local level, where governments are closer to the people. Moreover, many of the problems involved in informality exist only locally. Although some general laws will solve problems common to a large proportion of the population, there are a number of issues which can be handled or resolved efficiently only on a smaller scale. Finally, decentralization makes it easier to try out experimental solutions in order to grasp the nature of a problem and come closer to an overall solution.

Although the transfer was only a partial and limited one, the delegation of housing regulation to municipal governments in 1980 reduced the time required to acquire title to housing in the province of Lima by four-fifths.

Deregulation

By "deregulation" we mean increasing the responsibilities and opportunities of private individuals and reducing those of the state. Like democratic lawmaking, deregulation gets to the very roots of mercantilism. Deregulation involves depoliticizing the economy in order to protect the state from the manipulation of redistributive combines and the economy from politicians, just as the church was separated from the state. Although all economic, religious, and political systems are interdependent and go to make up a country's social order, each must have a large measure of autonomy so that none lives at the expense of the others.

The economic sphere needs to be freed from the grip of the political power brokers and from the influence of arbitrary lawmaking and parasitic interests. The political sphere, for its part, must be made independent of the economic power structure. Its efficiency and strength must be increased by limiting it to administering a manageable number of problems, free of interference by private selfish interests. We must have a state that is capable and strong, and this will be possible only when it gives up trying to handle all the details and instead tries to create the basic conditions for development.

In practice, deregulation would mean four things. It would replace the state's regulatory control of the economy by control expressed in judicial decisions. It means granting access to the market to all citizens and extending facilitating legal instruments to all. It means increasing the proportion of available resources so that the state can do what private individuals cannot do well. Last, it means delegating to informal organizations the responsibilities they can best meet.

The first of these would remove from the state's hands the power to restrict or confer access to production. This would reduce the state's power to decide who can produce and who cannot, what goods and services will be authorized, how they will be produced, and at what prices and in what quantities. This does not mean creating chaos—quite the opposite. Deregulation would mean freeing public resources so that the state could use them to ensure that strict, efficient rules of the game were imposed and that the freedom that individuals would then enjoy did not have adverse effects. The congestion, the unsanitary and dirty conditions, the disorder and lack of coordination associated with many informal activities show just how inefficient it is to try to control production directly and how much more important it is for the state to enforce a system of extracontractual liability in order to offset, correct, and penalize the adverse consequences of an individual's activities.

But to do so, the state must bring a swift, efficient system of justice within the reach of the entire population. Instead of controlling the economy primarily by regulations, the state should do so, after the event if necessary, through the judiciary. The state would thus be concerned less with administering resources and more with administering justice to ensure that laws are respected and that abuses do not go unpunished. The experience of developed countries shows that it is far more efficient to concentrate investment and public effort on creating an efficient, honest judiciary to administer justice among the private individuals who manage the country's productive apparatus than to try to turn the state itself into a good business operator. An interventionist state requires a bureaucracy, inspectors, penpushers, economists, accountants, and other officials who are not as necessary when the law is simpler to apply, because the judicial system functions only when there are litigants, who are relatively few in number, and not when unmanageable masses of citizens are involved.

This is why it is essential to reform and expand the judiciary, arbitration, the system of justices of the peace and, in general, all institutions which permit order without the immobility, corruption, and inefficiency that accompany direct state intervention in economic life.

The state must also provide the legal instruments that facilitate development. This means changing legal institutions so that ownership of property becomes widespread and that all Peruvians can be sure of having undisputed title to it and reap the legal benefits of investing labor or capital in developing it.

We have seen that the means of exchange are not always secure or universally accessible. Accordingly, the state must encourage and provide contractual mechanisms enabling everyone to pool labor, ideas, capital, and resources. Business and contracts must be made a simple matter, and the outcome of transactions must be made predictable in order to foster an efficient market.

We think that deregulation should also include delegating functions and coercive authority to those formal or informal private institutions which, as we have seen, are today operating better than the state. If they are given an appropriate legal framework, there is no reason why they should not be better placed than the state to undertake certain tasks.

Having assigned private individuals, the judiciary and informal organizations these new tasks, the state should then be able to devote more resources to doing those things which private individuals cannot do or do not do well—for instance, conservation of natural resources and public property, protection of the national heritage, personal safety, the control of monopolies and restrictive practices, transport, and education, for none of which the private sector suffices.

One of the state's primary responsibilities, however, is to redistribute resources to the poorest and least fortunate members of the population, although this must not be used as a pretext for granting privileges to a few and thwarting everyone else, including the poorest people. It is perfectly valid to want a state's many functions to include redistribution. The crucial thing is that resources be redistributed to the needy in ways which do not discourage production, labor, and saving. If redistribution remains a pretext to go on damaging property rights or imposing excessive requirements for their economic enjoyment and use, or for undermining the security of contracts, we will remain underdeveloped. By seeking to remedy the consequences of poverty in this way we will have only helped exacerbate its underlying causes. Redistribution should therefore take forms which do not distort economic incentives, as does the transfer of money through taxation, so that the understandable zeal for redistributive justice does not hamper productive justice.

As the reader will have realized, the aim of deregulation is the same as mercantilists claim to pursue, including land, labor, credit, education, transport, safety, and assistance to those who have the least. The difference lies in that fact that a deregulated state achieves these objectives by facilitating and controlling the functioning of the market, not be replacing it.

What is needed, then, is not to abolish informal activity but to integrate, legalize, and promote it. Private monopolies and oligopolies must be combatted by giving everyone access to the market, not by replacing them with state monopolies. Credit must be democratized by encouraging competition among financiers, not by nationalizing it or placing it at the mercy of politicians and bureaucrats.

In short, all of us, formals and current informals, need to be governed by just, efficient laws instead of by the arbitrary authority of the state.

Future institutional problems

The second way to adjust the legal system to reality is to make sure that when we enact legislation in the future, we do not repeat the errors of the past.

Accordingly, legislative procedures must ensure that governments justify the laws they plan to adopt, establishing the necessity and showing that their benefits outweigh their potential costs, so that they do not have to be simplified, deregulated, and decentralized at a later stage. Lawmaking must be transparent and properly monitored, which will mean subjecting it to control by the electorate through consultation with the people. The Instituto Libertad y Democracia (ILD) believes that this mechanism would require two procedures: the authorities would publish their draft legislation and then hear the general public's views, suggestions, and objections.

Unlike Peru, nearly all the developed democracies exert some kind of control over the way in which their governments make laws. For us, democracy means electing a new government every five years, giving it a blank check for its term in office, and refraining from all communication with it until there is another election. This turns bad lawmaking, lawmaking without popular consultation, into a series of surprises which we can barely observe. In a country where the executive branch produces almost 99 percent of all rules and Parliament only the remaining 1 percent, it is hardly surprising that, in the best mercantilist tradition, the legal system is divorced from reality and the needs of the market and favors redistributive combines and centralist voluntarism.

A democratic system of lawmaking, on the other hand, can respect, incorporate, and draw on the rules and positive practices spontaneously generated by formals and informals alike. Since such a system would make it possible to steadily absorb an order which is far from static, it would help laws to be attuned to reality. The purpose of such a system would be to build up an order based not on concepts pre-established by the central government but on the needs and aspirations of Peru's citizens. Another advantage of popular consultation is that the rule-making process would make much better use of the knowledge scattered throughout the country. In a society in which millions of people interact in billions of ways and execute thousands of contracts, in which a variety of cultures, life-styles, and viewpoints intermingle, it is inconceivable that an authority could, without consultation, have access to all the information it needs to formulate workable rules or norms.

We might even say that, just as there is a division of labor within the country, there is also a division of knowledge. It is thus far more efficient and worthwhile to make laws based on the knowledge scattered throughout the population than for small groups of public officials and their advisors to do so. When individuals make rules spontaneously, they base them on experience, their observation of what succeeds, and on past improvements, not on the reasoning of a closed circle. Democratic rule making also helps strengthen the position of society's less organized or weaker groups in relation to redistributive combines. It keeps the process transparent, making it difficult to surprise the general public with a rule which redistributes in favor of such combines. Unlike the members of redistributive combines, our population is heterogeneous and dispersed, and thus more vulnerable. A democratic system would force the government to justify, to the public, the need for a new law and to make sure that no group benefits at the expense of all. This would increase the political influence of the public in general, which, after all, loses the most by mercantilist regulations. It also means that rulers would be answerable to public opinion continuously, not just every five years.

If the legal system is to be democratized, two essential requirements must be met: the draft legislation must be published and its costs and benefits analyzed. Both requirements will improve the quality and reduce the quantity of mercantilist laws and regulations.

Publication of draft legislation

Economic and social legislation drafted by the executive branch would be published before it was promulgated so that anyone who might be affected by it could give their views, state their opposition, or make comments and suggestions. This makes it possible to mobilize public opinion against regulations which obstruct economic activity or create income for a specific group.

Advance publication provides the state with access to the public's views on each legislative proposal. If the lawmakers draft bad laws, public reaction will give them the information they need to enact better laws. This access extends the virtues of democracy from elections to the entire governmental process. When, as now, there is no such access, when the bureaucracy is almost the only channel through which those in power govern and receive information, governments ossify.

Cost-benefit analysis

Draft legislation would be accompanied by a cost-benefit analysis of its likely socio-economic effect. Public officials would have to demonstrate why their proposals are better than anyone else's, the purpose being to ensure that discussions of the relevance of the proposed legislation transcend purely legal criteria and consider the effect it may have even on third parties.

The requirement that the government justify each legislative proposal with a cost-benefit analysis will serve at least three purposes. First, it will identify and almost automatically eliminate laws which create unnecessary obstacles. Second, since many mercantilist regulations have no plausible basis, it will make it difficult to justify a harmful proposal to an informed and vigilant public. Third, it will be possible to discard laws which have some justification but whose costs far outweigh their benefits. The discipline imposed by the need to make a cost-benefit analysis should prompt the government department concerned to abandon any defective legislative proposal before publishing it. This would mean that when draft legislation is published, it will be because there is some basis for it, and interested groups will have a chance to confirm or reject the authorities' findings.

All the techniques we have described for democratizing the legal system meet the requirements of simplification, deregulation, and decentralization. The use of one technique often improves another.

Of course, many other changes would have to be made. The state has many responsibilities which need to be increased and enhanced. We could also discuss the level of state interference in different sectors. Broadly speaking, however, there is widespread agreement that state intervention in Peru is usually excessive and harmful. There is overwhelming evidence that it excludes most citizens from lawful activity and consumption and that it does not help promote economic activity, protect property, make contracts reliable, or administer justice. At best, it simply makes everyone's life more complicated. However, if we work on the proposed measures, some of the conditions for ensuring that the legal system makes a positive contribution to development could be created. Laws would be based on general behavior and the legal system could operate in such a way that spontaneously generated economic and social systems were incorporated into it automatically to strengthen the population's productive and regulatory capacities. As these objectives were achieved, good laws would begin to prevail.

Final Remarks

The issues dealt with in this book are inexhaustible and, as new evidence emerges, it will doubtless be necessary to rewrite it. However, we think it is essential to pass on to readers some of the basic conclusions we have reached as a result of this early research into informality in Peru. At best, these conclusions will serve to guide future research or analysis and, at worst, to field criticism and perhaps refute some prejudices. In any event, we think they provide an important starting point for a discussion which has yet to take place.

We are convinced that there exists in Peru an extraordinary reserve of productive human resources which each day demonstrates amazing energy and ingenuity. Its strength is tremendous, for it is overcoming centuries of mercantilist oppression. Its very existence is proof of the potentialities which the country has thus far failed to tap. We are convinced that, as the importance of the law becomes recognized, we will find that the real problem is not so much informality as formality.

There is almost unanimous agreement that the country's structures must be transformed. We believe that this transformation is already being made by the informals and that what our government must do is change the law so that this transformation is an orderly one that allows us to adapt peacefully and more productively to a new way of living in society. Sooner or later, our observation of informality will show us that, while reorganizing the legal system would appear to be a more modest task than revolutionizing the country's social order from the pinnacles of government, it is in fact a far more important and far-reaching undertaking because it is based on the energies of the entire population and their capacity to respond to opportunities.

We must begin to view the country's development in terms of profits and losses. We will find that most losses come from the public sector and the redistributive system to which it has accustomed us, and that the profits come from competitive individuals, both formal and informal. We must, finally, shake off all the prejudices which make some of us despise the informals and the view that, for racial or cultural reasons, our population is "different" and thus unable to take advantage of the freedom and the systems of the market economies of other countries. For years, these prejudices have been used to justify the discriminatory redistribution of what little we have to the advantage of small interest groups.

We are sure that once we have a thorough understanding of the adverse effects of our legal institutions, we shall be able to rid ourselves of our complexes about the developed countries. Many of our setbacks can be attributed to our anachronistic institutions. We believe that if we study our history from this standpoint, it will cease to be a conservative trap which makes us prey to eloquent dictators, and that we shall finally be able to transform our history into an instrument of progress which will help us to find efficient institutions and systems worthy of the effort and sacrifice of our people.

We hope that this research will help genuine left-wingers to see that concern about misery and hunger is not restricted to one political faction and that any of us with an awareness shares their anguish; that noble sentiments must be matched by effective action to combat poverty; and that to transform class struggle into a struggle for popular initiative and entrepreneurship is an intellectual challenge worthy of the best of us. The leaders of Peru's right wing may be able to play a significant role in the future if a fresh look at informality makes them realize that their prejudices have closed their eyes to poor people's problems and to the possibilities of attracting and helping the neediest classes.

The concepts of left wing and right wing in Peru sometimes confuse things rather than clarify them. We think that, more than the rhetoric which distinguishes them, what is important is the fact that both sides reward those who use their talents to obtain favors instead of encouraging those who create wealth and well-being. The conflict between mercantilism and a market economy helps to explain the apparent paradox whereby a large proportion of our middle class are pro-state and often socialist-leaning, while the popular sectors advocate private enterprise and cooperate in free, decentralized organizations. We are sure that if the right and left wings in developed countries were to evaluate the evidence correctly, both would condemn our system. The former might condemn its inefficiency, and the latter its injustice.

One of our rulers' most pernicious mistakes has been to concern themselves with the costs of production and not with those of transaction. We are convinced that they should devote their greatest efforts to the latter and use their lawmaking power to eliminate obstacles and provide more facilitative elements so that everyone, and not just an elite, can prosper. They should also leave the cost of production to individuals and give them the legal institutions to use competition and the market to reduce them.

It is obvious to us that the only way for Peru to resolve its present crisis and its problems of external indebtedness and inflation is through a process of economic growth which does not increase the deficit in our balance of payments. Appropriate macroeconomic policies and the corresponding investment are needed, but the most important element is the microeconomic measures to promote and protect property rights, facilitate access to business and transactions among individuals, and give people the necessary confidence to save, invest, and produce. Unless the microeconomic problems we have described throughout this book are solved, any macroeconomic policy or external financing will be so much wasted effort.

If some of our arguments prove correct, we will have begun to trace another path, one which will lead us away from violence as a solution to the disorder, poverty, and frustration caused by the perpetuation of mercantilism, one in which legal institutions are attuned to our reality and draw on its emergent social and economic forces, and one which enables us to join forces with that tremendous mass of Peruvians who currently do not believe in class struggle but rather in interchange and voluntary cooperation.

There is more than one country within Peru's borders. There is a mercantilist country which some are still trying to revive with various political formulas and techniques but which already shows all the signs of impending death. There is a second country, that of people desperate for solutions but caught between the destructive objectives of terrorist violence and the impractical exhortations of many progressives. And there is a third country, the one we call "the other path": a country which works hard, is innovative and fiercely competitive, and whose most conspicuous province is, of course, informality.

This third country is the alternative to subversive or criminal violence because it replaces the energy squandered on resentment and destruction with energy well invested in economic and social progress. The informals prove this to us daily: they are always prepared to engage in dialogue, show prudence, and adapt to society. People motivated by the desire for progress and advancement are always well equipped to live in a state of law. The hatred and rage of subversives find fertile ground only where informality has been unable to establish itself and mercantilist formality has already failed.

The real remedy for violence and poverty is to recognize the property and labor of those whom formality today excludes, so that where there is rebellion there will be a sense of belonging and responsibility. When people develop a taste for independence and faith in their own efforts, they will be able to believe in themselves and in economic freedom.

Epilogue

The forty researchers and workers currently employed by the Instituto Libertad y Democracia (ILD) are conducting the studies and designing the means to deliberately and resolutely transform a mercantilist, elitist society into a modern, democratic nation.

The evolution of the developed Western nations from mercantilism to their present systems was a spontaneous rather than a deliberate process, so much so that most jurists and economists in those countries are unaware of the important role played by their institutions in that evolution. It was only by studying Peru's informal economy where, despite the absence of such institutions, there is relative economic freedom, that we gradually came to realize their tremendous importance. Those who wish to offer their country the chance to become a modern society must direct their efforts not only toward eliminating certain conditions—the barriers to access to formal activity, the costs of remaining legal, the discrimination in capital markets, the state corporations—but also toward creating the basic institutions on which efficiency, social peace, and spontaneous cooperation are based in more advanced nations.

Accordingly, in addition to projects for simplification, regulation, decentralization, and democratic lawmaking, the ILD is designing other institutional mechanisms required in a market economy that could function without privileges and in a democracy that does not stop at elections but continues throughout a government's term of office. Let us mention some of these.

At present, for instance, we are trying to find efficient ways of controlling the exercise of power in order to limit abuse by government and redistributive combines—to establish a system under which people can

259

protect their property rights and the interests safeguarded by their contracts. For this, of course, we need an institutional context which ensures that government actions are clear. People cannot defend themselves, still less monitor the state, if they do not have access to the information the state controls. Nor can a market economy function in such circumstances, since the basic model for its operations presumes that information is free or at least universally accessible. In this connection, we are preparing the legal basis for obtaining access to public information and also seeing how efficient mechanisms of review can be created. The press and the judiciary must be strengthened so they can scrutinize the actions of government and combines, for the state's present control of the media of information—through credits from a largely state-owned banking system, the provision of news, the distribution of advertising and, in general, benefits and exemptions which can be revoked—seriously undermines their independence. The very limited number of lawsuits instituted against the state in Peru is evidence of the judiciary's lack of credibility vis-à-vis the administration.

To strengthen rights to real estate and improve the titling system in informal settlements, we are drawing up private instruments for insurance and mutual-aid associations, to help provide the security and credit required for investment in housing and other activities. Our immediate projects also include realistic alternatives for incorporating decisions made in ad hoc arbitration and enabling residents of settlements to participate in adjudicating lawsuits which for the time being cannot be resolved by the judicial system.

In the area of urban transport, we are designing laws and regulations to permit the proper functioning of a decentralized, competitive transport system with a large number of owners of vehicles. The ILD's analysis shows that our present problems of urban transport are due largely to the fact that the existing legal system is not adapted to widespread ownership. The project should permit the orderly participation of a large number of entrepreneurs on the basis of a legal system which provides the means to do so, for instance: traffic management and the coercive authority needed to resolve traffic congestion and aggressive driving; safety standards for vehicles; penalties to protect users; clear information about fares; a system of incentives based on private insurance; traffic courts and supervisory mechanisms for settling disputes and awarding compensation for personal injury and damage to property; and a system of fares and taxes to finance all of this and enable transport operators to provide an acceptable standard of transportation.

It can be seen that the ILD's projects range from the general to the specific and extend, literally, as far as our budget permits. Although we are trying to fit our projects into an overall framework and find an overall solution to problems, our strategy is more one of designing specific projects which are manageable and comprehensible. As soon as they are ready, we publicize them in the information media and through public hearings at which we test and enhance our proposals by opening them to public discussion and suggestions.

The idea is to open the debate now. We see no need to wait for a lengthy process, which might be painful and bloody, to lead us down the path of industrial revolution and social warfare to an unknown destination, as happened in Europe. We already know what institutions work, albeit incipiently, in Peru. As for international experiences, there is ample information about what succeeds and can be adapted. The ILD sees no reason why we Peruvians should not be able to trace a deliberate path which will enable us to escape from backwardness and advance toward a modern society.

Index